LETTERS FROM THE FIELD
1925 – 1975

WORLD PERSPECTIVES

Volumes already published

WORLD PERSPECTIVES · *Volume Fifty-two*

Planned and Edited by **RUTH NANDA ANSHEN**

LETTERS FROM

THE FIELD

1925–1975

MARGARET MEAD

The American Museum of Natural History
New York

1817

HARPER & ROW, PUBLISHERS

New York, Hagerstown, San Francisco, London

FIRST EDITION

Designed by Linda Dingler

Library of Congress Cataloging in Publication Data

Mead, Margaret, 1901–
    Letters from the field 1925–1975

    (World perspectives; v. 52)
    Bibliography: p.
    Includes index.
    1. Mead, Margaret, 1901–   2. Anthropologists—United States—Correspondence. 3. Ethnology—Oceania. 4. Ethnology—Field work. I. Title.
GN21.M36A4   1977   301.2′092′4   73–4110
ISBN 0–06–012961–1

77 78 79 80 81 10 9 8 7 6 5 4 3 2 1

Contents

Illustrations

These photographs, taken by different photographers to document specific occasions, have been selected in 1977 to illustrate the subject matter of the letters but in many cases do not document the particular events that are described.

New Guinea—Arapesh, Mundugumor and Tchambuli, 1931-1933

Bali and Iatmul, New Guinea, 1936-1939

Maps

World Perspectives
What This Series Means

It is the thesis of *World Perspectives* that man is in the process of developing a new consciousness which, in spite of his apparent spiritual and moral captivity, can eventually lift the human race above and beyond the fear, ignorance, and isolation which beset it today. It is to this nascent consciousness, to this concept of man born out of a universe perceived through a fresh vision of reality, that *World Perspectives* is dedicated.

My Introduction to this Series is not of course to be construed as a prefatory essay for each individual book. These few pages simply attempt to set forth the general aim and purpose of the Series as a whole. They try to point to the principle of permanence within change and to define the essential nature of man, as presented by those scholars who have been invited to participate in this intellectual and spiritual movement.

Man has entered a new era of evolutionary history, one in which rapid change is a dominant consequence. He is contending with a fundamental change, since he has intervened in the evolutionary process. He must now better appreciate this fact and then develop the wisdom to direct the process toward his fulfillment rather than toward his destruction. As he learns to apply his understanding of the physical world for practical purposes, he is, in reality, extending his innate capacity and augmenting his ability and his need to communicate as well as his ability to think and to create. And as a result, he is substituting a goal-directed evolutionary process in his struggle against environmental hardship for the slow, but effective, biological evolution which produced modern man through mutation and natural selection. By intelligent intervention in the evolutionary process man has greatly accelerated and greatly expanded the range of his possibilities. But he has not changed the basic fact that it remains a trial and error process, with the danger of taking paths that lead to sterility of mind and heart, moral apathy and intellectual inertia; and even producing social dinosaurs unfit to live in an evolving world.

Only those spiritual and intellectual leaders of our epoch who have a paternity in this extension of man's horizons are invited to participate in the Series: those who are aware of the truth that beyond the divisiveness among men there exists a primordial unitive power since we are all bound together by a common humanity more fundamental than any unity of dogma; those who recognize that the centrifugal force which has scattered and atomized mankind must be replaced by an integrating structure and process capable of bestowing meaning and purpose on existence; those who realize that science itself, when not inhibited by the limitations of its own methodology, when chastened and humbled, commits man to an indeterminate range of yet undreamed consequences that may flow from it.

Virtually all of our disciplines have relied on conceptions which are now incompatible with the Cartesian axiom, and with the static world view we once derived from it. For underlying the new ideas, including those of modern physics, is a unifying order, but it is not causality; it is purpose, and not the purpose of the universe and of man, but the purpose *in* the universe and *in* man. In other words, we seem to inhabit a world of dynamic process and structure. Therefore we need a calculus of potentiality rather than one of probability, a dialectic of polarity, one in which unity and diversity are redefined as simultaneous and necessary poles of the same essence.

Our situation is new. No civilization has previously had to face the challenge of scientific specialization, and our response must be new. Thus this Series is committed to ensure that the spiritual and moral needs of a man as a human being and the scientific and intellectual resources at his command for *life* may be brought into a productive, meaningful and creative harmony.

In a certain sense we may say that man now has regained his former geocentric position in the universe. For a picture of the Earth has been made available from distant space, from the lunar desert, and the sheer isolation of the Earth has become plain. This is as new and as powerful an idea in history as any that has ever been born in man's consciousness. We are all becoming seriously concerned with our natural environment. And this concern is not only the result of the warnings given by biologists, ecologists and conservationists. Rather it is the result of a deepening awareness that something new has happened, that the planet Earth is a unique and precious place. Indeed, it may not be a mere coincidence that this awareness should have been born at the exact moment when man took his first step into outer space.

This Series endeavors to point to a reality of which scientific theory has revealed only one aspect. It is the commitment to this reality that lends universal intent to a scientist's most original and solitary thought. By acknowledging this frankly we shall restore science to the great family of human aspirations by which men hope to fulfill themselves in the world community as thinking and sentient beings. For our problem is to discover a principle of differentiation and yet relationship lucid enough to justify and to purify scientific, philosophic and all other knowledge, both discursive and intuitive, by accepting their interdependence. This is the crisis in consciousness made articulate through the crisis in science. This is the new awakening.

Each volume presents the thought and belief of its author and points to the way in which religion, philosophy, art, science, economics, politics and history may constitute that form of human activity which takes the fullest and most precise account of variousness, possibility, complexity and difficulty. Thus *World Perspectives* endeavors to define that ecumenical power of the mind and heart which enables man through his mysterious greatness to re-create his life.

This Series is committed to a re-examination of all those sides of human endeavor which the specialist was taught to believe he could safely leave aside. It attempts to show the structural kinship between subject and object; the indwelling of the one in the other. It interprets present and past events impinging on human life in our growing World Age and world consciousness and envisages what man may yet attain when summoned by an unbending inner necessity to the quest of what is most exalted in him. Its purpose is to offer new vistas in terms of world and human development while refusing to betray the intimate correlation between universality and individuality, dynamics and form, freedom and destiny.

Each author deals with the increasing realization that spirit and nature are not separate and apart; that intuition and reason must regain their convergence as the means of perceiving and fusing inner being with outer reality.

World Perspectives endeavors to show that the conception of wholeness, unity, organism is a higher and more concrete conception than that of matter and energy. Thus an enlarged meaning of life, of biology, not as it is revealed in the test tube of the laboratory but as it is experienced within the organism of life itself, is attempted in this Series. For the principle of life consists in the tension which connects spirit with the realm of matter, symbiotically joined. The element of life is dominant in the very texture of nature, thus rendering life, biology, a transempirical science. The laws of life have their origin beyond their mere physical manifestations and compel us to consider their spiritual source. In fact, the widening of the conceptual framework has not only served to restore order within the respective branches of knowledge, but has also disclosed analogies in man's position regarding the analysis and synthesis of experience in apparently separated domains of knowledge, suggesting the possibility of an ever more embracing objective description of the meaning of life.

Knowledge, it is shown in these books, no longer consists in a manipulation of man and nature as opposite forces, nor in the reduction of data to mere statistical order, but is a means of liberating mankind from the destructive power of fear, pointing the way toward the goal of the rehabilitation of the human will and the rebirth of faith and confidence in the human person. The works published also endeavor to reveal that the cry for patterns, systems and authorities is growing less insistent as the desire grows stronger in both East and West for the recovery of a dignity, integrity and self-realization which are the inalienable rights of man, who may now guide change by means of conscious purpose in the light of rational experience.

The volumes in this Series endeavor to demonstrate that only in a society in which awareness of the problems of science exists can its discoveries start great waves of change in human culture, and in such a manner that these discoveries may deepen and not erode the sense of universal human community. The differences in the disciplines, their epistemological exclusiveness, the variety of historical experiences, the differences of traditions, of cultures, of languages, of the arts, should be protected and preserved. But the interrelationship and unity of the whole should at the same time be accepted.

The authors of *World Perspectives* are of course aware that the ultimate answers to the hopes and fears which pervade modern society rest on the moral fibre of man, and on the wisdom and responsibility of those who promote the course of its development. But moral decisions cannot dispense with an insight into the interplay of the objective elements which offer and limit the choices made. Therefore an understanding of what the issues are, though not a sufficient condition, is a necessary prerequisite for directing action toward constructive solutions.

Other vital questions explored relate to problems of international understanding as well as to problems dealing with prejudice and the resultant tensions and antagonisms. The growing perception and responsibility of our World Age point to the new reality that the individual person and the collective person supplement and integrate each other; that the thrall of totalitarianism of both left and right has been shaken in the universal desire to recapture the authority of truth and human totality. Mankind can finally place its trust not in a proletarian authoritarianism, not in a secularized humanism, both of which have betrayed the spiritual property right of history, but in a sacramental brotherhood and in the unity of knowledge. This new consciousness has created a widening of human horizons beyond every parochialism, and a revolution in human thought comparable to the basic assumption, among the ancient Greeks, of the sovereignty of reason; corresponding to the great effulgence of the moral conscience articulated by the Hebrew prophets; analogous to the fundamental assertions of Christianity; or to the beginning of the new scientific era, the era of the science of dynamics, the experimental foundations of which were laid by Galileo in the Renaissance.

An important effort of this Series is to re-examine the contradictory meanings and applications which are given today to such terms as democracy, freedom, justice, love, peace, brotherhood and God. The purpose of such inquiries is to clear the way for the foundation of a genuine *world* history not in terms of nation or race or culture but in terms of man in relation to God, to himself, his fellow man and the universe, that reach beyond immediate self-interest. For the meaning of the World Age consists in respecting man's hopes and dreams, which lead to a deeper understanding of the basic values of all peoples.

World Perspectives is planned to gain insight into the meaning of man, who not only is determined by history but who also determines history. History is to be understood as concerned not only with the life of man on this planet but as including also such cosmic influences as interpenetrate our human world. This generation is discovering that history does not conform to the social optimism of modern civilization and that the organization of human communities and the establishment of freedom and peace are not only intellectual achievements but spiritual and moral achievements as well, demanding a cherishing of the wholeness of human personality, the "unmediated wholeness of feeling and thought," and constituting a never-ending challenge to man, emerging from the abyss of meaninglessness and suffering, to be renewed and replenished in the totality of his life.

Justice itself, which has been "in a state of pilgrimage and crucifixion" and now is being slowly liberated from the grip of social and political demonologies in the East as well as in the West, begins to question its own premises. The modern revolutionary movements which have challenged the sacred institutions of society by protecting injustice in the name of social justice are here examined and re-evaluated.

In the light of this, we have no choice but to admit that the *un*-freedom against which freedom is measured must be retained with it, namely, that the aspect of truth out of which the night view appears to emerge, the darkness of our time, is as little abandonable as is man's subjective advance. Thus the two sources of man's consciousness are inseparable, not as dead but as living and complementary, an aspect of that "principle of complementarity" through which Niels Bohr has sought to unite the quantum and the wave, both of which constitute the very fabric of life's radiant energy.

There is in mankind today a counterforce to the sterility and danger of a quantitative, anonymous mass culture; a new, if sometimes imperceptible, spiritual sense of convergence toward human and world unity on the basis of the sacredness of each human person and respect for the plurality of cultures. There is a growing awareness that equality may not be evaluated in mere numerical terms but is proportionate and analogical in its reality. For when equality is equated with interchangeability, individuality is negated and the human person transmuted into a faceless mask.

We stand at the brink of an age of a world in which human life presses forward to actualize new forms. The false separation of man and nature, of time and space, of freedom and security, is acknowledged, and we are faced with a new vision of man in his organic unity and of history offering a richness and diversity of equality and majesty of scope hitherto unprecedented. In relating the accumulated wisdom of man's spirit to the new reality of the World Age, in articulating its thought and belief, *World Perspectives* seeks to encourage a renaissance of hope in society and of pride in man's decision as to what his destiny will be.

Man has certainly contrived to change the environment, but subject to the new processes involved in this change, the same process of selection continues to operate. The environment has changed partly in a physical and geographical sense, but more particularly from the knowledge we now possess. The Biblical story of Adam and Eve contains a deep lesson, which a casual reading hardly reveals. Once the "fruit of the Tree of Knowledge" has been eaten, the world is changed. The new world is dictated by the knowledge itself, not of course by an edict of God. The Biblical story has further interest in that the new world is said to be much worse than the former idyllic state of ignorance. Today we are beginning to wonder whether this might not also be true. Yet we are uneasy, apprehensive, and our fears lead to the collapse of civilizations. Thus we turn to the truth that knowledge and life are indivisible, even as life and death are inseparable. We *are* what we know and think and feel; we are linked with history, with the world, with the universe, and faith in *Life* creates its own verification.

World Perspectives is committed to the recognition that all great changes are preceded by a vigorous intellectual reevaluation and reorganization. Our authors are aware that the sin of *hubris* may be avoided by showing that the creative process itself is not a free activity if by free we mean arbitrary, or unrelated to cosmic law. For the creative process in the human mind, the developmental process in organic nature and the basic laws of the inorganic realm may be but varied expressions of a universal formative process. Thus *World Perspectives* hopes to show that although the present apocalyptic period is one of exceptional tensions, there is also at work an exceptional movement toward a compensating unity which refuses to violate the ultimate moral power at work in the universe, that very power upon which all human effort must at last depend. In this way we may come to understand that there exists an inherent interdependence of spiritual and mental growth which, though conditioned by circumstances, is never determined by circumstances. In this way the great plethora of human knowledge may be correlated with an insight into the nature of human nature by being attuned to the wide and deep range of human thought and human experience.

Incoherence is the result of the present disintegrative processes in education. Thus the need for *World Perspectives* expresses itself in the recognition that natural and man-made ecological systems require as much study as isolated particles and elementary reactions. For there is a basic correlation of elements in nature as in man which cannot be separated, which compose each other and alter each other mutually. Thus we hope to widen appropriately our conceptual framework of reference. For our epistemological problem consists in our finding the proper balance between our lack of an all-embracing principle relevant to our way of evaluating life and in our power to express ourselves in a logically consistent manner.

Our Judeo-Christian and Greco-Roman heritage, our Hellenic tradition, has compelled us to think in exclusive categories. But our *experience* challenges us to recognize a totality richer and far more complex than the average observer could have suspected— a totality which compels him to think in ways which the logic of dichotomies denies. We are summoned to revise fundamentally our ordinary ways of conceiving experience, and thus, by expanding our vision and by accepting those forms of thought which also include nonexclusive categories, the mind is then able to grasp what it was incapable of grasping or accepting before.

Nature operates out of necessity; there is no alternative in nature, no will, no freedom, no choice as there is for man. Man must have convictions and values to live for, and this also is recognized and accepted by those scientists who are at the same time philosophers. For they then realize that duty and devotion to our task, be it a task of acting or of understanding, will become weaker and rarer unless guidance is sought in a metaphysics that transcends our historical and scientific views or in a religion that transcends and yet pervades the work we are carrying on in the light of day.

For the nature of knowledge, whether scientific or ontological, consists in reconciling *meaning* and *being*. And *being* signifies nothing other than the actualization of potentiality, self-realization which keeps in tune with the transformation. This leads to experience in terms of the individual; and to organization and patterning in terms of the universe. Thus organism and world actualize themselves simultaneously.

And so we may conclude that organism is *being* enduring in time, in fact in eternal time, since it does not have its beginning with procreation, nor with birth, nor does it end with death. Energy and matter in whatever form they may manifest themselves are transtemporal and transspatial and are therefore metaphysical. Man as man is summoned to know what is right and what is wrong, for emptied of such knowledge he is unable to decide what is better or what is worse.

World Perspectives hopes to show that human society is different from animal societies, which, having reached a certain stage, are no longer progressive but are dominated by routine and repetition. Thus man has discovered his own nature, and with this self-knowledge he has left the state of nonage and entered manhood. For he is the only creature who is able to say not only "no" to life but "yes" and to make for himself a life that is human. In this decision lie his burden and his greatness. For the power of life or death lies not only in the tongue but in man's recently acquired ability to destroy or to create life itself, and therefore he is faced with unlimited and unprecedented choices for good and for evil that dominate our time. Our common concern is the very destiny of the human race. For man has now intervened in the process of evolution, a power not given to the pre-Socratics, nor to Aristotle, nor to the Prophets in the East or the West, nor to Copernicus, nor to Luther, Descartes, or Machiavelli. Judgments of value must henceforth direct technological change, for without such values man is divested of his humanity and of his need to collaborate with the very fabric of the universe in order to bestow meaning, purpose, and dignity upon his existence. No time must be lost since the wavelength of change is now shorter than the life-span of man.

In spite of the infinite obligation of man and in spite of his finite power, in spite of the intransigence of nationalisms, and in spite of the homelessness of moral passions rendered ineffectual by the technological outlook, beneath the apparent turmoil and upheaval of the present, and out of the transformations of this dynamic period with the unfolding of a world-consciousness, the purpose of *World Perspectives* is to help quicken the "unshaken heart of well-rounded truth" and interpret the significant elements of the World Age now taking shape out of the core of that undimmed continuity of the creative process which restores man to mankind while deepening and enhancing his communion and his symbiotic relationship with the universe. For we stand on the threshold of a new consciousness and begin to recognize that thought is as powerful an evolutionary force as teeth, claws and even language.

RUTH NANDA ANSHEN

LETTERS FROM THE FIELD
1925 – 1975

To my kith and kin, for whom I wrote these letters

Manus, 1929. Ponkob
plays at writing.

Sydney, 1971. Conversation with Bernard Narokobi, Arapesh law student. He is
now constitutional adviser to the government of Papua New Guinea.

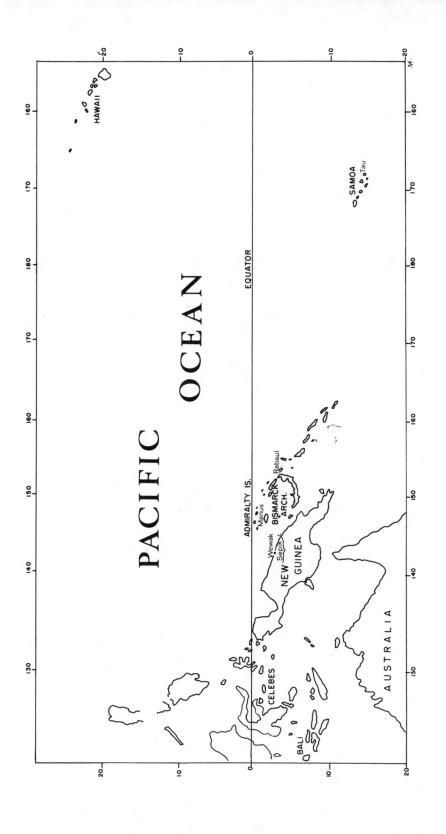

Introduction

These letters from the field are one record, a very personal record, of what it has meant to be a practicing anthropologist over the last fifty years.

Field work is only one aspect of any anthropologist's experience and the circumstances of field work—the particular circumstances of any one occasion—are never twice the same nor can they ever be alike for two fieldworkers. Yet field work—the unique, but also cumulative, experience of immersing oneself in the ongoing life of another people, suspending for the time both one's beliefs and disbeliefs, and of simultaneously attempting to understand mentally and physically this other version of reality—is crucial in the formation of every anthropologist and in the development of a body of anthropological theory. Field work has provided the living stuff out of which anthropology has developed as a science and which distinguishes this from all other sciences.

Field work is, of course, very ancient, in the sense that curious travelers, explorers and naturalists have gone far afield to find and bring home accounts of strange places, unfamiliar forms of plant and animal life and the ways of exotic peoples. Ancient records refer to the unusual behavior of strangers, and for thousands of years artists have attempted to capture some living aspects of the peoples and creatures evoked in travelers' tales or the sacred mythology of some distant, little-known people. A generation ago students still were given Greek and Latin texts through which they not only learned about high civilizations ancestral to our own but also gained a view of exotic peoples as they were described by Greeks and Romans in their own era. In fact, generation after

generation, philosophers and educators, historians and naturalists, polemicists and revolutionaries, as well as poets and artists
and storytellers, have drawn on the accounts of peoples who
seemed more idyllic or more savage or more complexly civilized
than themselves.

But only in this century have we attempted systematically to
explore and comprehend the nature of the relationship between
the observer and that which is observed, whether it is a star, a
microscopic particle, an ant hill, a learning animal, a physical experiment or some human group isolated for hundreds, perhaps
thousands, of years from the mainstream of the world's history as
we know it. Throughout my lifetime the implications of the inclusion of the observer within the circle of relevance have enormously
widened and deepened. Einstein lectured at Columbia University while I was an undergraduate at Barnard. I read Erwin
Schrödinger's *Science and the Human Temperament* when it appeared
in English in 1935. And of course I belong to the generation of
those who learned from Freud that observers of human behavior
must become aware of how they themselves have become persons
and respond to those whom they are observing or treating. This
kind of consciousness was systematized in psychoanalytic theory
and practice as transference and counter-transference; analysts,
attending intensively to the slightest change in the rhythm of their
analysands' speech or movement, learned to attend at the same
time to their own flow of imagery and to grasp the relationship
between the two.

As these insights became widely known and were incorporated
in scientific thought and practice, a counter-tendency also developed among certain scientists concerned with the study of human
behavior. Having discovered how deeply the observer is involved
in what is observed, they made new efforts to ensure objectivity
and to systematize methods of observation that would minimize
the effect of observer bias. Sophisticated statistical methods were
developed that effectively eliminate the individual observation as
well as the individual observer. Experiments were devised using
double-blind methods and observers were given formal check lists
on which to note, for example, the behavior of infants in such ways
that no hint of intuitive response would be preserved in the records that eventually saw the light of day.

In the natural sciences students were carefully trained to cast every experiment within a rigid framework that controlled the development of hypotheses, the use of methods of recording and analysis and the limits of the conclusions—a style of research recording that for a long time almost completely disguised the actual complexities of scientific advance under a mask of uniform orderliness. Following this precedent, social scientists elaborated the paraphernalia of objective social science. Their methods, identified as "science," were pitted against what were called "impressionistic" methods, in which the records of the human observer were presented without the sanitizing operations which appeared to remove the observer from the scene.

In this conflict between those who attempted to mechanize the intelligence and skills of the observer and those who tried to make the most of the idiosyncratic skills and intuitions of the observer, by enlarging and deepening the observer's self-awareness, anthropologists occupied a middle ground.

We were slowly devising ways in which our reports on the culture of a primitive people could be made objective in the sense that another fieldworker, comparably trained, might be expected to elicit the same order of data from members of the same culture. This was particularly the case in linguistics, since methods of standardized phonetic recording can be used to reproduce the regularities of an unwritten language in such a way that the data can be analyzed and used for comparative purposes by other linguists. In this work the sensitivities of the individual human ear are fully enlisted, both the ear of the native speaker of the language to whom the field linguist must present alternative sound sequences and the ear of the fieldworker who writes down the language. Today this can be supplemented by tape recordings of the process, which allow another listener to hear and compare.

With less initial precision—for language has the special advantage of being coded by speaker and listener in the same way—cultural anthropologists learned to record the kinship usages of a people by fitting the terms to the biological phenomena of reproduction, so that the terms for mother's brother, for example, or daughter's son can be as unequivocally specified as the method by which the outrigger of a canoe is lashed to the canoe can be described and diagramed.

Through the use of such techniques—and the training of students to use these techniques reliably and confidently—the ethnographic monograph came to contain a large body of ordered information which was reasonably independent of observer bias, whether that bias was owing to ethnocentricity, temperamental preferences, research interests or applied aims. Our methods of describing a ceremony or an economic exchange or the complex details of an agricultural process and of recording the texts of folktales and myths have become sufficiently formalized so that, if a large body of such diversified data is split in half, others trained in the same paradigms may be expected, by careful analysis, to arrive at comparable results.

But we were also developing a special approach to field work as a whole. That is, while we were learning how to apply the various formal techniques in the field—how to take down linguistic texts in phonetic script and how to learn a language and record it, how to trace socially contrived relationships through the ramifications of biologically derived relationships, how to relate a people's own color classifications to a color chart based on our contemporary understanding of the psycho-physiology of color perception and, especially, how to teach our informants how to teach us—we were also learning how to live in the field. This became known as "participant observation." It began as the observer moved from the mission compound or from the rocking chair on the porch of some inn or the office of a colonial administrator to the place where the people actually live.

However, this is only the beginning. Living in the village by night as well as by day and for long uninterrupted months, the field anthropologist witnesses thousands of small events which never would have become visible, let alone intelligible, at a greater distance. It is, in fact, a very peculiar situation, for while the anthropologist "participates" in everyday life he—or she—also observes that participation and both enters into genuinely meaningful and lasting relationships with individuals and learns from those relationships the nature of "relating" in that society.

It is sometimes assumed that participant observation means taking on a kind of protective coloring or even assuming a disguised or a fictitious role—an "as if" relationship to the people among whom one is living—as a way of observing them. Actually there is a kind of absurdity in this, as the fieldworker is always present notebook in hand, asking questions, trying to learn and to understand, and the field work becomes rich and rewarding to the extent that the people one is studying accept the legitimacy of one's work and at least some of them, in turn, begin to develop the second-level consciousness of self-awareness.

This new kind of field work, in which anthropologists live for an extended period in the midst of the people whose way of life they wish to understand, was just beginning when I entered anthropology. During the next decade it was developed, almost independently, in England by Bronislaw Malinowski and his students and in the United States by the students Franz Boas sent into the field to work on new kinds of problems in which an intimate understanding of many individual members of a primitive society was necessary. Our methods, which developed out of the conditions in which we worked, were grounded—as they still are—in certain fundamental theoretical assumptions about the psychic unity of mankind and the scientist's responsibility to respect all cultures, no matter how simple or how exotic, and to appreciate the worth of the people who are studied in order to increase our systematic understanding of the capacities and potentialities of Homo sapiens.

We knew that we had been bred in our culture and could never lose our own cultural identity; we could only learn about others through the recognition that their membership in their culture and our membership in ours, however different in substance, were alike in kind. But we did not yet recognize that every detail of reaching the field and of interchange with those who tried to bar or who facilitated our way to our field site were also part of our total field experience and so of our field work. This we have learned very slowly as we have learned to use our disciplined subjectivity in the course of a long field trip among isolated peoples distant in time and space from our own society. We have learned that every part of the field experience becomes part of our evolving consciousness—the impressions gained on the journey, our interchanges with government personnel at many levels, with missionaries and teachers and businessmen, the inaccurate as well as the accurate information accumulated from other travelers, the bright or the subdued light in which we first glimpse the villages where we intend to work, the letters that reach us, the books we read, the chills and fevers that accompany work in hot jungles or high, cold mountains.

When I started to write these letters, I had no sense that I was discussing the making of a method, that in making what I was doing intelligible to myself and to my family and friends I was recording steps in the development of a new kind of holistic approach. But I returned from my first field trip to Samoa to discuss the relationship between Samoans and the United States Navy not in terms of an ideologically defined separation of exploiting imperialists and an exploited people, but in the light of my own experience of the way both groups, through their perceptions of each other, were becoming part of a larger whole. However, it was only twenty-five years later—and only after the Manhattan Project had produced the atom bomb—that I realized the basic difference between such a project, which could be pursued in isolation from the rest of the society, and the applications of anthropological knowledge, which depend on the diffusion throughout the wider society of the particular findings about the capacities of our human nature and the constraints imposed by our shared common humanity.

From my own first field trip to Samoa participation has involved entering into many facets of the life of the people I have worked among—eating the food, learning to weave a mat or make a gesture of respect or prepare an offering or recite a charm as they had been taught to do, using the disciplined awareness of how I myself felt in the circumstances as one further way of coming to understand the people who were my teachers as well as the subjects of my study.

For the anthropologist living in the midst of a village, waking at cock crow or drum beat, staying up all night while the village revels or mourns, learning to listen for some slight change in the level of chatter or the cry of a child, field work becomes a twenty-four-hour activity. And everything that happens, from the surly refusal of a boatman to take one across the river to one's own dreams, becomes data once the event has been noted, written up, photographed or tape recorded.

As the inclusion of the observer within the observed scene becomes more intense, the observation becomes unique. So the experience of each fieldworker on each particular field trip differs from all other comparable experience. This, too, must be part of one's awareness. And the more delicate and precise the methods of recording—and I have lived through all the improvements from pencil and notebook and still photography to video tape—the more fully these unique experiences become usable parts of our scientific data. Equipped with instruments of precision and replication that were developed to meet the requirements of natural scientists for objectivity and replicable observations, human scientists are able to bring back from the field records of unique, subjectively informed experience which can be analyzed and later re-analyzed in the light of changing theory.

But the process of obtaining the information is very curious and exacting. Psychoanalysts, who must pay such intense and continuous attention to every slightest nuance in the communication process, at the end of the day can close the door of their consulting room, turn off their insightful attention and go out into the world to become, apparently, as unselfconsciously unaware as the least analyzed of their acquaintances. The field anthropologist cannot give the same kind of undivided attention to the full kaleidoscope of events, all of which together become the background experience which must be turned into data—the behavior of a woman with a fish to sell, the behavior of two children watching an old man who is preparing to tell a tale, the expression of a boy with a bleeding cut to be bound up. But field anthropologists never can turn off their attention. Visitors from outside this closed circle of attention are both a temptation and an interruption. Letters from home wrench one's thoughts and feelings inappropriately away.

Nevertheless, letters written and received in the field have a very special significance. Immersing oneself in life in the field is good, but one must be careful not to drown. One must somehow maintain the delicate balance between empathic participation and self-awareness, on which the whole research process depends. Letters can be a way of occasionally righting the balance as, for an hour or two, one relates oneself to people who are part of one's other world and tries to make a little more real for them this world which absorbs one, waking and sleeping.

Over the years I have come to realize that each generation of young anthropologists can only build on the present. They can't go back and they can't do it over again. They have to go on in a world that has changed, making observations and developing theory in ways that were not yet possible before their own teachers went to the field and that will no longer fully satisfy their own students when they, in turn, begin their field research. Books and monographs record the outcome of field experience. But we have very few records, written for others to read, of field work in process.

These letters constitute such a record. For from the very first letter, written when the whole adventure of my field work was still before me, to the most recent ones, which incorporate in some sense all my changing field work experience, they were designed to be read by a group of people, and a very diverse group at that, to whom for various reasons I wanted to remain explicable. When I wrote that first letter, in the summer of 1925, I was on the long sea voyage that was taking me by stages to Samoa, where my family and friends had never been and probably would never go. There was no way of knowing what lay ahead in the many months I would spend on those far Pacific islands, but I wanted them to share somehow in what happened so that, when I came home, they would know me better, not as a stranger but as myself.

I knew my parents would have no difficulty with the idea of field work. My mother, as a graduate student in sociology, had made a study of Italian immigrants and my father treated the troubles of small businesses, which his students in corporation finance brought to him for consultation, as so many short field trips into the real world. But neither my mother nor my father had ever been out of the United States or further west than Iowa. My grandmother had given me a sense of what natural science was about and had taught me botany, but she had no real feeling for studying strange and exotic peoples, who were stereotyped in some mental image of "the wild man of Borneo." And I think that in the beginning I saw my grandmother at the center of my audience—the one person whom I wanted most to understand what my work was about and the one it would be hardest to convince that I had chosen well in becoming an anthropologist.

My friends were a small close group. We were bound together by our interest in poetry and the theater and by the importance we gave to our personal relationships, our intense friendships, our love affairs and our struggles to relate ourselves to men and women in the next older generation who were close to us in mind but far removed in practice. What each of us was writing, who had fallen in love with whom, how we severally coped with miseries that kept us still together—these were our common preoccupations. There were also my student husband, Luther Cressman, who was traveling in Europe and who wrote to me describing paintings and places he especially liked, and my former college roommate, Louise Rosenblatt, who wrote to me from Grenoble, where she was preparing to write her thesis, *L'Idée de l'art pour l'art dans la littérature anglaise pendant la période Victorienne*. All these formed a second group. The third group included my parents-in-law, a country doctor and his musician wife, and my five brothers-in-law, whose interests then or later centered in the natural sciences.

Everyone for whom I was writing those field letters from Samoa was clear in my mind, as clear as if I were writing to each one alone. I could visualize how they looked, imagine what they were feeling and guess what their questions would have been had they been present. In fact, I hardly had to do so, for every six weeks while I was in Samoa a boat would bring the mail—a huge batch of seventy or eighty letters, which I would sit and stare at, spread out on my bed, bracing myself for whatever news they brought, whatever questions they raised.

Scattered through my earlier field letters are a handful written to individuals, people with whom I had a professional as well as a personal relationship—Franz Boaz, who was still my professor when I wrote to him from Samoa; Ruth Benedict, who had arranged for the summer field work on the Omaha reservation, about which I wrote to her; William Fielding Ogburn, whose student assistant I had been; and Clark Wissler, who was the chairman of my department at the American Museum of Natural History. I have included these few personal letters both for the sake of their content and because they touch on professional preoccupations.

Because I typed my letters, I could make several copies and I worked hard to make each letter intelligible to this varied, known and loved group of people. What I did not learn until I returned home from my first field trip late in 1926 was how many other people—relatives of relatives, members of my mother's little high-brow reading circle, neighbors, friends of friends and friends' lovers—read my letters or the copies typed by my mother, among others, to be passed on.

In this manner a style was set during my first field trip, in which I wrote for an intimate, identified audience that widened but without my willing it. As the years went by I adapted my writing to that knowledge by including as probable readers unknown others who were close to people who were close to me—an audience at one step removed from intimacy. This continued up to the war years.

After the war, when I returned to New Guinea in 1953, new methods of reproduction made it possible for me to have twenty-five or fifty or a hundred copies made at home to mail to an ever-widening circle. Then, as the group grew larger, the subject matter about which I wrote in my field letters became somewhat more formal. Later still, an occasional field letter was published or was used as the basis for an article or by a biographer writing for children. I myself published parts of several field letters in a chapter in *Women in the Field,* edited by Peggy Golde, a book designed to give women—and men, as well—some idea of what field work is like.

Through the years, as people who had read my first letters died and others came to take their place, field work became a commonplace among young anthropologists, who experienced hardships beside which my own discomforts and discomfitures appear trivial. And in these years the adventure of field work, of the attempt to enter deeply into another culture, became more rather than less exciting. Moreover, understanding of the relationship between what the anthropologist does in the field and the results of that research assumed new dimensions as books were published, books that appealed to a wide audience and in time became part of the undergraduate curriculum in many colleges—such books as Malinowski's *Argonauts of the Western Pacific,* Reo Fortune's *Sorcerers of Dobu,* Edward Sapir's *Language,* my *Coming of Age in Samoa,* Ruth Benedict's *Patterns of Culture* and Ruth Bunzel's *The Pueblo Potter.*

In the 1920s, when so few people knew anything at all about field work, it seemed to me necessary to describe in my letters each step in the process of groping my way into unknown territory. But writing from New Guinea on later field trips, I felt it was more important to document the series of accidents that determined the actual location of a field site. This was in response to an accusation anthropologists were beginning to encounter, namely, that we found what we were looking for. Those who had—and have—no sense of how highly and diversely cultures are patterned could not —and even today cannot—imagine how different one's research emphases would have been had the carriers or the canoe crew offloaded one's paraphernalia among another people only a few miles further on, but still almost as difficult to reach as the moon.

Although the number of those who read my field letters grew very considerably over time and the changing appreciation of anthropology among literate Americans led me to cast my preoccupations in a somewhat different mold, these letters still were addressed to readers who knew me—as I knew them—very well or at least to readers who were given the letters by someone who could describe the kind of person I am. Unlike a journal, they were never simply jottings for myself, which I then passed on to others. Nor were they the kind of self-conscious production in the form of a "private" diary which some writers construct for posterity—for an unknown audience of readers as yet unborn who, it is assumed, will be deeply interested in the agonies and ecstasies of creation.

In fact, I did keep a diary, complete but stripped of comment, as an index to events and records. This was an act of responsibility in case my field work was interrupted and someone else had to make sense of it. I also typed all my notes in the field so that they could be used by another person—and for this typing I came to use the best rag-content paper so that now, decades later, every page is intact. And I kept my private coding up to date just in case there might be a hurricane tonight or an earthquake tomorrow. My letters from the field were neither substitutes for proper field notes nor were they designed to orient some unfortunate successor who had undertaken to put my notes in order. They served another purpose.

Very rarely I have found a remark in a letter that somehow failed to get into my notes. The comment was then a useful supplement to the recorded state of my understanding of the culture at the date I wrote it. And once in a while in a letter I would describe some event with greater vividness—as I might later, writing a book —to convey the full sense of that particular occasion and at the same time to fix it in my mind.

But generally these letters were intended to convey to various people about whom I cared—in later years people with whom I had worked on committees, at conferences, on joint publications and in shared projects, as well as my family and old friends—what it was like on this trip, this year. Unlike an autobiography, in which one seeks to make oneself intelligible to an unknown audience, the letters were essentially a way of keeping up to date with the people who knew me best and with whom I liked to share some of my current preoccupations. Knowing this, the reader today may sense in these letters the kind of intimacy one usually experiences only in correspondence with one identified person, especially someone with whom the writer has had a long, complex relationship. Every word was measured for different people, each of whom was in some way close to me. The others, whom I did not know, remained accidental listeners at a conversation not expressly meant for them.

However, there were limits that I myself imposed. This collection might also be called "what I told my friends it was like to do field work." I did not tell them all of it by any means. There were fits of homesickness, the sudden conviction that a wrong choice of field site had been forced on us, tremendous difficulties both when I did and when I did not identify happily with the people I was studying, bitter arguments and sometimes, especially in the years before the war, frustration at being so far removed from events that were reshaping the world. Dashes in Ruth Benedict's diaries, published in *An Anthropologist at Work,* give some idea of the pictures she had in mind that developed out of the letters I wrote her from Samoa. But matters of this kind are best kept for letters to the one person who may be expected to understand and sympathize with some particular heartache. It would have made no more sense to broadcast one's miseries than to have cast messages onto the waters of the wide Pacific, hoping for some uplifting return three or four months later. Nor would it have made sense to write in detail about the day-to-day intricacies of field work. Who else besides a handful of fieldworkers who shared ways of thinking about theory and method and the exigencies of field work would respond helpfully? Most emphatically, these letters do not present a whole, complete picture of what a fieldworker feels, even about field work. It is certainly not a picture that has been touched up with brighter colors. But there are omissions related to the fact that what I wrote about was selected for those who were concerned and interested, but not desperately concerned or deeply professionally involved.

Field work is today part of our everyday life in many forms. Visual records of births and deaths and open-heart surgery are displayed for a general audience on the television screen, arguments take place in Congress as to whether pupils in the fifth grade should be exposed to a documentary film in which they can see Eskimo children watching a seal being butchered, and in many settings hot discussions focus on the question of whether anyone should be allowed to take notes about other persons to which those others will not have full access. We see in photographs and on television coronations and funerals, political celebrations and public hangings, natural disasters and battles while they are going on, conveyed to us by satellite, and we have somehow to reconcile in our minds our own beliefs and preferences, whatever knowledge we may have and the images presented to us by the persons controlling the camera's eye and the microphone.

Only during World War II did we begin to learn that anyone, anywhere in the world, might be listening. And from that time on the anthropologist had to assume a new responsibility to speak—and of course write—about every people in the world, however remote, in ways that they, their friends and their descendants would find bearable and intelligible.

But such an expectation of openness to the world did not exist before the war. Very few Americans had learned that mail could be opened by a government anxious to learn about one's political loyalties or activities. True, in Samoa, cables were subject to scrutiny by the Navy in the interests of intelligence and once I was commanded to put into "plain English" a message which I had phrased as "Reiteration."

For the most part anthropologists even then were careful in their books and articles and published reports to disguise identities and to protect those who might otherwise have come into conflict with officialdom over some colonialist government's regulations. But, in personal letters, the respect or the irritation, the affection or the plain-spoken dislike that shines through was private to the extent that it was not designed for, and seemed most unlikely ever to reach, the eyes of those about whom we were writing. This seemed to be equally true of the fieldworker's private diary, in which, having no one at all to talk to when he was angry or tired or depressed, he let himself go temporarily so that, the next morning, having faced his feelings, he was able to get on with his work in a reasonable frame of mind.

Fortunately, I never needed to keep such a diary. But there were other situations. I remember a photographer once asking: "Why don't you take some popular brand of soap along and photograph those people using it? You could bring the picture back and sell it. They'll never know!" It is true that they might not have then, but they would be very likely to today. Needless to say, this was not a kind of thing that appealed to me or to anthropologists in gen-

eral. But in the mid-1920s, even when I was writing a book, I did
not stop to consider, while I was disguising the names of the
Samoan girls whose love affairs I was discussing, how their grand-
sons fifty years later would feel about their grandmothers' behavior. Sometimes we were alerted by the comic, but almost invariably
denigrating cartoons in a magazine like *The New Yorker*. More often
we learned about misinterpretations and new kinds of resentment
from the hot political controversies of the war years and events in
the years that came after.

Nevertheless, in these letters, except when an individual might
somehow be harmed, I have let stand statements made in a way I
would not make them today. But my letters do reflect in various
ways the changing sensitivities of later years. And for good reasons
there may be no letters. In 1955, during my short return trip to Bali
with Ken Heyman, in the midst of the swirling uncertainties of
Dutch, Indonesian and Balinese politics, I wrote no letters at all
and did not even risk transcribing my notes until I returned home.

We live in a world today in which an apparent slip of the tongue
by a major political candidate and, equally, an imprudent remark
on an open postcard mailed home by a Peace Corps worker in a
Third World country can set off an international incident. In the
prewar years when most of these letters were written, the principal
hazard was that a lonely patrol officer might stop a police boy with
a mail bag, read one's correspondence and then forget to send it
on its way. But that was long ago. Now, in the face of the pride of
a very new country like Papua New Guinea, one must be prepared
to take full responsibility not only for all one says today but also
for everything one said—or is said to have said—in the past that
survives into the present.

I remember a sharp-tongued and very sophisticated old cousin
of my mother's commenting that she preferred the appendices to
the text of my books. "They really tell you something," she said.
And, if the circumstance that in these letters I could take myself
and my friends for granted proves to be difficult for some readers,
there are other forms of publication to which they can turn. There
is my autobiography, *Blackberry Winter*, in which I tried to describe
what there was about my upbringing that made it possible for me
to work with peoples who were, in those earlier days, very distant
from us in evolutionary time and with very young people today to
whom I have to try to speak clearly across the yawning generation

gap of the mid-1960s. Elsewhere I have published intellectual autobiographical statements. There are the books designed for general audiences and, in addition, monographs and specialist papers related to all the peoples among whom I have done field work, samples of notes, samples of the process of transforming notes into general statements and samples of a day's diary.

Because I think that field work—the intensive long months of trying to step as fully as one can into the reality of another culture —is a peculiar and tremendously exacting adventure, I have gathered together these letters from the field. I have not published all of them or, in some cases, the whole of long letters. In Samoa, my first field experience, where I was alone as a fieldworker, I wrote long and very full accounts in my field letters; only a fraction of them are included here. Where our working conditions were particularly difficult, as in Mundugumor, I did not write at length. And on almost every field trip, as the pace of work quickened and recording expanded with our growing knowledge, the gap between field letters grew. It is a pity that it is so, but it is also a realistic reflection of the field work situation.

These letters, then, are one record of the way modern anthropological field work evolved—a record, based on the experience of one fieldworker, of what goes into the making of a modern anthropologist and into the evolution of anthropological theory, which is both holistic and based on the analysis of the patterning of the finest detail. When the early letters were written, we did not even have a name for what we were doing, except the very general term "field work." The major shift came when anthropologists went to live in the community and shared, twenty-four hours a day, in the sights and sounds, the tastes and smells, the pace and rhythm of a reality in which every detail was not only different in itself but was differently organized as a perceptual scheme.

Only very slowly did we begin to take into account that we ourselves change with each step of the journey, with each new image presented to us in some casual comment and with each day in the field as we learned the language and as nonsense syllables and meaningless gestures resolved themselves into elaborate patterns of behavior. The development of intensive photography made it possible to record some of these changes in our ability to see and understand in the contrast between photographs and films made the first day and the last.

Visually, the illustrations may make a great difference to some readers. With one or two exceptions, I was never able to send photographs home from the field and so my family and friends, for whom the Pacific islands were far more strange and distant then than they have become now, had to create an image of their own with far less to go on. Other fieldworkers, reading between the lines, will know "what the jest is worth."

> *I have eaten your bread and salt,*
> *I have drunk your water and wine.*
> *The deaths ye died I have watched beside,*
> *And the lives ye led were mine.*
>
> *I have written the tale of our life*
> *For a sheltered people's mirth,*
> *In jesting guise—but ye are wise,*
> *And ye know what the jest is worth.*

By now almost all the older adults and a great many of the young people on whom I depended in the field have died. Fa'amotu, my Samoan "sister" in Vaitogi, died in San Diego in the spring of 1976. But I Madé Kaler, our gifted and indefatigable secretary during our whole time in Bali, who later became head of a school in Den Pasar, is still well and active.

After an interval of forty years, when I found my Arapesh villagers again, reassembled at Hoskins Bay in New Britain, where they were participating in the development of a modern oil palm enterprise, there were only two women who had known me as adults. The others, children when we were in Alitoa, knew of me only as a myth. But in my own memory, in photographs and in words, those I never saw again live on, transfixed in time. In the mind of one who studied them as children, they became more than friends, much more than babies who were dosed and nursed back to health. For even the small children were collaborators in an undertaking that transcended both me and them—the attempt to understand enough about culture so that all of us, equally members of humankind, can understand ourselves and take our future and the future of our descendants safely in our hands.

I.

SAMOA
1925–1926

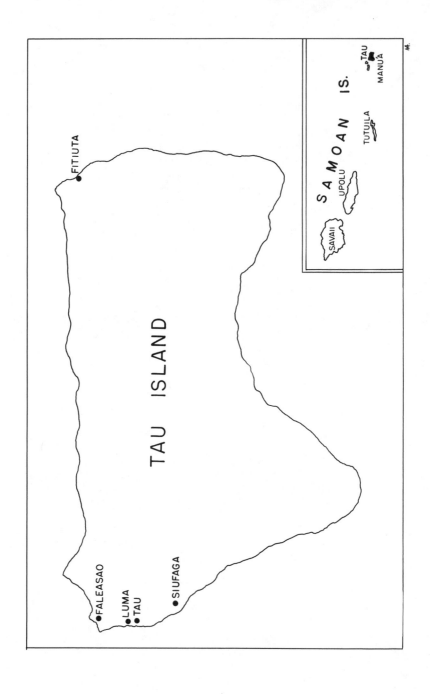

In the summer of 1925, when I said goodbye to my family and my student husband, Luther Cressman, at the B and O railroad station in Philadelphia and boarded a train that would take five days to reach San Francisco, I had all the courage of almost complete ignorance. I had read everything that had been written about the Pacific island peoples who had become known to the Western world through Captain Cook's voyages, and I was deeply interested in the processes of change. But I myself had never been abroad or on a ship, had never spoken a foreign language or stayed in a hotel by myself. In fact, I had never spent a day in my life alone. The Social Science Research Council had declined to give me a grant because I was too young. The National Research Council, which had awarded me a fellowship in the biological sciences, trusted me with no more than one month's stipend—$150—at a time.

Luther's traveling fellowship was taking him to Europe. Mine was taking me to Samoa to carry out the task given to me by my professor, Franz Boas—to investigate to what extent the storm and stress of adolescence in our kind of culture is biologically determined and to what extent it is modified by the culture within which adolescents are reared. I imagine that my age and physique—at 23 years old I was 5 feet 2½ inches tall and weighed 98 pounds—had something to do with his choice. I had wanted to do my initial field work in some much more remote and "untouched" place in the South Seas. But Samoa proved to be a most felicitous choice. From no other Polynesian culture would I have returned with results that challenged so completely the prevailing belief that adolescent turmoil is wholly biologically determined and therefore inevitable.

In Samoa I had the full cooperation of the medical branch of the United States Navy. My father-in-law, a physician, had been a medical school classmate of the Surgeon General of the United States; this made possible tutoring in the language, my residence in the household of Edward Holt, a pharmacist's mate, and the right to purchase supplies, which I needed as gifts, from the commissary.

The Samoans appreciated my seriousness and scholarship in such matters as learning about oratory and dancing, and during the few weeks in which I worked on formal ethnography we developed a productive interchange, in the course of which I learned a great deal about the intricacies of Samoan etiquette and my mentors profited by the many gifts courtesy required me to give. For the rest of the time, living as I did, I could work freely with children without any bother about status.

On my way home, in 1926, the ship on which I traveled from Pago Pago to Australia encountered one of the worst storms of the century, in which many ships were lost. From Sydney, I sailed for Marseilles on the maiden voyage of the S. S. *Chitral.* Reo Fortune, a young New Zealand psychologist, was a fellow passenger. His work on Freud's and Rivers' theories of dreams had won him a fellowship to study in England. We talked nonstop for six weeks, fitting all that each of us had learned into a new approach to the study of primitive peoples.

At the end of a summer in Europe I met Ruth Benedict at the meeting of the Congress of Americanists in Rome and came home to take up my new life at the American Museum of Natural History.

S.S. *Matsonia*
Last day at sea
August 10, 1925

The trip has been unfestive and uneventful, even the phosphorescence was chary of its company and only a few red-winged flying fish have danced for us. The ship's company is motley and disconnected—a few working people touring for a three weeks' vacation and anxious about volcanos, wives and children joining husbands and fathers, island people returning for the winter, large numbers of native children shouting over the deck, three Roman Catholic priests and one dissenting minister, a Salvation Army family which was seen off by all the Salvationists in San Francisco, a rather hefty Sadie Thompson seen off by all the U.S. Navy and other such unrelated voyagers. . . .

My table has been fun. At first I sat with the three priests and a pious and gay Catholic lady. The conversation turned mainly upon various minor ecclesiastical dispensations and her 21 Catholic first cousins in Washington, D.C., where one of the priests is professor of moral theology at Catholic University. I play bridge with them in the mornings and once I made a grand slam. Although far from proficient and finding it a great labor to keep my mind continually on the game, still I shall now face bridge without undue qualms.

The third night I moved from that table to sit with Eleanor Dillingham and her father, who is professor of chemistry at the University of Hawaii and a perfect lamb. Eleanor is plump and fourteen and enthusiastic. I dressed her for the masquerade as my mother, in Mother's white organdy which hasn't yet been shortened, my black hat made into a poke, Mr. Banks' flowing black tie and the Catholic lady's pink rose. She had never been to a masquerade before and was most properly excited. I went as her child in the bridesmaid dress, which *is* too short, socks, a borrowed doll, and a most fetching hair ribbon made from a pink handkerchief. . . .

Honolulu
August 11, 1925

We woke up this morning at five with land in sight and everyone excited except me. I was blue and disgruntled because I was blue. It seemed a poor fashion to be greeting the Paradise of the Pacific.

Eleanor Dillingham and I watched the ship come into harbor, rounding point after point of rugged clay-colored mountains. There was no color in the landscape, occasional patches of green showed as pale gray. The city itself was hardly resting on the sea, and the wandering mists, which seemed extensions of the clouds which covered the tops of the mountains, hid all the signs of industrial civilization. Two huge straight smokestacks became silver towers with white highlights on one side.

Reception of guests is entirely a matter of flowers, leis, necklaces of flowers strung variously so as to fall halfway to the waist.

Mrs. Frear met me, as did Professor Gregory, Director of the Museum, and Miss Jones, Secretary of the Museum. And I'm staying in Mrs. Frear's house, in a great gracious room with a bookcase filled with my favorite books, and wide lawns and pleasant distances. Mrs. Frear is away most of the time, up in the mountains, a 20-minute drive from the city, and another girl and I and the Japanese servants have this great house pretty much to ourselves. It's like being invited quite casually into heaven—for I'd expected first a hotel and then a furnished room, both unappetizing. So picture me for these next two weeks the most fortunate of mortals in charming surroundings with all my needs noiselessly supplied. . . .

I had lunch with Dr. Gregory and the Museum's official reporter. Then Dr. Gregory took Miss Winnie, whose family have lived here for four generations and who has done a lot of work on Polynesian music, and Dr. Shafer, an Austrian geologist, and me for a 40-mile drive across the island. The principle of this country is endless folds, folds of rock and folds of red soil, and perpendicular mountains that look like stiffly folded green velvet. The roads wind so that each turn holds infinite possibilities of green transparent rice fields, banana groves, sugarcane plantations or pineapple plots. I had my first lessons in Hawaiian botany and now I can locate the breadfruit, koa, kukui, mango, live oak, alligator pear, poinciana, noni and ti trees, so I feel as if I'd made a start. The island people's speech is full of native terms and so far I am holding my own, though I have to catch the word, keep it carefully and match pronunciation with rules and then remembered spellings. My head reels a little with the minutiae of Hawaiian botany, industry and geology which have been poured into my head. It is hard to give it significance without translating it into foreign terms or at least into analogies. It is like an elaborate jeweled costume standing quite alone waiting for the wearer to appear. . . .

S.S. *Sonoma*
5th day at sea
Nearing the Equator

It's no use, dear friends, I just can't write you a nice long descriptive letter on this ship, it rolls too much. To summarize: I had a lovely time in Honolulu, with a whole group of people to see me off and so many leis around my neck that I had to stagger up the gangplank. I got the structure of the language, met all the proper people and was loaded down with more letters of introduction and numerous presents ranging from the picture of a statue of Duke Kahanamoku, the Olympic Games hero, which I am taking as a gift to Tufele, the high chief of Manu'a, to a slip of a palm tree which I am taking to the captain of the *Lady Roberts*. . . .

Pago Pago, Tutuila, Samoa
August 31, 1925

We got in this morning at daybreak, a cloudy daybreak, with the sun appearing sullenly for only a moment and the surf showing white along the shores of the steep black cliffs as we entered the "only landlocked harbor in the South Seas." The harbor is the one-time crater of a volcano and the sides are almost perpendicular. It is densely wooded down to the sea and ringed with palm trees along the narrow beach. The Navy have really done nobly in preserving the native tone; their houses are low green-roofed affairs which cluster under the trees much as the native houses do; only the radio stations and one smokestack really damage the scene.

The presence of the fleet today skews the whole picture badly. There are numerous battleships in the harbor and on all sides of the island, mostly not in the harbor because they make the water oily and spoil the governor's bathing. Airplanes scream overhead; the band of some ship is constantly playing ragtime. All the natives on the island and many from Manu'a and Apia are here, laden with *kava* bowls, tapa, grass skirts, models of outrigger canoes, bead necklaces and baskets. They are spread out in the *malae*—market place—with whole families contentedly munching their lunches around them. I've already planned all my Christmas presents.

I met Mr. Walters, the head of the bank and incidentally the Controller of Customs, when I got off the boat and he brought me out to the hotel (THE hotel where *Rain* was staged) where I left my baggage and went back to the boat for breakfast. Then Miss Hodgson, the head of the native nurses' training school, who had come down to the boat to meet me, but missed me, had me up there for lunch, a large and festive lunch in honor of the nurses from the hospital ship. Surgeon General Stitt had the Superintendent of Nurses write Miss Hodgson asking her to help me. She's going to let me put my evening dresses in her dry closet, which is the greatest help of all; otherwise they rot or get rust stains from cockroach bites. . . .

September 2, 1925

. . . The ceremonies in the *malae*—market square—were depressing. Tufele, governor of Manu'a, Mauga, governor of Tutuila, and a visiting chief from Apia presided at the *talolo*—formal gift giving. They were gorgeous, in full regalia, high grass headdresses, elaborate grass skirts and naked above the waist with their bodies oiled till the skin glowed. The *malae* was crowded with sailors from the fleet, all the visiting natives and the people from the *Sierra*, which got in at noon and stayed till five. With the exception of the three chiefs and the natives who were dressed for the *siva* dance and a visiting chieftess, the daughter of Maletoa, the last king of Upolu, the other natives were in the nondescript dress which they all wear, the women barefoot and in light shapeless dresses (some wore overblouses fitted in under the breasts in a most ungainly fashion), the men in white cotton shirts and lava-lavas—cloth caught at the waist with a belt and falling a little below the knee—of various hideous striped American stuffs. And almost all carried black cotton umbrellas to make the scene finally ludicrous. I tried to get some pictures but I know they won't be any good; the brightest costumes melt into a background of endless umbrellas, and even the children carry them, so they graduate from very near the ground.

Tufele, orator's staff in hand, made a glorious speech, his retainers sitting behind him, under umbrellas, and presented a composite gift of coconuts, fine mats, strings of beads and pieces of tapa to the Admiral. The Admiral replied through an interpreter saying what a nice harbor this is, how nicely the Samoans were behaving, how much improved they were since his last visit, how he'd tell the President and the Secretary of the Navy what a good time he'd had and how, being specially fond of coconuts, he meant to eat all the coconuts himself. . . .

September 4, 1925

. . . Yesterday I began my lessons in Samoan. My teacher is one of the head native nurses. Her name is G. F. Pepe. She is of chiefly family and a cousin of Tufele's. She dictates to me in Samoan and then I try to give it back to her with correct pronunciation, phrasing and cadence. Her English is perfect and though she has no grammatical knowledge, she gives me just about what I need. And what is most excellent, thanks to the Surgeon General's letter that the nurses were to help me, her services are free. I have to pay $28 a week at this hotel so I haven't much money to spend on interpreters and this way I can afford to stay in the port till I get a good hold on the language. I have already learned about 200 words and quite a few phrases and I can take dictation almost without errors. (That isn't a great boast for the missionary orthography makes very few fine distinctions.)

I am now the sole occupant of this hotel and my meals are served in solitary state. I moved into a new room today; it's one with practically a four-sided exposure, opening on two sides with screen doors onto porches and having windows on the other two sides. I have Samoan mats on the floor, a bureau, table, armchair, washstand and bed. Louise Bogan sent me an *International Studio* containing some excellent prints and with these on the wall, books on the table and my green steamer rug on the bed, I feel very civilized. Making a room look livable in this hotel is no mean feat either. My cook-boy, Falavi, takes great pride in my progress in Samoan and gloats over my ability to say thank you and please. . . .

Tutuila, Samoa
September 27, 1925

If modern wanderers are to repeat the thrills which early travelers experienced, they will have to cultivate the much neglected senses of taste and smell. The movies and the phonograph have effectually eliminated the other two senses and touch doesn't seem to have much of a role here. But taste and smell are still untampered with by *Asia* and Pathé News. And here alone I get my real sense of being in a strange land. The morning I landed in

Honolulu, I had papaya for breakfast and Honolulu will always taste like papaya with Chinese oranges. Samoa tastes like papaya without Chinese oranges. There is a great difference here. Papaya and coconut oil and taro, that tasteless yet individual carbohydrate, serve for taste and the frangipani blossoms with their heavy oppressive odor for smell, mixed on the warm breeze with the odor of slightly fermented overripe bananas, an odor which is like bee-stung grapes.

. . . Last Thursday I went on my first *malaga*—journey—to my first feast, given by the girls' boarding school of the London Missionary Society. We were taken in cars, obligingly provided by the Naval Station, to Leone, two miles away, and walked the rest of the way. The feast was elaborate, neat and tedious. On a large terrace below the school building a square was enclosed by upright palm leaves. At the foot of this green lattice were spread green leaves containing the "covers"—a coconut, a piece of baked taro, a large piece of almost raw pork and some boiled bananas. At one end a narrow arbor was built, heavily freighted with strings of flowers. Under this the Americans sat and ate foreign food. Then there were endless speeches and the children sang and danced in their neat, ill-tailored white muslins which hit their knees at just the wrong place. . . .

October 11th

Yesterday I went out to Leone to call on Mrs. Wilson, a half-caste woman. The bus is a rattletrap affair and goes over fiendish roads. When it is packed with Samoans, baskets of food, ice, pigs and chickens in sacks and baskets, riding in it is a tiresome business. I had been told that Mrs. Wilson was married to a white man, that her mother, Mrs. Ripley, was very old and would probably be able to tell me a lot about old customs, that Mrs. Wilson spoke English well and lived in a big *papalagi*—foreign—house. And that was all. I was quite unprepared for what I found.

When I left the bus, I was greeted by a slim attractive half-caste boy, who said he was Mrs. Wilson's nephew and took my things with quite a gesture. Mrs. Wilson herself was a delight. A woman of about 35, the wife of an ex-Navy man who was a captain in the merchant marine during the war. She was educated in Honolulu and had two years of life at the Station as companion of a former governor's wife. Her knowledge of white standards is so exact, the precision with which she pigeonholes people as to birth and breeding is so acute that her social comment would be a delight anywhere. And still she is a Samoan by sympathy—"with European training," she always adds—and makes tapa and eats Samoan food and lives in a great patriarchal household with her much more native relatives.

Her mother, a full-blooded Samoan of noble birth who fled from the onerous duties of a *taupou*—a village girl who is given a high ceremonial title—is a tiny little old lady who kisses your hand and whose kiss assures you of benediction. We had luncheon *fa'a* Samoan in her mother's great Samoan house, a house larger than our house and two stories in height, partitioned by huge tapa curtains of gorgeous design. Her mother was the originator of colored tapas and makes her designs by quite conscious conventionalizations of Samoan fruits and flowers. Our luncheon was spread on banana leaves, around which we sat cross-legged and ate delicious roast chicken with our fingers.

Mrs. Wilson told me of comments that had been made about her when she lived in Michigan with her husband, how she had been called a "squaw," a "brown thing," etc. Her feelings are raw and bleeding under insults from white people and with shame for the commercialization which has overtaken her own people. Her three little three-quarter-white children are an almost impossible problem. They are very poor, despite the huge estate, because there is no man in the family to direct work on the copra plantation.

And with her perfect manners and acuteness of social sensitivity went terrific American slang, "Nix on that," and so on. It is distressing to see the good breeding of the Samoan obscured in the general difference of cultural level between the white man and the native, so that well-born Samoans marry uneducated enlisted men and Samoan women who would never err in using the right word for the meal of a chief, of a talking chief or of a common man, say "chow" for any meal in English. She is intelligent, an excellent interpreter and thoroughly conversant with Samoan custom. She can answer most of my questions herself and there is the safeguard of having her mother always there to confirm doubtful points.

October 13th
Steamer departure day

. . . For the next four or five weeks I shall probably be out of the port on this island. This will still be mainly practice in the use of the language and collecting some ethnological information for relaxation. Sometime in November I am going to Tau, one of the islands of the Manu'a group. There is a radio station on Tau and my cable address will be Tau (Samoa) and just Mead will be enough. I shall cable home when I go and don't try cabling me until you hear I'm there.

Tau is the only island with villages where there are enough adolescents, which are at the same time primitive enough and where I can live with Americans. I can eat native food, but I can't live on it for six months; it is too starchy. In Tau I will be living at the dispensary with the only white people on the island and right in the midst of the village. I can be in and out of the native homes from early in the morning until late at night and still have a bed to sleep on and wholesome food. The food will be much better than the hotel food because the Navy people have canteen privileges. Mrs. Holt is a sweet woman, was a school teacher, and I think I shall enjoy living with them. I shall probably not come back to Pago Pago until I am ready to leave next spring. It is really optimum in every way because I will have infinitely better care than I could possibly have in one of the remote villages on Tutuila.

Mrs. Holt has two babies—at least she has a two-year-old and the other one is to arrive next week. I am going back with her on the *Tanager*. She likes to read, so old novels and magazines will be doubly welcome on her account. Nobody need send me any clothes; I shan't need them. I'm going to leave all my good clothes with the nurses here on the Station. But imperishably packed foods will be acceptable.

From a letter to Franz Boas
Pago Pago, Tutuila, Samoa
October 11, 1925

I have now visited almost every village on this island. They are divided into two types, those which are along the bus line and those which are practically inaccessible except by difficult mountain trails or by water. The villages along the bus line have been very much influenced by American goods and American visitors and do not present a typical picture of the original culture. The villages off the bus line present two disadvantages: they are very difficult to reach and very small. No one of them boasts more than four or five adolescents, and so the difficulty of getting from one to the other makes them impossible places to work. To find enough adolescents I would have to spend my time climbing mountains or tossing about in the surf in an open boat, both extremely arduous and time-consuming activities. . . .

Because of these disadvantages I have decided to go to Tau, one of the three small islands in the Manu'a group about 100 miles from here. The Manu'a islands are included in the American Concession and a government steamer goes back and forth every three weeks. They are much more primitive and unspoiled than any other part of Samoa, being equalled in this respect only by part of Western Savai'i. There are no white people on the island except the Navy man in charge of the dispensary, his family, and two corpsmen. There is a large village, or rather a cluster of four villages there within a few minutes' walk of each other. The chief, Tufele, who is also district governor of Manu'a, was educated in Honolulu and speaks excellent English and is probably the most cooperative chief in American Samoa.

Furthermore, this is the only place where I can live in a white household and still be in the midst of these villages all the time. This is the point about which I am particularly anxious to have your advice. If I lived in a Samoan house with a Samoan family, I might conceivably get into a little more intimate touch with that particular family. But I feel that such advantage as might be reaped would be more than offset by the loss in efficiency due to the food and the nervewracking conditions of living with half a dozen people in the same room, in a house without walls, always sitting on the floor and sleeping in constant expectation of having a pig or a chicken thrust itself upon one's notice. This is not an easy climate to work in; I find my efficiency diminished about one-half as it is, and I believe it would be cut in two again if I had to live for weeks on end in a Samoan house. It is not possible to get a house of my own, which would of course be optimum. . . .

By the time I go to Tau I will have made a fairly comprehensive survey of the life of the Samoan girl, ceremonies and observances surrounding birth and marriage, her theoretical functioning in the community and the code of conduct which governs her activity. In the course of gathering this material I have of course collected a good deal of information of value ethnologically but not bearing with particular force on my problem. . . . Most of the observances which I am recording are still going on; my informants are of the chiefly class and well informed. How much checking should you consider it necessary and legitimate for me to do?

My knowledge of the language is progressing more slowly than at first. I take texts several hours a day, have one definite lesson and then prospect about for chances of conversation. For the next five or six weeks I hope to divide my time between a Samoan girls' boarding school where no English is spoken and a half-caste family in Leone where I can hear Samoan most of the time. These two places are only three miles apart. But I can't be sure about going to the school until the teacher returns from Australia next week.

I am quite well and standing the climate with commendable fortitude.

Tutuila, Samoa
October 31, 1925

First by way of news be it said that Mrs. Holt's baby is safely born, the new station gunboat has arrived and we shall go to Manu'a on the 9th of November.

. . . A half-caste acquaintance here had told me about taking some Americans out to a village which they had cried to leave. I was most thoroughly skeptical about the crying, but pared down to plausibility, it sounded a feasible place to live and I was determined to get away from the port and out in the bush where I would have to talk Samoan all the time. The village in question proved to be Vaitogi, the famous village of the Turtle and the Shark, which is one of the few things the Navy takes the trouble to go and look at. The village is about three miles from the bus line and about twelve miles from the station. Legend has it that an old woman and a child, neglected by their relatives in a time of famine, jumped into the sea and were transformed into a turtle and a shark. The children of the village stand out on a rocky bit of the coastline and

The "iron-bound coast," Vaitogi, where the turtle and the shark come up.

sing to the turtle and the shark, and sure enough, always one and sometimes both appear. I saw both the same day.

Vaitogi is on what is known as the "iron-bound coast," for it is edged with recently cooled lava against which the surf dashes sometimes 15 feet high, with frequent little caves and blowholes. There are no *papalagi*—foreign—houses in the village, which skirts the sea on a wide clearing sparsely dotted with coconut palms. Along the sea front stand five great *faleteles,* the round guest houses of the different chiefs. Above these the houses of the chiefs and the meaner dwellings of their various relatives are scattered inland on the gently rising ground. But this anticipates, for I had never seen Vaitogi, but I knew it by reputation. I went to collect a letter of introduction from the Secretary of Native Affairs and he told me that Ufuti, the county chief whose guest I was to be, was one of the most intelligent chiefs of the island. I was told that Ufuti's *taupou,* Fa'amotu, spoke a little English, and thus I set out.

I never spent a more peacefully happy and comfortable ten days in my life. Lina—Ufuti's niece—simply took me into the house and announced that I had come to stay for a week and went away and left me. Immediately, a great tapa curtain, some 12 by 20 feet, was stretched across one end of the oval house to make a room for me, and my bed and Fa'amotu's were made behind it. For my bed some twenty fine mats, mats which it takes a woman a year or more to make, mats from the Ellice Islands, the Gilberts, the Tokelaus, were spread upon the floor and then one blanket covered with a sheet for a mattress. Fa'amotu's bed was beside mine and one mosquito net was let down over us both at night and secured at the corners with smooth round stones. This kept out dogs and chickens and cats, all of which roamed over it in the daytime. There was a cupboard, made like an icebox with the feet set in cans of water, about two feet from my head. All the animals came to drink out of these cans.

When I arrived I presented Ufuti with cloth for a lavalava and his wife, Savai'i, with cloth for a dress and Fa'amotu with perfume. Ufuti is about forty, a slender, delicate-featured, very handsome man, keenly intelligent and surpassingly kind and gentle. He speaks no English at all nor does his wife. They have three children; the oldest, Alo, is a perfect little peacock of a boy who is studying for the ministry; then the *taupou* daughter and a 19-year-old son, Liu. Two younger cousins, Tulipa of nine and a little boy of five, and a sister of Ufuti completed the household. This sister's name is Pupa; stout, jolly, a little apologetic, she did most of the hardest work. The first night after we had gone to bed, I asked Fa'amotu whether Pupa was married. The softest, saddest voice in the world whispered, *"Ua uma"*—it is all ended—and added that her husband had gone to Upolu and never returned and that her three children were dead. And the kind consideration with which the children insisted on Pupa's dancing was sweet to see. These people and the little grandmother, who is the sister of old Mrs. Ripley in Leone (see my last letter) and a famous tapa maker, two girl cousins, numerous relatives of both sexes, a visiting chief, Fuimaono, and two *tulafales*—talking chiefs—Lolo and Ofoio, were my chief companions.

Lolo spoke no English and he took it upon himself to teach me to speak the chiefs' language and to act as a Samoan lady. Ufuti conferred upon me his *taupou* name, which makes me a member of the family and *taupou* of the village. When the other chiefs learned that I could talk politely, which means being master of three sets of nouns and verbs and using the proper terms of address to each rank, they all came to see if it was true. Solemnly they

In Vaitogi with Paulo, child of Ufuti's household.

addressed weighty questions to my royal highness and I answered each lord and duke as best I could, with Lolo watching for mistakes with a hawk eye.

The food was wonderful. Fa'amotu had been trained by Mrs. Wilson and anyway breadfruit was in season. They killed two young chickens a day for me and then there were mangoes and limes and papayas and a coarse woody pineapple, and Ufuti walked to Leone early Monday morning to get me tea and coffee and bread. Once a young member of the extended family caught an *i'a sa,* a fish sacred to the high chief, and he brought it to me as *taupou* of the village.

The chiefs were so tickled over my taking the trouble to learn their ways that they got up a *talolo*—ceremonial food offering—for me and had three *fiafias*—dances. I was most perfectly healthy, getting up at five, resting during the heat of the day, sleeping virtually out of doors, bathing in a lavalava knotted precariously beneath my armpits, beneath the village shower or in the high surf. Withal an idyllic existence. It didn't rain the whole ten days but once, which was a godsend, for the entrance of wet animals is bad. I got them a hanging lamp for a *tofa* gift—my goodbye present— and the whole family cried when I made my farewell speech. Because it may amuse you to see how I'm getting on linguistically, I'm going to quote the speech—in English. I wrote it in English and Liu translated it and then I learned it verbatim in half an hour:

"Your highness Ufuti and the noble wife and the whole household of the chief. Today is the day when we must separate. I wish

Lolo, visiting talking chief in Vaitogi, who taught me Samoan etiquette.

to express my thanks for your kindness and affection for me. I wish to add a few little words to make known my great happiness here. America excels in the making of machinery. France excels in the making of clothes. From Italy come the greatest singers. But the Samoan people excel the whole world in hospitality. I will remember these ten days when I lived in Vaitogi and the kindness of Ufuti and Savai'i and all the household of the chief to me when I am old and bent and wrinkled is my skin. . . . "

This waxes tiresome. There was about three times as much again. You have to make these speeches on every occasion, and it's no picnic. Can you imagine making them in a strange language in which the slip of an accent changes your meaning and all your Samoan extended family are proud of you and want you to show off well?

Comfortable and happy as I was, I could not live like that and do my problem, because I was too sheltered. As a *taupou* I could go nowhere alone nor could I enter the houses of common people. But it was like visiting at a royal court and excellent for getting practice in the language.

Letter to Franz Boas
Pago Pago, Tutuila, Samoa
November 3, 1925

This is just a note to report that I leave next Monday, November 9th, for Tau. Most of this steamer interval has been spent in a native village where I have had an opportunity to test my proficiency in the language and get a great deal of additional practice. I think I shall be able to manage.

Tau, Manu'a
November 14, 1925

As far as I know now I will be here the rest of my stay in Samoa. The whole location is ideal for my problem. Tau is an island 8 miles by 11 miles and 32 miles in circumference and 12 miles from the other two islands in the group, Ofu and Olesega, which rise sheer from the sea and look as if they were about a mile away. There are four villages on Tau: Fitiuta, 8 miles away at the other end of the island, and three villages right here, Luma (where I live) and Siufaga and Faleasao. The first two touch boundaries at the common church and Faleasao is about half a mile away over quite a steep trail. The dispensary is the only *papalagi* (foreign) house here. Even the church is built in Samoan fashion with the addition of whitewashed wooden walls. There is a store which charges exorbitant prices for bad food and that is all. There are between 900 and 1000 people in these villages which are right at my very doorstep.

Our little household here consists of Mr. and Mrs. Edward Holt, Arthur, who is two and gabbles Samoan and English with cheerful unpreciseness, the new baby, Moana, who cries quite a bit but is otherwise a blessedly inconspicuous addition to the household, and "Sparks," the radio man, a young sailor whose chief preoccupation is the fact that he had only a third-grade education. He spends his days fooling with new types of radio apparatus and reading radio magazines and only appears for breakfast and supper. Mr. Holt is a tall fair man—reminds me quite a little of Dick in his appearance—intelligent, goodhumored and efficient. He still does most of the cooking, and what time is not consumed by that and his clinic duties goes to disciplining Arthur, who is slated to have a strong character some day; . . . a most conspicuous presence. Then there is the present Samoan maid, Leauala. Arthur

A chief's meeting house on Tau, Manu'a.

shouts her name all day long; it serves variously as a call for help, a curse and a prayer. Her husband has deserted her, her baby is dead; she twists her hair into a negligent knot and makes faces behind the *fo ma'i*'s (doctor's) back. The washing is done by the wife of a chief, To'aga by name, who gathers any amount into a sheet and ambles over to Faleasao to beat each piece separately and destructively clean on the stone wall around the village shower. There is no water in this village except what we catch in the dispensary tank. There is a brackish spring which is uncovered at low tide and the natives have to depend on that for fresh water. However, they scarcely ever drink water, only an occasional coconut and *kava* for the nobility.

This whole island was devastated by a hurricane ten years ago and when the coconut palms were replanted, they were planted in rows, so a long stone-bordered sandy walk runs the length of these two villages with rows of palms on either side. The bush does not rise as steeply here as on Tutuila and as a result there is no sense of being boxed up beside a sullen sea, which is the way one feels on rainy days in Pago Pago when the clouds hang low over the harbor.

My room is half of the back porch of the dispensary quarters building. There is a loosely woven bamboo screen which divides my room from the porch outside the dispensary and here the Samoan children gather to peek through the holes and display their few English words or chatter endlessly in Samoan about Makelita's various belongings. It is really an excellent arrangement. At night I push back the curtain which divides my room off at the other end, put away the chairs, push back the tables and there is plenty of room for a small *sivasiva*—dance. The young people bring their guitars and ukeleles and dance for me. A few new ones come every night and it gives me an excellent opportunity gradually to learn their names. . . . The boys paint beards and mustaches of blue or red on their faces, tie ti leaves around their wrists, put an *ula*—necklace—or two on their oiled naked chests and dance endlessly. They never seem to tire of it and it is practically their only amusement. Out in Vaitogi they would hold a big *siva* in the chief's house, where a huge chest served as a sort of property box from which tapas and *siva* skirts were produced for visitors of rank, a bottle of coconut oil was kept handy and a whole assortment of *ulas* hung over a line in the center of the house. The performer retired outside to readjust his lavalava, and rub on some oil and returned to select a necklace. Although the dance itself is often an attractive and finished performance, usually heavily spiced with burlesque and uncouth cries, the beginning and end are strangely unfinished as the performer becomes overcome with embarrassment and retires suddenly with a scanty bow and a half-concealed agonized smirk.

Solomona, pastor and political boss of Faleasao, has presented me with one of his "good Christian girls" to be my girl. She appears on the scene every morning promptly at eight. As she speaks no English she is very good for me; at present I am extracting family histories and relationships of every household in Faleasao. She stays until about 11, when I sink exhausted on my couch and work is over until about 3.30. It's much hotter here than in Tutuila and it is practically out of the question to do anything in the middle of the day. We have lunch at 12 (the food by the way is excellent) and then a dead silence prevails for a couple of hours. Supper is at 5 and then very often I work ahead until midnight. A curious working schedule, but the only possible one. As you see, it leaves very little time for reading or writing letters. All those nice little extra hours go into a sort of drunken sleep.

This is Sunday so the schedule is varied a little. I was wakened at 6 by two maidens who insisted that it was time for church, which really starts at 7.30. After church, late breakfast, and it is now 12.30, zero hour for heat. At 1.30 my "good Christian girl," Felofiaina, will arrive to escort me to the afternoon service in Faleasao, an abominably hot walk, and Solomona warned me to start early because we would be so wet when we got there!

I am writing on the front porch. A whole procession of girls with wet lavalavas tied as sarongs under their armpits and pails of water slung on poles over their shoulders are returning from bathing in the sea. The costume problem is blessedly simplified here. I wear only a combination, a slip and a dress and Keds when I go out and walk barefoot in the house. Two little girls have just come in and two more, I see, are coming. Letter writing is over for now and conversation is in order.

Tau, Manu'a
December 11, 1925

. . . There is probably going to be a boat next week and then there will be none till after Christmas and perhaps till after the next up-mail. At any rate I have to act on that assumption. The mail which came last week I had waited five weeks for, and when it came we had only a couple of hours to do what answering we could, to unpack packages and repack Christmas presents for people on Tutuila, to search violently to see whether the bank had sent checks and the post office, stamps. (It had not.) And no food came on the boat at all. That is the reason we hope for another, for we've had no supplies for a month now. And it was the hottest day of the year and washday, so millions of flies.

Woman scraping mulberry bark to make tapa.

There is the most peculiar sensation one gets here from even a few hours in a native house, a different taste in the mouth, a sense of heavy, almost sticky heat, a feeling as if one's skin were going to fly off in thin gossamer layers and a curious buzzing inside one's head, mostly from the strain of listening. I don't know exactly what is responsible for it, possibly the food and sitting cross-legged and the flies.

The pleasantest time of day here is at sunset. Then accompanied by some 15 girls and little children I walk through the village to the end of Siufaga, where we stand on an iron-bound point and watch the waves splash us in the face while the sun goes down over the sea and at the same time behind the coconut-covered hills. Most of the adult population is going into the sea to bathe, clad in lavalavas with buckets for water borne along on shoulder poles. All the heads of families are seated in the *faletele* making *kava*. At one place a group of women are filling a small canoe with a solution of the native starch—arrowroot.

And perhaps, just as we reach the store, the curfew-angelus will stop us, a wooden bell that clangs mellowly through the village. The children must all scurry to cover—if we're near the store, it's the store steps—until the bell sounds again. Prayer is over. Sometimes we are all back safely in my room when the bell sounds, and then the Lord's Prayer must be said in English, while flowers are all taken out of their hair and the *siva* song stops in the middle. But once the bell sounds again, solemnity—never of a very reliable depth—is sloughed off, the flowers are replaced in the girls' hair and the *siva* song replaces the hymn and they begin to dance, by no means in a puritan fashion.

Their supper comes at eight and sometimes I have a breathing spell, but usually the supper hours don't jibe well enough for that. They dance for me a great deal. They love it and it is an excellent index to temperament as the dance is so individualistic and the audience thinks it is its business to keep up incessant comment. Between dances they look at my pictures—I am going to have to put Dr. Boas much higher on the wall, his picture fascinates them —and converse with one another about many and sundry things.

I've typed the end of this standing up at the sideboard for I was shooed out of the dispensary. Now breakfast is ready.

Tau, Manu'a
January 10, 1926

Christmas was hectic. All day Christmas Eve, while Sparks helped me tie up soap and combs, mirrors and hairpins—four "combies" and one "glassie"—in little red, green and blue packages secured with rubberbands, which are in great demand, the procession of gift givers came and went. In the front room Mr. and Mrs. Holt were also wrapping, wrapping, stopping to say, *"Lelei tele, fa'afetai"*—Very beautiful, thank you—and write down new names and wonder desperately where another gift was to come from. *Ulas,* shell and seed necklaces, are the Samoan Christmas cards; they differ from ours only in that a gift is expected in return. But each more ambitious gift was accompanied by an *ula,* and if the Holts were brought a present by someone I didn't know, I got an *ula.* They are fragile affairs, strung on weak insufficient string, easily broken and easily tangled. However, each half dozen reposed about my neck for a bit and then joined their sisters on the wire across the end of my room. They made a curtain of themselves and every visitor stopped to admire them. Christmas Eve the traffic grew fast and furious. The Ash Can Cats sent me a red paper wreath inscribed "Home is where you hang your halo," and I hung this against my screen with the electric candle Deb contributed beneath it. That was an excellent talking point to visitors for they all inquired about it. The table was piled high with tapas, *siva* skirts and fans, and each visitor wanted to know who had given me what till my head reeled. . . .

Christmas over, the Samoans began immediately to prepare for New Year's, a much more popular feast, known as the "year of eating." They sat on my floor and waxed absolutely lyrical over the noise that was to come. And the racket was deafening. Companies and companies of little boys with tin cans slung around their necks beating tattoos of deadly monotony in perfect time. I promenaded until about 2 A.M. It was a curious scene there at midnight on the edge of a fretting sea, raining a little, at times a sickly moon, the sand sticky and yielding under foot, tiny children escaped from home scurrying here and there, adults with blackened faces in strangely uncohesive groups that scattered when anyone approached, shrinking indecisively behind the bordering coconut palms. I had to skip, an unknown accomplishment in Samoa, to the tune of the deafening tin cans on that pulpy sand, and then of course there were hundreds of salutations, some respectful and some not, it being New Year's Eve. The cut of my dress betrayed my identity, even at midnight.

New Year's morning dawned wet and ominous. We took the

stormy portents as the special intervention of the Most High in our favor, for after church the whole of the three villages had planned to assemble and dance for food, and it takes quite a little food to feed three villages. Mr. Holt had set his jaw and announced that this year he would give them no food and rumor had it that they would dance until they got it. But as they scuttled by under umbrellas, their fringed tapa dresses and paper necklaces already drooping pathetically, it looked as if there would be no New Year celebration. I sat in the dispensary and wrote my report to the Research Council. After church I had visitors from Faleasao, for I had promised to sleep that night in Faleasao. Instead, I wrapped up tobacco and salmon and bully beef for Solomona and sent my regrets. So they put a wreath of orange seeds and pieces of blue Medical Department paper around my neck and left me. Leauala drifted in and out, the storm was getting worse and she began muttering about hurricanes, but I only half listened.

But the storm was getting too noisy for consecutive work. Pieces of tin banged on the roof and the palm over the engine shed lashed its tin roof in a perfect fury of chastisement. My room was being gradually flooded and I had to make periodic excursions to pile more things on top of other things. Finally Sparks and I went swimming, but the undertow was very bad and the air seemed almost a solid substance, it was so full of flying sand. I got my raincoat wet in that excursion, which was a bad move.

Then we had dinner and I made the hard sauce for the fruit cake while the Holts anxiously lit and relit the flames of the oil stove, which as promptly went out again. There was lots of butter which hadn't seen ice for weeks and it made marvelous sauce. I made more sauce than there was cake and was completely absorbed in the enormous and satisfying extravagance of that proceeding. Dinner was at four o'clock. It was a little noisy for conversation, the roof leaked in half a dozen places and the rain came in in two. But still, no one really got excited, except Leauala, who had a child over the hill in Faleasao. In the last storm Faleasao had been hit worse and the county chief came all the way over to tell Mr. Holt that the people were very much frightened; the wind was rising and what should he do? The storm must have risen all through dinner, but we, absorbed in the unprecedented hard sauce, had not noticed.

After dinner we all went out on the front porch and then Mr.

Holt began to chew three matches, a sign that he was worried. The wind was coming from behind us, where a huge hill broke its force. Even so, the Samoan hospital, just a Samoan house where the week before we had our Christmas tree, began to reel unsteadily and finally collapsed entirely. A minute later the schoolhouses and the singing house went down. The church at the other end of the village had already gone, kneeling down very decorously in a long thatched line. But these were all just a little further to seaward than we were. If the wind didn't change—

And then came the calm. It only lasted about a minute, but the air seemed choked full of coconut leaves so stiff they might have been wired. Even the sand was suspended in the embrace of that calm. And then the other edge of the storm, charging straight over the sea from Ofu, hit us, tearing that little calm into a thousand pieces. After that it was just a question of how long before the house went. The two-months-old baby was the main point. One would be safe enough out in the open spaces between the houses. But it was pouring rain and the air was full of flying sand, coconuts, parts of tin roofs, and so on.

Wiezorek, the Polish sanitary inspector, was scared blue and moved out into the backyard where he could intensify his fright by watching large pieces of roof coming towards him. Sparks made momentous excursions up to the Soatoa'a to look at the barometer and communicated the results in low, portentous tones to Mr. Holt. I got out flashlights, candles, matches, wool socks and sweaters for Arthur, coats for Mrs. Holt and me, and amused Arthur. We had all retired to the diningroom by now. The porch was off and all the front doors down. The electric candle was the only thing it was safe to have as a light. Mr. Holt had dramatically slipped Sparks a hatchet and carried out a bottle of alcohol to sustain Wiezorek. The back screen door was fastened open with obvious implications. And so we sat, four square, occasionally adding an extra piece of wool to Arthur or putting a can opener in the tobacco can. The presence of the baby made us take the thing seriously. Outside in the howling, wet darkness Sparks and Wiezorek hacked their way into the cement water tank, a 4-by-5-foot affair, and let the water out.

Then came the announcement that we were all to be put into the tank, and I was to go first and receive the baby. Mr. Holt gave me its bathtub to receive it in. The tank had a tin roof now bent back in a half circle. Up the side and over the edge I climbed and down into several inches of water, pitch darkness and very little idea of my bearings. The tank is out in a corner of the backyard, back of the bathroom. I'd never even looked at it before and had no idea of its size. However, they had stuck in a couple of boxes and I balanced the bathtub on one. Then from Mr. Holt, "Here comes the baby and she's upside down," and a large blanketed bundle was thrust into my arms. I stuck it in the tub, other side up and made a frantic search for the baby's head. She was too big for the tub, so I held one hand under her neck. Then, "Here comes Arthur," and in the pitch dark arrived Arthur to be stood on an overturned dishpan and supported with my other hand. That was the only moment of the hurricane I minded, while I had those two babies and no light in the bottom of a tank with the rain pouring in. Afterwards arrived Mrs. Holt and Sparks with a flashlight and Wiezorek with his bottle, and Mr. Holt kept appearing over the top to hand in another box, dry clothes for the men, a whole roasted chicken which some Samoan had sent us, a loaf of bread and so forth. Finally we were all in, the baby in the bathtub under the only dry spot, a box in the center for our feet. Mrs. Holt held Arthur, I held the chicken, a fat red candle, extra batteries and the electric candle, a loaf of bread and a large basin to catch some of the rain water from the roof of the tank. Wiezorek kept apologizing for drinking, but "Gosh, I'd be sick if I didn't—"

When the wind went down, part of our side of the house was quite whole and we crawled in between wet blankets and slept a little, while all night—or rather morning—Samoans crept in to ask us how we were and commiserate with us. Only five houses stood in Luma.

This morning we walked abroad to view the ruins and the people stopped long enough in the desperate work of salvaging their belongings to offer us a ceremonial food gift. Now the whole village is building and weaving furiously, although the woman I visited this morning, having a house over her head, was weaving very difficult fans. At present it rather interferes with my work, but later it will help for there will be no copra to cut and consequently more leisure. They have just put a new roof on my room and also I have a swimming and a fishing date.

Tau, Manu'a
January 16, 1926

My stay in Samoa is more than half over.

These last two weeks, since the hurricane of blessed memory, have been devoted to the ethnology of activity. The whole village is busy building itself new houses or weaving itself new walls and floors, according to the sex of the workers. Informants are not to be had for love or money, so I wander about, sometimes engaging in useful activity and sometimes merely sitting on the floor and looking on, taking notes on where the woman puts her foot when she weaves a fan, and so on. Also I help sweep the village up. Doesn't that sound well, like sweeping cobwebs out of the sky? You take a marvelous broom (the *papalagis* call them "witches' brooms" and they are worthy of the name) with a handle five feet long of bamboo and a bristly end of the spiky ribs of coconut leaves. Each prong of the broom is a different length and it works like a charm. You sweep the floor of a house, composed of small coral stones, or the half-grassy, half-stony yard and all the rubbish comes away and never a stone or blade of grass.

Last Wednesday I went fishing on the reef by torchlight. It would be worth looking at if nothing happened at all. The edge of the reef, a white line far away, the whole curving shore dotted by torches, the reef itself an amazing world of strange shapes and different densities of darkness. And in addition there are crabs to be had for the grasping and little fish to be cut in two with a swift stroke of a knife and great puckering things like pincushions—all to be jumbled in a basket. I carried the basket. Dotting the reef were the *vannas*, giant spiky black balls, sometimes with a band of white near the ends of the spikes. And flat rubbery creatures lying everywhere and brown pudgy worms plastered to the stones. The fishing is all very inefficient and festive. Some have knives and some have not, so when a fish is seen there is much hallooing and the fish, tiny creatures about four inches long, are usually half a mile away before the boy-with-a-knife arrives. It is likewise with the basket. Crabs must be dashed about to silence their struggling and fish have their heads bitten off with great dispatch. Then there is the boy-with-the-torches. These are pieces of dried bark about three feet long, a bunch of which are used together. The boy-with-the-torches is very stingy with them; he holds his bunch tight and

Wearing a dress woven by Makelita, last queen of Manu'a.

you have to pull hard. The sparks from your torch fall on the water with a gentle hiss. You have quite forgotten which way is towards the land, but the roar of the reef warns you back towards the shore if you wander too far. . . .

The two big boys I went fishing with are my chief male stand-bys. They are bosom friends, named respectively, Falepogisa, House-of-midnight-darkness, and Vimotu, Broken-vi-tree. Fale is of a chief's family, Vimotu of a talking chief's, and the relative rank is duplicated between them. Vimotu it is who must propose for Fale should Fale decide to wed, and when Fale makes me a fan, Vimotu braids the sennit and receives in return from Fale a can of salmon, the perquisite of the *tulafale*. It is curious to see these two and half a dozen other boys, clad only in lavalavas, with hibiscus behind their ears or a graceful fillet of leaves on their hair, sitting on the floor of my room, tremendously at ease amid its various sophistications. The Santa Claus which is weighted at the bottom so that it always stands upright is their favorite plaything or they musingly turn over the pages of a *Dial* or a *Mercury* with an air of detached tolerance. But when one of them discovered a letter of Louise Bogan's about the style of Henry James, all neatly typewritten and legible, he admitted himself stumped. . . .

Thursday I went swimming with the younger children. The only good swimming place is about two miles away, where a stream of fresh water flows from underground into the sea. There is a long walk under arching coconut palms, through which you run very fast because a coconut might fall on your head. The children like best what they call their "jumping hole," a hole some twelve feet in circumference with steep slippery sides of lava into which the sea washes through a narrow aperture changing the level about ten feet with every wave. The braver ones of nine years old and older stay in all the time, bouncing about like corks, being alternately washed almost to the top or sucked down into the vortex. Younger ones jump into their sisters' arms, are held for a wave or two and are flung on the rocks when the water rises again. Even two-year-olds are hurled in. Afterwards you bathe in the fresh water pool, with half a dozen handmaids to pour cool fresh water over you from coconut shells and wash your clothes, fetch your shoes and dry your hair. It's altogether too elaborate an affair to attempt often but it's great sport. I find I am happiest here when I am alone with the natives, either bathing or lying on the floor of a Samoan house watching the sea or making long flowery speeches to some old chief. . . .

Gradually I am becoming part of the community. Have I not three dark spots on a white dress, spots come from the blood of the pig which was sacrificed for the birth feast of the tenth child of Mealeaga? Have I not woven *polas* for the great guest house of Siufaga and argued with the members of the *Aumaga*—the young men—on the advisability of burning down what is left of Ofu, because the people of Ofu stoned the meddlesome pastor of Tau out of the village? And has not Talala, Tufele's royal mother, the only woman *matai*—chief—in all Samoa, put her arm lovingly on my shoulder, and Pal made me a dress from material stamped on her hoarded tapa pattern-board? And does not everyone else know these things and many others? And already wherever I go they say: "God love you, you are going away!"

And now I am caught in the toils of high rank again. I suppose

I should give most hearty thanks to have escaped it for two months. Vaitogi taught me just how inconvenient it is to have rank and when I came over here I purposely deprecated my *taupou*-ship in Vaitogi so I could be plain Makelita and wander at random over the village. I emphasized the fact that Mr. Holt was the chief of our little *papalagi* household and that I had to obey him, and then any whims of mine could be conveniently attributed to his orders. It wasn't as much fun in some ways, but it was far more practicable and a less expensive procedure.

But now, alas, it is all over. A *malaga*—a ceremonial visiting party—has arrived from Upolu, the mother of Tufele, a chief in her own rank, the only woman chief in all the islands at present. She has come for the imminent arrival of Tufele's first-born son. With her she has brought her talking chiefs, male and female (talking chiefs all ought to be nosy old women), her *taupou* and several ladies of her age. A *malaga* in Samoa is of first importance. This one occupies the great guest house of Siufaga and all the men go to pay tribute. Talala possesses the double advantage of having been the wife of the last Tufele, who was an outstanding character in Manu'a, and of being the mother of the present one and, in addition, has all the prerogatives of a visiting chief of high rank.

So as is right and proper I go to visit her, bearing a gift of four

Tufele's mother, Talala, a visiting high chief from Western Samoa, with her two female talking chiefs.

yards of old-rose calico, and I tell her with all the courtesy phrases I have not used since Vaitogi why I have come to Samoa. And, being pleased and flattered, what must she do but make me a *taupou,* her *taupou,* of the village of Mulivaesafalo in the district of Tuamasagasafata. My *taupou* name is very nice, Fuailelagi, Flower-in-the-heavens, and the name of my cup in the *kava* ceremony is O Fa'avivi-a-poa-vivi, etc. And then I must make a feint at dancing, with a *tulafale*—talking chief—on either side, and then Talala presents the talking chief with a piece of tapa. And there's the rub. Whenever a festival is made in the house where there is a *taupou,* the chief must give a gift to the *tulafale* and of course I must now provide the gifts.

Today at high noon, an honor reserved for half a dozen high chiefs, but of doubtful value as it's much cooler at night, they made the *kava* to celebrate my installation, *and* I gave gifts to each and every one of them. Each beneficiary went outside the house and shouted long ceremonial phrases to celebrate my generosity.

The intricacies of the gift reciprocity in Samoa are graceful but bewildering. The chief pays the *tulafale,* who in return renders all manner of ceremonial and personal service. Then I—as *taupou*—bring gifts for all the retainers of the visiting chief. These they give to the talking chief of their host and the family of their host, Tufele. Then they present me with a lusty meal including a whole chicken, and knowing that I probably will not want to eat it, they tactfully suggest that they send it as an *alofa* from me to my *matai* and to our visitor, Chaplain Edel. So that food gets down to the Holts' house by these devious means.

It's all very elaborate and time consuming, and my chief gain will be a traveling party when I want to go to Fitiuta and most splendid entertainment in Fitiuta, Tufele's home village. As my main reason for going to Fitiuta is ethnological and not to capture adolescents, this is all to the good. Fitiuta is the stronghold of original custom and also a very polite place. When I go there I am to receive another *taupou* name. It is very wearing.

Tau, Manu'a
February 9, 1926

There is no mail except a few things that went to Apia by mistake. Mrs. Holt got her first letter from her family since September; the letter had been to Australia and Apia. My wandering mail consisted of tickets to a lecture on January 14th at the Museum and such like ironies.

My room is very dressed up, as I've received so many flowers today that I got tired of hunting vases. So Papa Franz's picture is wearing a huge red hibiscus and Pelham blooms between two cerise ones at a fairly unclashing distance. On my bed is a beautiful new mat which my *tulafale* has just woven for me. It's a very nice mat edged with black and old-rose wool by my prescription, but she says that for the next mat she is going to choose the colors. And she came at daybreak to bring it.

Ethnological methods in the South Seas are most curious. Perhaps it isn't fair to say "ethnological methods," for if I were doing straight ethnology I wouldn't have to be quite so sociable or quite so circumspect. But for this particular type of problem one can't rely on a few informants or on paid informants. Furthermore, when I do use real informants and sit down and ask questions by the hour, I can't pay them, for they are too haughty. Instead I have to give gifts. And there's a limit to that because they have to give a return gift in addition to the information. So gift-giving becomes a subtle way of impoverishing someone—especially me. So my noble and commoner informants all prefer endless little favors.

In the last two weeks I have given away, separately, some 100 envelopes and 200 sheets of paper, dozens of cigarettes, boxes of matches, onions in threes, needles, thread, ink, loaned pencils, carbon paper to trace embroidery designs, scissors. It's endless. Perhaps a dozen people come within 15 minutes. And this is quite aside from the children who bring shells or flowers and must be given candy or crackers. These are the material things. But then there are a multitude of commissions. Solomona has lost his wife's wedding ring; will I send to Honolulu for a new one? Fa'amotu wants a bathing suit, Fale a fountain pen from the commissary store; Fa'apua'a writes me from Fitiuta for powder and soap. Someone else—everyone else—wants pictures taken and pictures of all their relatives. Fale wants me to type a love song he has written to his sweetheart; Vimotu wants me to write a long sanctimonious letter of repentance to the head of his pre-ministerial school from which he was expelled; Lilia wants the address on her letter to her daughter typed, as does Leauala, and Leauala wants a bobbin for her sewing machine of prehistoric model. She will bring me a chicken for it, and what do I want with a chicken? Lole and Avea, being married, have now become church members. They must have hats and the mats at the store are very expensive. Will I order hats for them from Tutuila, and they will weave me beautiful mats in return. And to crown it all, Felofiaina and Fa'apua'a turned up last Monday with a request I go over to Faleasao in the bright morning sun on the hottest day we've ever had and take a picture of a corpse. . . .

Yesterday it poured and I had a couple of hours when no children came. I spent it taking stock. And that resulted in a feeling of intense relief, for if anything should happen to my work now I'd still have a sizable amount of material to show for these months. Which relieves my mind immensely. For it seemed such a gamble to put a long trip and all the time it took to learn the language into a doubtful venture which might have been hopelessly cut short by illness or hurricane or what not. And when I add to this the assurance which everyone gives me that the last few weeks are always the most fruitful, then truly I have cause for rejoicing.

We had a lovely instance of professional pride the other night. There was a new baby and one of the nurses got Mr. Holt to come over and look at it. When he entered the house the old Samoan midwife, who is by the way the high chief's sister, turned her back on him and sat in haughty, offended withdrawal until he left. . . .

Tau, Manu'a
March 7, 1926

Ever since I have come to Tau I have known that sooner or later I would have to make the trip to Fitiuta, the little village of some 350 inhabitants at the other end of this island. Many of the natives from the villages here have never been there. The sanitary inspectors and other government officials who have to make the trip dread it articulately for a week before and come back to be nursed and sympathized with for a week afterwards. It's supposed to be one of the two worst trails in Samoa. But going by boat would mean even more hours in the boiling sun and two bad channels over the reef. So I procrastinated. And then Tufele's mother proposed a *malaga*, which was too good a chance to miss. Dr. Cook,

Mr. Judd and a young shell collector from the Bishop Museum were here for a week collecting land shells and Tufele invited them to join the party. It is an awful trail, miles of mud to your knees. I take these coast trails in a sort of semi-delirium, apparently bending all my attention to where I am to put my next foot, while my mind twists and repeats and rearranges two or three simple sentences the way it does when one has a high fever. But I arrived with only a headache.

The village itself is charming. A high stone road, grown over by grass and moss, runs the length of the village. The houses are set along this road so that to the left one must climb down stiles to the level of the land and to the right one must climb up even higher. The houses are built on double stone platforms on the steeper side, the circle of the outer terrace sweeping imperceptibly into the level of the hillside.

In Fitiuta as nowhere else in American Samoa is the flavor of native courtesy preserved. The first three days were consumed by ceremonies. The *malaga* must present its great ceremonial *kava* root and the *kava* must be drunk in the guest house. Then all the high chiefs of the village must come and drink it over again, this time from their *kava* root. And many speeches must be made over each root, and after I had drunk chief after chief would call out with flowery additions, "Bring me the cup of Fuailelagi." Then the case of salmon I had brought was presented to the village and the youths of the village brought us our ceremonial food offerings—platters and baskets of coconut leaves piled high with chickens and fish, land crabs, octopus, pieces of pork and pieces of breadfruit and taro, all smoking hot from the oven. . . .

At night the same procedure was repeated, except that I had to dance in native dress and then presents had to be distributed, as they must be whenever the *taupou* dances—great pieces of tapa and soap and tobacco. After the chiefs left, the *Aumaga*, the young men of the village, came and I had to go and sit among them at the end of the house, flirt and banter and play *Sweepy* (Casino) to the tune of several ukeleles while at the other end of the house the girls of the household made up the beds and hung the mosquito nets. . . .

The second day all the ladies of the village—the wives of chiefs and talking chiefs—came to do us homage. Dressed in their gayest

garments with necklaces and wreaths of flowers, they sat in state
around the circular guest house at the posts at which their husbands had the right to sit, and we had another *kava* ceremony.
Only this one was a much gayer affair. After the talking chief who
sits beside the *kava* bowl had called out, "Bring me the cup of
(naming a chiefly title)" and had properly named the recipient,
someone else called out, "Stop her!" and the girl who was passing
the *kava* would stand, her arms raised, by the center post. Then
the recipient would have to sing or recite a poem or dance. Usually
she attempted to recite a poem, but whether it was correct or not,
the others would pound with their knuckles on the mats, crying,
"Mistake, mistake!" and the unfortunate one had to dance as pen-
alty. The unmarried girls and wives of untitled men, who had been
doing the serving and were sitting modestly outside, were got in
to provide a chorus for the dancing. First danced the *taupou* of the
malaga; last danced the *taupou* of the guest house. And for each
dance many presents had to be given. It was a very dignified and
festive proceeding and any woman in the group could give cards
in spades to any of our club women. Without hesitation or embarrassment they threaded their sedate way through all the baffling
intricacy of the ceremonial language. And this is the more amazing
because the principal speakers were chosen not for their speaking
ability but because they were the wives of talking chiefs of a certain
rank. Their husbands had been selected to become talking chiefs
with prayer and meditation from among all the available young
men in a large family connection to hold a title which demanded
the eloquence of Demosthenes. But the wives had been trained
after marriage. And the young girls sat outside and listened.

    This Samoan scheme of organizing both young girls and young
men into groups with definite ceremonial connection to the adult
life is an educational masterpiece. Among themselves the *Aumaga,*
officially convened, treat each other with grave ceremonious good
manners, and should a chief be in the guest house when the
Aumaga come to pay court to the *taupou,* he also says, "Most honor-
ably be welcomed, o ye sons of chiefs and sons of talking chiefs,
the *Aumaga* of this our village." So there is no abrupt transition
from the little girl who bobs awkwardly to the young lady who is
expected to be at the center of the ballroom or from the boy to the
man—as in our society. And when the *Aumaga* come to call, each

one brings a small food gift, one of the "made dishes" in a little square basket lined with a banana leaf, and all rank is again observed, with the *manaia* (the male counterpart of the *taupou*) sitting in front and dancing last as a great honor.

All this ceremonial took up a great deal of time but it was well worth it for the firsthand knowledge it gave me of the workings of a *malaga* and because it gave me position and popularity, so that I could get informants, high chiefs, whom I could not have bought. But now Pomele, huge, indolent and unbelievably wise, with his close-cropped black hair just white at the tips, so that his lion's head looked as if it had been touched by a September frost, would sit and talk to me by the hour, immensely proud of the speed with which he understood my peculiar questions and the amount of detail with which he could answer them. Or else some half a dozen chiefs, after the day's work was done, would gather in the guest house and we would discuss judicial procedures as of old. In almost all cases a group of informants is better than one here in Samoa, especially when you understand the language and can follow the arguments closely. And Pomele would lean back and wait until as many people as possible had assured me that there was no taboo peculiar to Fitiuta, and then he would say in his soft, strangely powerful voice, *"E i ai se tasi"*—There is one.

I only tried an interpreter once and that was to use the native nurse, Mele, with an old midwife. But the old midwife stayed behind to tell me some stories she wouldn't tell Mele because she came from another village. So I gave up attempting interpreters and worked on everything from religion to medicines without them. There is no real esoteric knowledge here except recipes for medicines and charms, but the Samoans like to think there is. So all the stories one can get on Tutuila are taboo here because the "men of Tutuila and Upolu and Savai'i boast of their beginnings, but the men of Manu'a—of the island which was made first of all —keep silent and do not boast." Then each village thinks it knows stories another village doesn't and each family likewise is deluded, so the variety of stories which may or may not be esoteric is amazing.

A Samoan house is an excellent place to do ethnology for the floor is covered with small stones of all sizes and descriptions and the informant simply puts them in rows as chiefs, raises them aloft as cups or piles them ceremonially as food. A Samoan never points within a house; instead he tosses a small stone towards the post or person he is discussing. . . .

I've really been very lucky. In this village, living with white people and because of the very *papalagi* character of the chiefs at this end of the island, I've escaped high rank entirely. The children call me Makelita and treat me as one of themselves, which is just what I needed for my problem. Then in Fitiuta, where I can get all my richest ethnology, I have rank to burn and can order the whole village about. It couldn't have worked out better. I've now got only eleven more weeks in Samoa, four of which I shall probably have to spend in Tutuila as the boats run so irregularly. But school has begun and it's practically impossible to get hold of the children any more. Anyway my problem is practically completed. So I'll spend the rest of the time filling in gaps in the problem and getting ethnology.

School opening made me homesick for the United States. I've been homesick for New York or for the farm or for bathtubs or beefsteak, but never just collectively for America. But the first day of school here with school gongs and slate pencils gave me a peculiar feeling. When the teacher asks the children, "Do you understand?" they have been taught to answer, "Yes sir, but not very much." What effect will that have on the psychology of the future?

Tau, Manu'a
March 24, 1926

This will be my last bulletin from Manu'a and very probably the last from Samoa. I'll probably leave Manu'a in about three weeks. And oh, all the holes there are to patch—the width of a basket, the height of a post, the name of a feast, how they burn scars, what you really do call your mother's brother and how many fires there were at a death feast. At this stage my work looks exactly like a beaded dress only partly beaded. So there will be no more bulletins. But I have a temporary lull for this one because I've had tonsillitis and am forbidden to walk about until tomorrow. . . .

At dawn on March 8th, a boat arrived from Ofu and lured by thoughts of ethnological gain I decided to go back with the boat —a 15-foot rowboat. At the last minute Fa'apua'a, Tufele's *taupou*, and another Fitiuta girl came tumbling head over heels into my room and announced they were going with me. I decided it would be expensive but pleasant. So we set out in the broiling sun with a crew of some nine Samoans. The girls were desperately seasick, but I rested my head on a burlap bag of canned goods, and with my ear on a tin of salmon and my temple on a can of prunes enjoyed the three-hour pull in the open sea. The swell is impressive when viewed from such a cockleshell of a boat. The Samoans chanted and shouted. After a little it poured and we could not see land at all, and then there was an hour of thin rain with the portals of the sunset all about the horizon. Finally we reached Olesega and the "Maga"—a long jagged promontory on the end of which stands the figure of a man with uplifted hands and just behind him the stone figure of a child, the pair looking for all the world like an early British bishop and his acolyte. On the high cliff behind them is their stone castle where they retire at nightfall. Legend says it is the figure of a man who wanted to go back to Tau, but the god Tagaloa prevented him and he died standing on the outermost point of land staring toward the land of his dreams. We got to Ofu after dark, scrambling in over the reef to seek refuge in a strange village.

Life in Ofu was complicated by the fact that there is a famine and I had to provide food for my court as well as for myself. But then there is a bakery on Ofu and I reveled in yeast bread for a whole ten days. . . .

On Thursday I went to the other island, Olesega, in a boat with the Navy men and while they returned, we—my talking chiefs and I—stayed the night. But it was a dreary business. Olesega was wrecked by the hurricane. There will be no copra for years. And there is nothing to eat except *masi* (decayed breadfruit, which smells worse than Limburger cheese) and the rice and salmon famine ration. And a Samoan knows no courtesy unaccompanied by food. So the village was churlish, took our short stay in ill part, and tried to hide its poverty-stricken shame under vehement protestations. But I found a most excellent and wise old man and got all I wanted, so we decided to sleep the next night at Sili.

Sili is a charming, tiny village of 80 people tucked under a tremendous cliff. It has one great disadvantage. Pieces of the cliff, weighing five to ten tons, come off occasionally. And the sea has a way of coming right into these houses. But neither of these disasters greeted us. Our gracious hosts killed a pig for us and the whole tiny village made merry, while the high chiefs told me anecdotes, illustrated, of the days of cannibalism, and a most gaunt and pitiful madman, who believes he is Tufele, danced and sang for us.

The walk back to Ofu the next day was sheer delight. First the trip from island to island, going one at a time in a *poapoa,* a canoe just 18 inches wide. Then a long walk skirting the sea, at places racing the tide or leaping between high waves from one wet rock to another, but mostly following an easy trail under a weak complacent sun.

The whole conduct of the *malaga* was charming. My two companions were my talking chiefs, functionally speaking. They made all the speeches, accepted and dispersed gifts, prepared my meals, etc. For this I bought them each three new dresses. For the talking chief who accompanied his lord need take nothing with him, neither food nor raiment, for he believed and enforced the adage that the laborer is worthy of his hire. But it is all much pleasanter than having a real servant. And these were merry companions. Even when they went to wash my clothes, one carried the clothes but the other carried her ukelele, and they must play at least a couple of tunes before sitting up in the morning. Fish was my chief prerogative, other foods being scarce, and there were lovely scenes when one side of the house was piled high with flowers, from which the girls were sewing *ulas* and on a mat on the other side my host would pour a mass of many-colored, glittering fish. There were some slight difficulties. Once I killed 35 mosquitoes *inside* my net *in the morning,* and all had dined liberally—a quaint way of dipping one's hands in one's own blood. Then there was warring as to what house we would grace with our presence. And it took much dusting to get all the ants off the bread. And crowning disaster, I dreamed Fa'apua'a had twins, the very night before we left. That is an "octopus dream"; had we gone fishing, untold devil fish would have rewarded us. Instead, we sailed away on the station ship. . . .

II.

PERÉ VILLAGE, MANUS

ADMIRALTY ISLANDS

1928–1929

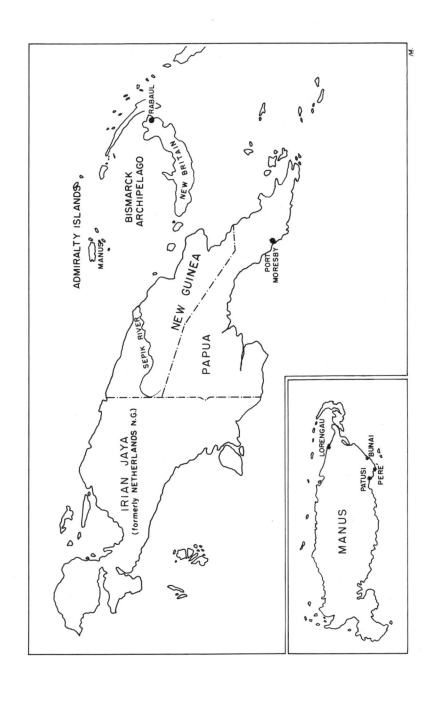

In Samoa I found I could not understand adolescents without studying pre-adolescents. For my next field trip I decided to study even younger children. The problem I wanted to investigate had to do with animistic thinking in young children. More particularly, I asked, if Freud, Lévy-Bruhl, Piaget and others are correct in claiming that primitive people, civilized children and neurotics are alike in their patterns of thought, what is the thought of *primitive* children like?

As Assistant Curator for Ethnology at the American Museum of Natural History, I was responsible for all the cultures of the Pacific area and I wanted next to go to Melanesia. Since my research problem did not call for any particular people or ecological situation, I left the choice of location up to Reo Fortune, whom I was planning to marry. He was already in Melanesia, working under A. R. Radcliffe-Brown as a Fellow of the Australian National Research Council. In consultation with Radcliffe-Brown, Reo decided on the Admiralty Islands because no modern ethnological research had been done there. Narrowing down his choice through discussions with an officer in the New Guinea Service whom he met in Sydney, he selected the sea-dwelling Manus people of the South Coast. In turn, we decided on Peré because Banyalo, the schoolboy interpreter lent to us in Rabaul, originally came from this village.

I traveled alone across the Pacific. Reo met my ship in Auckland, where we married. From this time on my intellectual life became a cooperative enterprise and the excitement of intellectual discussion was part of my life in the field itself, not something to be shared in letters or much later, after the event. But our first joint enterprise in the field as we approached Manus was learning simultaneously Manus and Pidgin English, the lingua franca, from Banyalo, who spoke very little English.

On our return to Rabaul at the end of our field work, we were invited to lunch with the Acting Governor, F. B. Phillips, who later became Chief Justice, Territory of Papua and New Guinea. Reo was planning a short return trip to Dobu to take photographs, as his camera had broken down on his first trip. Judge Phillips persuaded me to remain behind and spend the six weeks working on a life history with one of the great early settlers of New Guinea, Phoebe Parkinson, the half-Samoan wife of Richard Parkinson, the German author of *Thirty Years in the South Seas*. The story of Mrs. Parkinson gave me vivid insights into ways of life both in Samoa and New Guinea to which no one of my generation could have had access.

We returned to the United States by way of San Francisco. Reo assumed a graduate fellowship at Columbia University and I returned to the Museum.

Lorengau, Manus
Admiralty Islands
November 22, 1928

The *Marsina,* the steamer coming up to Rabaul from Sydney— a voyage that took twelve days—was a tiny, evil-smelling little tub; the menu boasted eighteen curries, different in name only. We stopped an afternoon at Samarai, where Reo collected a group of his natives and elucidated an obscure point in the Dobuan kinship system.

From Samarai we went to haul a stranded ship off a reef and spent a dull day in a bay off the New Guinea coast waiting for high tide. Natives in flat wide canoes, bound together, floated about idly and at night built a fire in the center of the canoe and spread the sails over themselves as they lay in a circle, feet inwards. They were tied up to the ship's side and a whole hose of water was debouched over them by accident, spreading disaster over the twenty sleepers. We pulled the *Morinda* off the reef, went to a concert on the *Montura,* which was also standing by, climbed over the rail aboard the *Morinda,* which had tied up alongside to fill her water tanks from our supply, and maundered back to Samarai and so on to Port Moresby and Rabaul.

Chinnery, the government anthropologist, took us in charge in Rabaul. We stayed with the Deputy Governor, a charming gentleman with a game leg and a gift for mimicry and housekeeping. And so here, with many government documents attached. The documents were all O.K. Here we are being entertained by the District Officer, pay no customs duties, have access to all records, etc. Oh, and the government in Rabaul has lent us a Manus boy from the government school who can read and write and typewrite. His name is Banyalo.

Lorengau is the government station and will be our metropolis for a year. There are some two dozen white people. Everyone speaks to everyone else and hate is rampant. It was really better at Pago Pago where they didn't speak to each other. The District Officer, Mr. Mantle, is a strict, reserved Englishman. He has a grand house, left from the old German days, with great verandas. His wife is away and he keeps solitary and disgruntled state, reiterating how much he prefers his pipe and his books to the society of vulgar people. There is the Patrol Officer who has been in the Territory for nine years and has just brought up an Australian wife. There is old Charlie Munster, who was a famous blackbirder; when the war came, he produced Australian citizenship papers from somewhere and so he stays on with a plantation which doesn't pay and a pearl shell trade which pays so well that he can afford a refrigerator—the only one on the island. Munster lives two miles from the station, but the government is now out looking for prisoners to build a good road to Munster's place so that all the staff can have a pleasant little walk over in the afternoon, after tennis, for some good beer.

There is Mr. Burroughs, the storekeeper, who makes 100% on every sale, and his Australian wife who talks like a gramophone. And Mr. Burroughs' partner, Kramer, who trades about for tortoise shell and pearl shell. There is the pompous, but likable "little doctor"—the Medical Assistant—who has almost finished medical school and knows a lot about tropical medicine. And his assistant, Dunstan, who asks whether it is quicker to go down a river than up. And the *kuskus*, chief clerk, who is teaching us to develop pictures. An hour's sail in one direction is Father Borchard, who has been here for fifteen years without intermission and whose great interest is a Pidgin-English dictionary. On the other side is a pale German Protestant mission, six adults and two children, who live on £15 a month and haven't converted many natives. Then there are the planters here and there and the Chinese and Japanese plantation managers.

Such flimsy structures of a hundred or so white men govern

and exploit this vast country—find gold, plant great plantations, trade for shell, hide their failures in other lands, drink inordinately, run into debt, steal each other's wives, go broke and commit suicide or get rich—if they know how.

The recruiting system, which began as blackbirding—straight out-and-out kidnapping and slavery—now consists of a milder form of forcible persuasion and long contracts, three and five years, enforced by law. Boys can be signed on from twelve years old up. The policy is to have boys from faraway islands and from as many different parts as possible. Then they will be unable to steal and pass things on to their relatives—the theory goes—or plot in their own language or fall in love with girls of their own people. The recruiter gets £15 to £20 per boy; the boy gets £4 or £5 per year, his food—rice and *bulmakau* (beef)—and tobacco.

These natives become very traveled people. Many houseboys are taken to Sydney to look after the children when their masters go on leave. They are not allowed to own motor boats or automobiles or to wear shirts or carry firearms. Yet they handle all of these. They pour out liqueurs from the south of France, wash rare china, take care of the children and understand what they are doing only in human terms—and then with the continuous qualification that all white men are *longlong* (crazy) and a shrug at the complete incomprehensibility of *fashion belong white man* (the ways of Europeans). And they have developed a perfect lingua franca in Pidgin, a flexible, flowing language with a cadence of its own, which they are coming to speak to one another in preference to their own *one-talk* (mother tongue).

For Melanesia is split up into thousands of tiny communities, each speaking a language incomprehensible to others, practicing different customs and living in fear and terror of all neighbors as well as all enemies. This island, 40 miles long and about half as wide, with about 14,800 natives, has at least eight language groups on the mainland and little bordering islands. The little islands are specialized according to material culture: some make carved bowls, some betel sticks or obsidian spears or great carved crocodiles, painted red and white. There are no great language groups, no politically integrated groups to withstand the onslaught of another way of life. Fifty people here, two hundred people there, disintegrate and go to pieces entirely because government or the mission has forbidden some particular custom. A few miles away, three hundred people stagger under the attack; their birth rate falls, then slowly, before they have all died out, comes up again.

And meanwhile this new social system, in which almost every ablebodied young man goes away for three to five years to work for the white man, is growing up. He goes away as often as not to earn his bride price and comes back, having mingled with natives from all parts of the Territory, with new black magic, new love charms, new drugs for producing barrenness and abortion and a new language in which he can converse with the young men of other tribes. The women (in Pidgin all native women are called *maries*), on the other hand, seldom go away from their villages and speak very little Pidgin. A few white women have *maries* as servants, but it is said to be virtually impossible to keep both boys and *maries*. It is interesting to speculate what the position of women will be when all the men speak a common tongue and the women still speak a dozen mutually incomprehensible ones. . . .

So in Pidgin, it's possible to see a new language—a perfectly good, adequate language—in the process of formation, adapted to half a hundred varying Melanesian grammars and drawing its vocabulary from all sides.

On Monday, Gizikuk, chief of the *sodawater* (sea) boys—the *Manus-true*—is coming to get us and our gear in a fleet of canoes. We'll have an all-day trip along the coast. By next letter we'll be in the thick of it. I've already got a fair start on the language. Boat every three weeks.

> *Kwe bo kwa*—You may go.

Peré
December 16, 1928

I am writing on the porch of the *house-kiap*—government rest house—in Peré, the largest village which is *Manus-true*. Beside me sits the father of a new baby, clad only in G-string, bracelets, armlets and woven belt, with a bag for his betel nut and pepper leaf slung over his shoulder. He hasn't seen his new baby and will not until the mother's brother has collected a great sago feast; only then can he go back to his family. Meanwhile he and another new father have nothing to do but loiter about, play at darts or carve toy canoes for the children.

Manus house built over the water, at low tide.

Dismantling the thatch of a Manus house.

Government rest house where we first lived in Peré.

The village is a primitive Venice—the streets are waterways, the houses set on high posts over the water. The only land is found in a few tiny islands, inundated at high tide, some tiny volcanic islands and the mainland a quarter of a mile away. All life is conducted by means of canoes. Children of three and four can pole canoes ten times their size, handling a pole ten feet high. The three- and four-year-olds have tiny canoes of their own in which they paddle about half under water, upsetting every other minute, perfectly at home. On the ends of the little high islands long swings are hung from the tops of trees and the children swing out over the water. The house floors are made of strips of wood, short and smooth and unevenly placed, so that there are frequent gaps. The little children have to exercise nearly as much care as if they lived in trees above the water.

Paddling about in the village one suddenly looks down and sees the head of a woman with a two-months-old baby on her shoulder, projecting above the water in which she is standing chin high. Even the pigs have become water animals. During the day they are kept fenced up in small pens on piles, but at night they are let out and wallow and swim peacefully about in the low water, only to be hoisted back into their pens, amid much grunting of pigs and shouting of men, in the early morning.

The houses are fifty to sixty feet long, with small enclosed verandas with windows at each end. They are large and high, but dark and smoky and cluttered up with shelves containing pots and baskets and food. Below the house floor proper is a low front platform where visitors must wait until invited in and where firewood is stacked, pots are made and nets dried. The women wear long grass tails before and behind, secured by woven belts. When these are new they are bright green and offer a pleasant relief to the brown-gray tones of the village. The thatch is red-brown when it is new, gray when it is old. The long pieces of cloth which the women wear over their heads, Eastern style, are usually faded to a nameless color. Even the minnows and the jellyfish are a pale gray. Occasionally a canoe loaded with sago done up in bright green packages invades the dull tones or someone may place a row of coconuts across the front of a house to sprout in a sort of elevated window garden.

It's a paradise for children. They have no work except to run errands and that involves paddling about in the water. The women take care of the babies, so that the children are free. At low tide in the early morning they course about shooting fish with tiny bows and arrows, dragging the water for minnows with a long piece of bark used in imitation of a net, or practicing just missing each other's feet with a piece of coral hurled through the water. Although little girls wear the two long tails, before and behind, just like their elders, they are not seriously hampered by them. In low water they walk about holding them aloft so that they won't get wet. At high water they discard them altogether.

The houses are so close together that voices carry easily and there is continual shouted intercommunication between house and house. Disputes over sago, conducted between a man in a canoe and a man standing on his house platform, ring through the village. The code beating of the signal drum announces all important events.

There are forty-three houses in the village, including a men's house and two fairly good-sized houses which are play houses for the children, particularly the little girls. This makes a large enough community for something to be happening all the time. Since we arrived three weeks ago we have seen a ceremony to bring an unconscious woman back to consciousness by sending good spirits out to capture her spirit, which had been carried off by an angry ancestral ghost; a ceremony to make a boy, grown up now, a virtuous member of the community; a ceremony to insure the successful outcome of a first pregnancy, in which sago is thrown to the ancestral spirit; two ceremonies in which the relatives who slept with the corpse of a dead relative were paid; and a turtle dance in the house of the chief man of the village. In one evening sometimes half a dozen disputes and wailings ring over the water, the drum beats to announce that a sick man is summoning the spirit of his father, a crowd gathers hurriedly to listen to a woman who, although she professes to know no Pidgin English, is talking it fluently in a delirium, while a canoe moves noiselessly about distributing pieces of a new turtle catch to the women who washed the bones of the fisherman's dead father.

Our house is situated on the edge of a tiny island which boasts two trees and a small pagoda. Here the inhabitants of one village division come to build fires to straighten their bamboo torches, to singe a newly-caught possum or to hew out a house plank. Here the children gather to play games or watch an older man carve a toy canoe. There are two such "social centers" in the village and the head man of the other division is building me a house on the other one, so we will have a house on both scenes of activity. These little houses, which they have learned to build for the patrol officers, are very comfortable—a veranda all around and the cookhouse set off at one end of the veranda. An open space at the top of the walls, sheltered by the sloping veranda roof, four windows and two doors. This house is now rimmed with cupboards for stores, but my house, prepared for the invasion of children, will contain only locked cedarwood boxes and baskets slung from the ceiling.

Food has turned out much better than we had dared to hope. From the village people we buy fish, from the land people papaya, pineapple, taro and various unknown vegetable-like fruits. Occasionally, Reo goes out and shoots a wild duck or some pigeons. A cook-boy who was a terrific thief temporarily marred the placidity of our household, but a new one is supposed to arrive presently.

Marie's first aid kit saved the day about a week ago. A child had fallen, cut his head on a stone and lost consciousness. When our canoe arrived outside the house, the terrible din inside—a combination of women's voices wailing, "My mother, my mother, my mother!" (the ever-present cry of distress or surprise), men's voices shouting commandingly to their particular ancestral spirits and the sound of sticks beating on wooden bowls—informed us that the child was unconscious. Reo went in, armed with iodine and bandages, while Manuwai and I came back for the tiny bottle of aromatic spirits of ammonia left in Marie's kit. When we got back, I clambered up into the house filled with people and found Reo in complete exasperation. There was a crowd ten deep about the child, the heat was suffocating and they would have none of his ministering. We smashed the ammonia bottle and he slipped forward and thrust it under the child's nose. The child, who was very slightly hurt, came to at once. The effect was too instantaneous to be ignored and Reo was permitted to wash and bandage the wound. Afterwards, we sent off post haste to Lorengau for a whole bottle of aromatic spirits, praying frantically that no one would lose consciousness in the interval.

The whole society is run by the spirits of the immediate ances-

Our new house and the adjacent islet at the beginning of a ceremony.

tors, who preserve exceedingly human characteristics—easily angered, easily solaced. Each house has a special guardian spirit of the owner's father or uncle and this spirit both punishes and protects. If a man disobeys his elder brother, the spirit of the dead father makes him sick, and then the elder brother has to hold a séance and call him off. They are genuine séances with whistling and calling until the medium calls up the spirit of a dead relative, always the same one, apparently, a true "control," and then the one desiring information can talk directly with the control. Sorcery takes second place, although there are occasionally inter-village sorcerers' contests.

They are a gay and open-hearted people, almost as light in color as the Samoans and as friendly in feeling, though unmannerly. The light conversation turns on betel nut; those who have plenty in their bags hide their own supply and beg from others who are equally well supplied. These in turn say they have no betel. The beggars reply: "You're a liar!" The others insist: "No, I speak the truth!" This is often followed by a friendly bit of violence in which the bag is searched and the betel nut found. The children are present on every occasion, dance on the feast place, cling lovingly to the leg of the father who is engaged in violent wrestling for an absent spirit or peer under the arm of the midwife who is massaging a woman in labor. The adults also are always ready to join in the play of the children, to carry them on their shoulders in the water or to direct their sport.

The language is enormously difficult, hard phonetics, a mass of sounds which are intermediate between sounds familiar to us and a great deal of individual variation. One man will pronounce a word *worol,* while another pronounces it *wolor,* and each refuses to recognize our imperfect rendition of the alternate pronunciation. . . . I can manage simple dialogue in which I am participating myself, but I can't follow conversation yet. It's much harder than Dobuan or Samoan. . . .

Altogether, however, it's as delightful a place as we could have found in New Guinea, a people with a good material culture and an elaborate economic life. Their legends end with this phrase: "This belongs to legend. It has come down, it has come down, it has become human. It comes down, it appears on the scene, it becomes mortal."

With Kawa.

Reo Fortune with Ngalowen, about 4 years old.

Peré
January 10, 1929

I am alone for the first time. It was more complicated to plan for than in Samoa because here we have so much worldly wealth which couldn't be transported about easily. The house is lined with shelves filled with tins and stationery and photographic material. I couldn't leave it and go to a native house to sleep because no native would be willing to sleep here and guard it, for they are very frightened of houses without guardian ancestral spirits.

Meanwhile Reo went off at short notice to witness an inter-village row on a nearby island. I think I've mentioned the child betrothal through which sometimes four- and five-year-old children are betrothed and paid for. The "paid for" is the principal point. Marriages are usually arranged between cross-cousins—the son of the sister having a right to demand from the son of the brother a girl-child for marriage with his own son. The relations between cross-cousins are very complicated anyway. They stand in a joking relationship to each other and on every solemn occasion take it out on each other.

Now the son of the head man of Patusi, the next village, was betrothed to a Loitcha girl, and the cross-cousin (on the other side) of the fiancé had seduced the girl. In former days the alternatives were a fight or a propitiatory payment; today the alternatives are to *make court* (have a court case) or demand a propitiatory payment. The Patusi boy was sulky and furious and demanded court action against his cross-cousin. But as he, like all Manus boys, had been "paid for" by an older male relative, he had nothing to say in the matter. And the relatives declared for the *kano,* the propitiatory payment.

Reo and his chief informant, the head man of Pontchal, the tiny village cheek by jowl with Peré, have gone with representatives of Patusi and several other villages to collect the payment or help with the fight, as the case may be.

So I surveyed my household and its retainers. Our usual menage consists of Banyalo, the schoolboy from Rabaul, who is five feet six of sulky uselessness most of the time. Still we keep him because he is useful at working out texts; he's on call in a way that the older men are not and he's responsible enough to be left in charge of the house if we go away in the daytime. He wears a shirt

Manuwai during his ear-piercing ceremony.

Piwen of Patusi, during her month-long "coming-out" party.

and khaki shorts which impair his character still more. But Banyalo wanted to go to Taui with Reo so he was out of the picture. Then the head cook is Manuwai (Bird), a charming, indolent youth of sixteen who was our original houseboy. Since he has become cook his *laplap* has become incomparably longer, his dignity extraordinary, his aloofness incomparable. But three days ago he had his ears pierced and so is *hors de combat* for five days. Five women of his father's family have come from Loitcha to cook his food over a special fire. He wears tents of pandanus leaf over each ear and looks very solemn and impressed by the fact that his ears are in great danger. Any relaxing of the taboos means a club ear, an unthinkable future to one as vain as he. So he is paddled about in a canoe by smaller boys gravely ministering to his infirmity and only turns up once a day or so to beg newspaper for cigarette papers. Since his ear-piercing ceremony, Kilipak "Go to Pak" (an island), has been head cook. Kilipak is possibly thirteen, quick as a flash, son of the ruling family, a natural leader of men. Kilipak's promotion to cook promoted Sotoan, formerly mere kitchen knave who worked for his food alone, to the position of waiter and head *valet de chambre*. Sotoan is possibly twelve, mild, without authority, deprecatory in manner. And a new *monkey* (small boy), who had not haunted the premises before, became assistant *valet de chambre*. They are so tiny that it takes two to fold a blanket. An even smaller *monkey*, Kapeli, also joined the forces. So the household headed by a boy of thirteen got under way. The procedure of the absent Manuwai was imitated faithfully by Kilipak; Sotoan strove to take on some of Kilipak's authority as butler and never forgot the vinegar, the quinine, the salt, and the hemoglobin bottles. And Kilipak next organized a band of ten-year-old girls to fetch the firewood which he and his fellow *monkeys* had formerly fetched for Manuwai. Five tiny girls, wearing their little grass tails before and behind, set off in two small canoes, one outriggerless, fastened together to contain the firewood. On their return he shared a tiny bit of his tobacco with them and begged cigarette paper for the whole crew. So by the time Reo left, the child household was in good running order. No one had more than a minimum of work to do, everyone was gay and happy, serious about their tasks, running away to run canoe races while I slept in the early afternoon. For water, wood and cooking I was well equipped, but now for a sleeping companion.

Our female retainers are three in number, two *wash maries* (who do the laundry) and my lone "widder" woman, Main. The *wash maries* are two girls of sixteen or so, both engaged to be married soon and able to devote only a small fraction of their time to their work because some man who is taboo to them is always passing in a canoe, or coming on the little island or coming into the house. All the girls and women wear cloth over their heads in which they can muffle themselves when a taboo relative passes. Married women have only to worry about brothers-in-law and fathers-in-law, but unmarried girls are taboo to all the men of the clan into which they are going to marry. These two girls, Ngaleap and Ngaoli, have worked in a most desultory fashion, sometimes not turning up at all. It was a long time before I could get any response out of them, but since Ngaleap trimmed my hair and Ngaoli got a thorough blowing up for refusing to wash on the proper day, they have both been devoted. Before that they talked and sulked and demanded, "Betel, betel," with lowering brows. But Ngaleap is *hors de combat* because one day when they had planned to wash and I declared it unnecessary, they went off to swing on a nearby island.

Small girl assistants supervised by Nauna.

The swings are thirty feet long, long creepers fastened in tree tops. Ngaleap's broke and she fell, not on the water, which would have been quite safe, but on land, and hurt her leg; so she was out of the running. I decided to ask Main, my "widder" woman. She's particularly "lorn" having seen five husbands into the grave and she not yet turned fifty. I pay her three sticks of tobacco a week and it's her business to come and fetch me whenever anything is on foot in the village either in the way of women's industrial activities or of feasts. She demurred heartily from the proposition that she should sleep here but finally consented if she might have Ngaoli and another young girl with her. So it was arranged. And yesterday I went off to a turtle feast and a terrible storm came up. All my *monkeys* kept house in fine style, lowering canvas, barricading doors with the ironing board, etc. I came back to find them thoroughly domesticated and proposing to stay the night en masse. They added that the reason Main was so frightened was that one of her dead husbands belonged to this division and she was afraid he would catch her. So I sent word to Main she needn't come. In the end Ngaoli turned up and slept by my side, while five *monkeys* made a room of canvas on the veranda and sang their frightened little selves to sleep, waking up at intervals to declare that a ghost was nearby. In the evening, which, owing to the storm, had all the appearance of a shut-in night at home, I gave them pencils and paper and they did their first drawing. I'm starting with the older ones, so that the little children will draw under conditions similar to those surrounding small children's spontaneous drawing in our culture—that is, after having seen older children draw. At their own request they took new paper and their pencils to bed with them and were up at dawn drawing away. The arrival of a man with fresh fish finally recalled the cook to his duties and the day began. It's altogether a jolly household, infantile, happy, with Kilipak, a genius at organization, at the head. I am as much a figurehead as an English queen when it comes to practical arrangements.

January 16, 1929

Reo is back after a long trip which ended in a fiasco. The man who had paid for the girl as a bride for a boy in his family got cold feet because once before he had accepted *kano* from the same people and a pig had died. The guardian spirit, their common ancestor, was evidently displeased, and this time it might be a child he would kill. So the party came home again. Pokanau, the *Kukerai* (Pidgin English for government representative in the village), was furious because he had hoped to share in the *kano*.

The *Kukerai* is Reo's righthand man. He's as good an informant as the heart could wish—a pure introvert, skeptical, scornful, with a wonderful memory and an excellent mind. Reo takes him along to a feast or a quarrel and when they return the *Kukerai* dictates every speech that was made. His skill with the kinship system is incomparable. He's not over-given to work, fond of cruising about, proud of his position as chief informant and easily offended on points of pride. He's daggers drawn with Main all the time.

We have also attached to ourselves Paleao, the *Tultul* (government interpreter) of Peré. Paleao is building the new house; he shoots all our ducks for us; he takes the mail to Lorengau and fetches our supplies. His wife is making bead armlets for me. He is the prime extrovert, the man of affairs, buying sago at native rates and selling it to a trader, hiring a canoe from his cousin for a stick of tobacco and insisting that we pay him the thirty sticks for his canoe voyage in the dark or on a canoe at sea. He's as scornful of the ceremonial aspects of his culture as the *Kukerai* is respectful towards the structure and scornful towards all the individuals in it. When Paleao receives a large payment from the family of the girl whom one of his "sons" is to marry, he flips off at the native system of endlessly moving about unconsumed pawns by remarking in his formal speech: "This food which you have brought will move on to Patusi tomorrow to pay for someone else in my household." And the *Kukerai* gives Reo the text of his speech, in which, moreover, he has not bothered to invoke his guardian spirit, and says scornfully that Paleao "talks like a child, without understanding."

And Paleao in an aside tells Reo that the reason all Pontchal men are dying is because of the guardian spirit of the *Kukerai* and that everyone is beginning to avoid the *Kukerai*. But when the *Kukerai* is present, Paleao says the reason all Pontchal men are dying is because they have all been Main's lovers. (If one commits adultery here and does not confess, one is supposed to die, killed by the outraged spirits. If one confesses, propitiatory payments are made. Note how well the culture is arranged to make spirit dovetail with the workaday world!)

Yesterday a wail rang through the village. "What's that?"

"*One-fellow mary i-cry now*. Her baby is dying. I think it will soon die."

The dying child turned out to be a child in the house of Main. We rushed along with aromatic spirits and found the child in a delirium from malaria. Reo went back for the quinine. Quoth the *Kukerai*: "This baby isn't sick. The trouble only has something to do with the *palit* [spirits]." It seems that the father of the child is planning to make a big payment of 1,000 dog's teeth to the relatives of his wife, without waiting for his wife's younger brother to return from work in Rabaul. Presto! the grandmother of the child is angry and is causing its death! However, we forcibly fed the child quinine and this morning he was all right.

There have been a few minor casualties in the kitchen nursery. Once two *monkeys* got into a fight and all the saucepans went into the sea. Our dinner was late that night and the little head cook was sadly harassed. But on the whole they are a contented crew. As are we likewise.

Peré
February 14, 1929
St. Valentine's Day

The natives say: "*Kor e palit*"—that is, the place is full of spirits and it behooves all men to walk warily. This three-week interval began with a wedding but ended in two deaths and one dying.

The wedding was a gay affair badly mutilated by a rain storm. In the general scramble for positions, I found myself in the house of the bridegroom and Reo went to the house of the bride, which was the result of the taboos governing our various informants, but it turned out to be quite right for all the men fled the house of the groom after he had been ceremonially prepared for the great ordeal with elaborate anointing with red paint. The titular father of the groom remained simply to hand the bride hastily into his house. Then he left in the bridal canoe which had brought her and was poled away. The little bride, so laden with shell money, dog's teeth, beadwork and feather combs that her person was hardly visible, sat at the top of the ladder with her back to the groom, who waited a moment and then made a rush out the back door. Where-

Bopau, son of Sori, practices
the men's phallic dance.

Men in war regalia dance on a
carved dancing pole at an
affinal exchange ceremony.

upon all the groom's paternal aunts rushed at the bride, took the combs out of her hair and dug in her armlets for the several pipes which were concealed there.

The girl was half dead with embarrassment. Betrothed years ago, she had never been able to enter the village of her future husband. When she passed a Peré canoe, she was forced to muffle her face in her cloak or pandanus rain shelter. Now, at seventeen or so, she was brought to the house of relatives at the far end of the village and decked out in all her finery, her ears heavy with bead earrings, her nose weighed down with a long dog's teeth pendant. All the women of her betrothed's clan came to fetch her in the evening and carried her away to sleep with them this last night of her girlhood. She sat in the great canoe laden down with chattering women who had come to fetch her and she looked at the water and said nothing. The next day she was taken back to her relatives, re-decked in finery and brought to the bridegroom.

Lomot, Talikai and their young son, Matawai, in their canoe loaded with pots and grass skirts for an affinal exchange.

After the bridegroom ran away, she was taken out again, placed on the carved table which is the essential part of all such proceedings, and paddled to the islet which abuts on our new house. Here all the foreign cloth, all the beadwork, the pots of oil, the grass skirts of her dowry were spread out in fine array. The village band assembled in the unthatched scaffold of our new house and set up a deafening racket on slit drums of all sizes. And then the rain came down in torrents. Everyone rushed for shelter except the bridal party, who remained huddled under the little canoe house as there was no house which they might enter.

The next day was the house feast for our new house, which was enlivened by discussions of the bride—who was said to have web fingers and breasts like an old woman. All the men of the village, who had never before been permitted to see her, were eagerly scouting about hoping that she would emerge from her house. General gaiety reigned in the village, tinged by angry mutterings over a suspected intrigue to which neither of the principals had confessed.

On Monday my merry widow came to take me to the ceremony by which her nephew would acquire sufficient magical power to wheedle property out of his relatives. Solemnly the head magician painted him, dipped his *wanke*— made of the bones of a dead man —in red paint and hung them about his neck and stretched his raffia basket at all four corners until its capacity was magically increased. Then we all set forth, Nane—the nephew—and his wife seated on the front of the canoe platform with a great carved bowl in front of them. We went from house to house where he had relatives and everywhere the magic worked; dog's teeth, shell money, tobacco flowed into the bowl. This was the beginning of a long series of collecting trips which Nane would make to gather together enough property to make a *metcha*—a great ceremonial payment to his wife's relatives.

The next morning he set out again to go to another village, but the canoe had barely left the village when a great wailing called him back. His middle son, a child of ten years, had fallen down in a fit. We worked over the child for two days with quinine and ammonia, but he never recovered more than to open his eyes unseeingly. And meanwhile the seers, soothsayers and diviners worked also. Some stood tall and vigorous, dwarfing the crowds that sat on the floor, stirring water in wooden bowls and calling their own spirits to go and seek the absent spirit of the child. Others sat in corners trailing the divining bones over their shoulders and addressing long, complicated problems to the bones, which answer yes or no by scratching one side or the other. As night drew on, the mediums got to work and low sibilant, uncertain whistles hissed through the village. From time to time, as a new theory about his illness was announced, a payment of propitiatory property was made to the offended people or the mortal wards of the offended spirits. By next day a half-dozen theories about his illness had been concocted and rejected either because the child seemed to rally as they were mentioned and the spirits involved were invoked or because a payment made on the basis of the theory brought no results.

Suspicion turned chiefly upon Noan, our rascally ex-cook-boy, and Lauwiyan, a tall stately girl who was said to have had an affair with him. The natives firmly believe that sickness follows close on the heels of adultery and death on a stubborn refusal to confess. Both boy and girl had been charged with their sin the previous week and both had denied it. Now little Popitch, the cousin of both of them, was stricken. The young *Kukerai* of Peré, a cross-cousin of the girl, set out to get a confession. First he approached the girl, who remained steadfast in her denial. Then he left her, poled the canoe out into the middle, waited half an hour and returned to her, telling her that Noan had confessed, whereat she broke down and provided the details. And the father of Noan paid a cedarwood box and other things to her father. But the child got no better.

Then the theory shifted. If it were not adultery on earth then it must be adultery in heaven. And so it proved. The medium, who is, incidentally, the mother of the offending maiden, disclosed that the dead brother of the child had committed adultery with the dead wife of his father's dead brother, the guardian spirit of his grandfather. Cause enough for death, indeed—adultery and incest.

Meanwhile another theory was advanced. The old grandfather, who was said to be so old that he no longer cared about anything, killed a taboo fish called *pitch* and took it to market, trailing it underneath his canoe so that none could see. But he bartered it for betel in the usual way, by throwing the fish down on the betel, and some of the betel found its way to the brother of the widow of a man whose guardian spirit was Popitch. More séances revealed that it was not this Popitch, however, but his son by a spirit wife after his death—also named Popitch—who was avenging the insult to his name. This second—or rather third—Popitch is the eight-year-old guardian spirit of Kilipak, our prize *monkey*. So the distracted father prepared to make propitiatory payments to his father, whose spirit was offended by the spiritual adultery, and to help his father make a payment to the family of our *monkey*, that is, the brother of the medium and the father of Lauwiyan, the sinning girl. Both payments were brought down onto the platform ready to be taken away. But in the night little Popitch died and the payments were taken back again.

And while the women mourned and mourned, taking turns lying on the corpse and wailing long stereotyped laments, the search for the cause of the death went on. None of the former suspicions could be true. All had been dealt with, yet the child had died. The old father of Noan set off to walk a day's tramp up to the Usiai country where he paid a dreamer to reveal the truth. Meanwhile at the exchange following the death, Lorengau, a ceremonial friend of Nane's, had officially stated his intention of bequeathing a coconut grove to Nane's surviving sons and asked that the child might be buried there. Perhaps the Usiai heard of that speech, for his dream said that Nane had been eating too freely of Lorengau's coconuts and Lorengau's spirit was cross.

And then sullenly, secretly, another accusation broke out. The true murderer was the spirit of Panau, a former doctor-boy of Peré who was now the guardian spirit of Paleao. This was known to be so because now the grandfather remembered that the stricken child had pointed to the back of his neck, which meant that a spirit had cut him there. And the medium spoke gruesomely of some blood which had appeared that day on Paleao's floor—obviously brought by the spirit trailing his bloodstained way back to his resting place beside his skull in the bowl among the rafters. And why had the doctor-boy committed the murder? Because he died before he made a *metcha* and was jealous that Nane should make one. This all came out in the house of death where dozens of people had gone to sleep. The medium thought all Paleao's people were asleep, but the widow of the accused lay awake and she roused her children and fled the house.

Now half of the village is on each side. Nane and his brother are going to break down their houses and move away from the close vicinity of the doctor-boy. Accusations made during the lifetime of a sick person are fairly innocuous; the mortal ward of the spirit rushes about calling on his spirit to desist or payments are made. If the person recovers, the spirit gets the credit; if he dies, it was obviously not that spirit. But from an accusation made after a death there is no such easy acquittal.

Meanwhile the general fear and terror which was spreading over the village intruded practically into our lives, as well as damping our spirits. I caught cold and was sick enough to stay in bed. Then Kilipak came down with fever. The next night a solemn deputation of three called upon us, headed by Paleao, who was seriously worried for fear we would not move bag and baggage into the new house he had built for us. They had divined, they had held a séance. It was the spirit of Sori, the guardian of our friend the *Kukerai* of Pontchal, Paleao's chief rival, who had made both me and Kilipak sick. Neither of us would recover until we moved.

But the new house had no steps, the cook-house had neither walls nor floor, the veranda was only a scaffolding. Sick as I was, I dreaded the moving which was to be the occasion of a drastic reorganization of stores and household arrangements. I temporized. In my country it was very dangerous to move at night. If I was no better the next day, we would move. The next day I got dressed and had my meals at a table on the veranda. Paleao went off on some business of his own and the matter rested.

The next night Loponiu, another of our *monkeys,* came down with fever. And the next day Kapeli, the third one. Both Kapeli and Loponiu had gone the long hot journey to Bunai to see Popitch buried, poling several miles in the hot sun on empty stomachs and sick with fear. For it is upon those of his own age that the spirit of the recently dead preys before he has become accustomed to his spirit life and is reconciled to it. But whatever our opinions were about the children's illness, the natives knew it was Sori and the next day we moved at an hour's notice.

The new house is charming. It has a bedroom filled with shelves and the beds can remain all day instead of being folded up; it's a place to retire into to open treasure chests or take a sponge bath. There is also a big livingroom which I have decorated with native things. Round black water pots stand in pairs by two of the doors; two carved crocodiles sit up on the ridgepole and chat together, so the natives say, whenever we go out. On the green bamboo shelves are ranged carved wooden bowls. The shelves are curtained with pandanus mats and the doors with mats, also. The only foreign things are a few books, our tables and chairs, which are natural wood and so blend well, a lamp and a tinkling glass Chinese gong which tinkles in the wind and delights the natives. We tell them that it corresponds to their pig-tusk fetishes, which insure them plenty of food and property. There is a wide veranda flanked by huge slit drums. The floor is made of flexibly split wood with the rounded surfaces, about three inches wide, upward. All rubbish slips through it and glass falling on it bounces and does not break. There are cedarwood chests on which the children draw. On my shelf is a basket which belongs to the children. It contains pencils, crayons, erasers, scissors and cigarette papers— the much valued newspaper for the older ones and discarded slips of white paper for the younger ones. The pre-school child smokes like a little fiend. Reo works in the old house which is now bare and neat. It is simple to load a table and chair on a canoe and pole across.

From morning to night this place is full of children drawing, chattering, spatting, begging cigarettes from each other until one

Wife of Ngamel prepares to bathe her infant.

Carrying Piwen, about
2 years old.

cigarette has gone the round of twenty. When the drawings are
finished, they come to me to be dated and named, and then they
are deposited in a great wooden bowl, which is already full to
overflowing. At sunset I sometimes make bread or roast a chicken
in a camp oven on the little islet with twenty eager helpers shriek-
ing, exclaiming, running to throw rotten eggs in the sea or to fetch
firewood for a dying fire.

Peré
March 27, 1929

This is going to be my last bulletin letter, I am afraid, for work
is getting faster and more furious as the end of the trip approaches.
Also buying material culture takes a lot of time. These people love
trade better than they love anything in the world. Every event is
cast in terms of economics. If you ask a girl to describe her puberty
ceremonial, she says: "All my relatives made a great excitement by

throwing coconuts into the sea. Then my relatives sent a canoe load of steaming food to the relatives of my betrothed. Then after five days another big feast was made and my relatives sent many bowls of cooked food to his relatives, and later his relatives will give bead belts back to my relatives," etc., etc. If you ask someone whether So-and-so is his sister, he says: "Yes, I give her food and she gives me beadwork."

The most dreadful quarrels in the village are the noisy ones between two wives of one man because he has given one more fish than the other and the silent, bitter quarrels between a man's wife and a man's sister because he has given his sister more fish.

The spirits take a constant interest in property, sending sickness and death if exchanges aren't made promptly or if property is misused. One poor woman has been dying of puerperal fever for the last five weeks. And as if her illness were not sufficient penance, one brother had an attack of cerebral malaria, the whole family drifted away in a canoe with a broken mast and only got back after days of hardship and living on birds' eggs. En route they took some coconuts from the island of the Taui people, and two days after the shipwrecked people got back to the village, while feasts and wailings were still in progress for them, the Taui people arrived in force to claim payment for their 60 coconuts. A week later another brother went mad and tried to break into a trader's house in Lorengau.

All of these calamities are due to two basic causes—in native theory. Because there was a division of opinion in the family over the remarriage of a widowed daughter who had been paid for by Pataliyan, the principal sorcerer in the village. The lady was unwilling and eloped in the night. Meanwhile the pay remained with the Kalo family. The dead father was outraged at such behavior and proceeded to punish all the members of the family who had helped the daughter to elope. But his punishment was to make another daughter sick and this softened the heart of the head of the family, who promptly forgave the young rebels for helping the lady to elope. This made the dead father angrier than ever—and thus the shipwreck which involved the head of the family.

On top of this, the head of the family took a lot of property and paid it to his wife's relatives instead of paying his younger brother's bride price for the girl whose seduction was the cause of the death of Popitch, described in the last letter. This younger brother had "made court" against the seducer of his fiancée, and everyone had lied nobly to save the seducer (our former thieving cook-boy). The outraged fiancé was fined for bringing a false accusation and went mad and broke into the trader's house.

But this is only one theory of the disaster. Another theory traces it all to Pataliyan. Pataliyan is my favorite sorcerer, in fact, the only important sorcerer in the village. These people had no sorcery of their own, it is all imported by work-boys from foreign parts. Pataliyan long ago, as a young boy, was seduced by the widowed mother of this Kalo family. He ran away to avoid marrying her and stayed away ten years working for the Germans and then for the English on the mainland of New Guinea. He saved his pay and with it he bought charms to keep away harm, charms to kill a pregnant woman, generalized charms for evil, charms to keep a new baby well. Fighting with the Germans he lost one eye and finally, after ten years, he came back to the village, a scarred and rather frightening figure with a great head of hair which he keeps dyed dark red. He married and then was almost immediately widowed. Then he asked to marry the daughter of the woman whom he had fled from years before. Hence the rift in the family. For the old widow insisted with a lewd and lifeless chuckle that he who had rejected her should not marry her daughter. And according to some people Pataliyan's charms made Alupwa—the woman dying of puerperal fever—sick, made the brother sick, made the eloping sister sick, made another woman who eloped with her sick, made the boy in Lorengau go mad! And so Pataliyan has been dashing about performing counter-charms with a great sense of importance and collecting wooden bowls and strings of shell money and dog's teeth for his medicining. The wooden bowls find their way to us.

Pataliyan found out other things while he was away, for instance, that the white man said that New Guinea and Australia were once one place. When he came back he told all the young men and some believed him and some did not, and two of them had a hard fist fight over the truth or falsehood of Pataliyan's tale.

Pataliyan has great respect for the white man. He says: "*You-fellow*, you write something down on paper and it's there to stay. We don't know how to do that; we're stupid (or ignorant). *You-fellow*, you teach the dog, you teach the horse, you teach the pussy, you teach the *monkeys* [the little boys]—they all have to learn how to do some kind of work, work on the road or work on paper. And if the master says anything, they have to listen. But we're too ignorant. We don't know how to teach like that. Here, where we live, the pigs, the dogs, the cats go about doing nothing! *You-fellow you number one!*"

They are great dialecticians and will argue for an hour over the difference between a word which means "borrow to return the same object" and one which means "borrow to return another of the same kind." Or whether a certain fish has teeth. And later the jawbone of the fish will be produced. At present there is a great argument on as to whether fishnets have souls. The *Kukerai* claims that if they didn't, the spirits would have to take the whole net, whereas now the spirits are able to make the net impotent, just as the spirits can make a man sick. The opposite side feels that nets shouldn't have souls and puts the discrepancy upon the powers of the spirits.

While Reo was in Lorengau giving evidence as to the inherited streak of madness in the Kalo family, Paleao and his family moved in with me and this house became a native house, filled with taboos. One girl had to be fed in the bedroom, as she could neither eat with her future husband's younger brother in the cook-house, with her future husband's paternal aunt in the livingroom nor with her future husband's paternal aunt's husband on the veranda. Pataliyan could not come near the house because long ago he was accused of having an intrigue with Paleao's wife. Our new cook-boy arrived, but he could not start work because his adopted brother's wife was living here.

Now that Reo has returned, the new cook-boy is here, but he is brother-in-law to three of our boys, so his name can't be mentioned and he must be referred to either as "Son-in-law of Kemaï" or as "Husband of Pondret." These crazy circumlocutions become standardized like names; one of my pre-school children calls his own mother "Grandchild of an Usiai woman"—using the term his father uses. If a group of youths painted up with feathers in their hair appear on the islet, our *wash-maries* flee, because who knows what terrible love magic they may not be sending towards them on the wind or in their cigarette smoke? And a really good girl doesn't want to be seduced by love magic; she wants to marry her "husband," whom she probably has never seen but who has paid for her properly.

The pre-school children swarm happily about the place, drawing pictures, fighting, crying, pleading, having his and her own way upon every possible point. A mother will hardly dare to take an injurious fruit from a two-year-old's hand. It is a perfect tyranny of childhood, and the virtues of childhood are illuminating: A good child is one who doesn't destroy property, doesn't beg food or tobacco from other houses and can talk well. No mention of fighting, deference or obedience. Boys up to their marriage work only when the spirit moves them; the rest of the time they loll about in the boys' house, singing and cracking jokes. Children of whom an adult asks information reply: "Who's grown up around here? Who should know? Am I grown up that you should bother me?"

We will be leaving here in July, so send all letters to the Department of Anthropology, Sydney University, Sydney.

"Go with a fair wind."

Peré men with their catch. The net is made of twisted bark cord.

III.
OMAHA RESERVATION
SUMMER
1930

Like all American anthropologists I was reared on American Indians—their past, their languages, their myths and ceremonies. But I had very early begun my field work in vigorous, ongoing South Sea cultures. Soon after my marriage to Reo Fortune I suggested to Boas that we be allowed to work, in a joint professional enterprise, among the Navaho, one of the few lively, evolving American Indian cultures. He refused. The Navaho "belonged" to Gladys Reichard and Pliny Goddard.

But in the winter of 1930, while we were preparing for our next trip to New Guinea, Dr. Wissler, the chairman of my department at the Museum, asked me to do a brief summer study on the changing life of American Indian women. In 1929 Mrs. Leonard Elmhirst's Committee had contributed a small grant to our department for an investigation of the family life and social setting in a tribe of American Indians and—an unusual state in those days—there was no one to carry out the research. At that period few anthropologists were interested in studies either of women or of change. Then Ruth Benedict offered Reo Fortune field funds to work on a special and difficult problem among the Omaha.

This determined our choice of the Omaha Reservation in Nebraska, where we spent three strenuous, grueling months caught in a style of work—without the language—we were not used to, watching the sorrows of a fading culture. In *The Changing Culture of an Indian Tribe* I used the tribal alias of "Antler" to protect the people we had studied. The recent renewed pride of American Indians in their special identity has made proper identification desirable and necessary.

From a letter to Ruth Benedict
Omaha Reservation
July 21, 1930

This is a very discouraging job, ethnologically speaking. You find a man whose father or uncle had a vision. You go to see him four times, driving eight or ten miles with an interpreter. The first time he isn't home, the second time he's drunk, the next time his wife's sick, and the fourth time, on the advice of the interpreter, you start the interview with a $5 bill, for which he offers thanks to Wakanda, prays Wakanda to give *him* a long life, and proceeds to lie steadily for four hours. This is the more usual procedure interspersed with demands to feast a hundred people before anyone will open their mouths, and one or two cases where people will talk through corruptibility. But they know so little. Practically everything stopped in the days of the old men's fathers. There was no long ritual which would be intact despite disuse. The only interesting points, such as the mechanisms by which a man had the same vision experience as his father, are quite unprovable. If everyone who knew a thing talked, the conditions would still be so aberrant in several cases and the cases too few to prove anything. There is a belief that death follows divulging sacred things; Joseph La Flesche died ten days after he told Alice Fletcher about the sacred white buffalo robe. And the devil of it is that when they do talk it's nothing. Just little one-line songs. "I'm the tobacco, that's me." It would have been an interesting culture to study with its dynamics because the emphasis on form rather than content would have come out then. But it's no culture to excavate in. What any *one* old man tells you isn't worth beans. . . . They are rich, know very little and fear death if they tell. And anyway, it's not worth getting. The head man of the Marble (Pebble) Society is a Carlisle *graduate.* He's seventy-odd. . . . Would you please write us what you think in terms of worthwhile investment of time and money. The feasts cost a lot to give not only in money, but in time, and spending a whole day at a feast. The conventional thing is to feast everyone from whom you want anything FOUR times. And there is no guarantee that they will tell you anything at the end, no way of checking whether they are telling the truth, and no way of making the stuff coherent and integrated anyhow.

I know you think we are spoiled and will, as you said, be harder too on the conditions than other people will be. But that's a two-edged sword. We are also able to value what we get nearer to what it would be worth gotten in a going culture. If I were going to be an Americanist I would stay in the library most of the time and only emerge to try to verify the most key points after a long search of the literature. For instance there is a place in Texas where the Indians go to pick peyote. If someone who knew a lot like you could go and camp there for four or five weeks, you'd get informants from every tribe in the middle U.S., according to accounts we get here.

. . . I see no way of checking up on material obtained from indifferent, unwilling and frightened informants for money, on what their fathers or grandfathers told them. It isn't the kind of material which ever carries the marks of authenticity on the face of it as verbatim ritual can. It's a case of "You belong to the same society as your father?" "Yes." "Did you have a vision of that society?" "No, no one had visions when I was a boy. The country was all settled and there was no place for a vision." "Who is older, you or S.W.?" "I am." "Well, S.W. went out and looked for a vision." No answer from the informant.

This is a culture in which many people refused to give their visions to their own son, but died without giving them; where patients were pledged on pain of death never to repeat the vision which the doctor told them when he doctored them. And they aren't poor enough to be tempted by anything less than $25 or so, and then there is no check on their telling the truth. . . . It may be this is what all Americanists are up against, and all of them overcome these insurmountable difficulties and emerge with something, but I am not convinced this is true. And anyway if this is the kind of material they have it is not worth much. After all kinship and social organization can be checked, material culture is tangible if enough survives, but religion of this sort could never have been gotten properly without a mass of detailed evidence, without say a hundred visions of fathers and sons, and material on what they did with them. . . .

Later. More light. Gilmore has been here, financed by Heye, and paid $50 a bundle, insisting on having song and vision. He refused to buy a bundle without the song and vision, so they reckon it is valuable. Now could you see if that information is recorded at the Heye Museum. . . .

Don't think I am a thankless wretch, please. And scold me if you think I still deserve it and am overestimating the difficulties. It costs $100 here to join Peyote. Do you think that is worth doing? It seems dull. We've seen the peyote death ritual. I feel as if I had no sense of values left, when I try to evaluate this work. It has rained after a month's drought. That is one of the mercies.

IV.

NEW GUINEA—ARAPESH
MUNDUGUMOR
AND TCHAMBULI
1931–1933

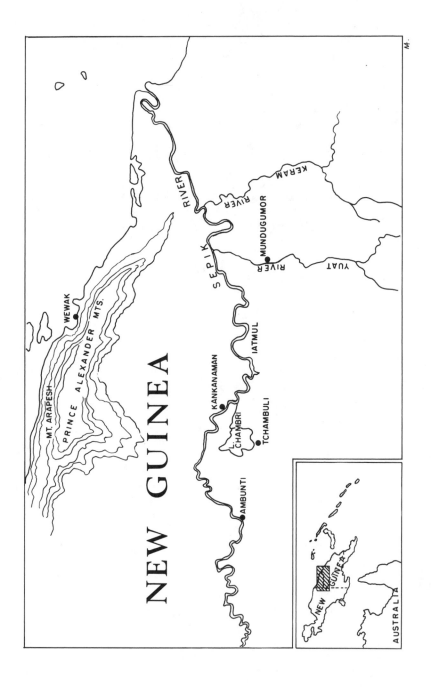

When we returned from our short field trip to the Omaha, I wrote *The Changing Culture of an Indian Tribe* and Reo wrote *Omaha Secret Societies* and the first draft of *Manus Religion*. We intended to leave for New Guinea in the spring of 1931, but just at that time a review of *Growing Up in New Guinea* appeared in the *Saturday Review of Literature*, in which it was alleged that I did not know the Manus kinship system. This so angered me that I decided to postpone our field trip until I had written "Kinship in the Admiralty Islands," which was the most detailed monograph on kinship published up to that time.

As my field funds came from the Frederick F. Voss Anthropological and Archeological Fund of the American Museum of Natural History, I could state my field expectations very broadly, instead of narrowly specifying a research problem, as in the past. What I planned was research on the way sex roles are stylized in different cultures, as a necessary prerequisite to any study of innate biological differences between the sexes. And this time I expected to include the whole life cycle, beginning with birth.

In September 1931 we were able to set out from New York.

Our initial choice for a field site was the Plains people, later called the Abelam, about two days' walk inland from the northeast coast of New Guinea, across the Torricelli range. We had seen pictures of the splendid ceremonial houses and we hoped for an elaborate culture. But the carriers recruited by Reo on his first trip inland from Karawop plantation all came from the villages across the mountains and they refused to carry our equipment and supplies beyond the mountain village of Alitoa, among a people we later called the Mountain Arapesh. So we found ourselves with an exceedingly simple culture, one in which the personality and roles of men and women alike were stylized as parental, cherishing and mildly sexed.

For the second part of the trip we decided to go up the Sepik River and choose the first group off the river on the first tributary above the Keram River, where Richard Thurnwald had worked before World War I. This proved to be the group on the Yuat River we called the Mundugumor, about whom we had no ethnographic information. Although they had very recently come under government control, theirs was already a broken culture. But they provided a contrast to the Mountain Arapesh for, while men and women were expected to display like personality traits, they were stylized as fiercely aggressive, highly sexed and noncherishing of children.

At this point I felt I was getting nowhere with my principal inquiry, although many other fascinating problems were emerging. Fortunately, we still had several months' field money and we finally selected a site on Tchambuli Lake, where I found a revealing reversal of the expected personality of the two sexes. The women were brisk, businesslike and cooperative and they dressed up the men and the children; the men were catty, exhibitionistic and preoccupied with decorative and artistic activities.

Gregory Bateson was working in the Iatmul village of Kankanamun and, intermittently, in Aibaum on Tchambuli Lake. Iatmul men were active, dominating and proud, while the women were shy, meek and responsive.

The combination of these several findings provided me with the theme of *Sex and Temperament in Three Primitive Societies,* a discussion of the way temperament transcends sex and different societies emphasize the same or contrasting temperaments as the basis of the expected personalities of women and men.

At the end of this field trip we each went our separate way. I returned to the United States and the Museum. Reo Fortune went to the London School of Economics. Gregory Bateson returned to Cambridge.

Alitoa
January 15, 1932

Our itinerary was as follows: New York to Panama, Panama to New Zealand, New Zealand to Sydney, Sydney to Madang, where we had to change boats and stayed with the District Officer. Then from Madang to Wewak, up the Sepik River as far as Marienberg, sleeping one night amid the cannibal mosquitoes. Then a week at the government station in Wewak, reading reports and making maps. Then by pinnace to Karawop, a plantation owned by the Cobbs. He is an Englishman, a Leeds University man trained as a wool buyer and now making the best of the price of copra by recruiting.

I stayed there while Reo went inland to scout about. The chances of getting our stuff moved in looked very poor. The country is mountainous, there are only native trails, running up perpendicular cliffs or along the beds of streams. The natives have practically everything they need of white goods, knives, blankets, kettles. They cannot be compelled to carry, and they don't like carrying. Reo was pretty hopeless at first, but he went about from one village to another, unearthed their darkest secrets which they wished kept from the government, and then ordered them to come and carry. This for some villages, and the others came by contagion. Reo came back to the Cobbs' not knowing whether any carriers would turn up or not, but the next day 87 came. In all it took about 250 to get our stuff up here to Alitoa, which is three days from Wewak, the government station, and two days from the Cobbs'. Mr. Cobb lent us six strong boys from his plantation line to carry me in. We had brought one of those string hammocks and they strung it on a pole and laced me, with banana leaves over me to keep out the sun and rain, for all the world like a pig. It was a little sea-sickish being handed up and down some of the mountains, but it was a great improvement on walking.

Reo had only been in this village overnight. He had made a speech telling them that he approved of all their old customs and that if we came to live here the village would always be full of matches and salt—the two great desiderata. So they said we could build a house and Reo marked out a place the right size in the spot they assigned to us and told them to build a house. Then he left a boy in charge of all our stores, piled up in two natives' houses, and came down to get me. We didn't have any idea whether we would find a house here or not, but when we got here they had the framework up and the floor down, a big fence about the whole open space, and the village paths were spread with sago-leaf thatch shingles. We lived in a native house for a week while they finished the house.

The way they built the house was amusing but difficult to follow. At least 100 men, most of them from surrounding villages, must have come in and done a little work, put up a post or put on a bit of thatch, and then drifted away, often never to return and claim any remuneration. If one went to the house at hour intervals one found entirely new faces among the workers. No one supervised, although there was one man, the *tultul* (man with the government hat, who is official interpreter), who had helped to build at the government station. He did the skilled jobs, but as far as directing the work, he would only remark vaguely: "We need more light wood." Then in half a day or so if no one had got any, he would go off himself and get some. We contributed half a bag of rice, on condition that they send carriers down to bring up a whole bag, and our shoot-boy finally shot a pig in the nick of time. This was for the big feast the day of the thatching. Then all those who had worked for three days got a knife. The house complete with big veranda, center room, bedroom, storeroom and cook-house cost, at the present rate of exchange, about ten dollars. We are now moved in and very comfortable. At night it is cool enough to sleep under two blankets and it is never unbearably hot. Our big door looks out on a high mountain across a steep valley. . . .

Salt is our chief currency. We can buy ten sweet potatoes for a tablespoon of salt and their appreciation of salted food is strong enough to make salt good currency day after day. They will walk two days to trade a big bag of taro or four mud-hen eggs for tinned meat or fish. And they are hospitable to a degree—easy, unexacting, not keeping careful count of food given and received. Each village has a *time hungry,* but it varies from village to village and one can always borrow. They are very quiet and unaggressive, laughter and a sort of lilting shout are the most frequent sounds. We are right in the village, in a fenced-in spot between two divisions of the village, but often it is as quiet as the grave. The night they finished building our house everybody went off to their farms and there were only three families left in the village. It is an excellent place to work on the language without too much pressure of people and consequent interruption.

The language is the most complicated thing about these people. It has eleven genders and twenty-two third-person pronouns and a different set of numerals for each gender, and the plural of at least half the words is completely irregular and unguessable. If

Our house in Alitoa. After the feast for the house, the women bid us goodbye while the men still are thatching the roof.

In Alitoa, houses and palms crowd together on the mountain ridge.

An Arapesh garden ready for planting.

you use the wrong adjective ending, they just look blank and refuse to supply your meaning for you. You have to learn the whole grammar before you dare say more than a few words. However, the people seem to have exhausted all their inventive capacity upon the language. They have big House Tambarans (men's ceremonial houses) and initiation ceremonies sometimes; but if they don't feel like having them, they just circumcise a boy or two casually.

If this letter sounds rather scrappy it is because I am writing it in intervals in linguistic work when Jack (our linguistic boy and boss-boy) goes off to chew betel nut or a boy comes in to tell Reo that there is a pigeon on a nearby tree. Our boys object to having their own names shouted through the village and so insist upon white names. So permit me to introduce Jack, large, opulent, tireless, intelligent, always preening his feathers but preening them with reason, endlessly good-humored in the face of being asked to pronounce the same word twenty times. It takes good nature and patience to stand being asked first for a word, then for its plural, and then to say: "I see it" and "I see them"—which has to be done for every noun to determine all its forms. Jack is also boss-boy, chief carpenter and general factotum. He has a fine animal lustiness which, combined with intelligence, is very pleasing and he is a delight to work with after our sullen little Manus schoolboy.

Next in age and rank of the houseboys is Tommy. He is married to a small solemn-eyed child of ten or eleven who is, it appears, but not clearly, his wife in name only. He ploughs his way vaguely through his tasks and provided there is nothing new or unusual about them does quite well.

Then there is my small *monkey*, Billy, a delicate little boy whom Reo sent me at Karawop, where he became tremendously impressed with the rituals of bed-making and table-setting. We like to eat on the open veranda, which is too cold for the natives, so I have fashioned Billy a smart jacket from an old cotton flannel pajama top. He walks cat-footed about the table, a necessary skill on the uneven, shifting floor of split flattened-out logs. But the minute he gets two paces away he streaks for the house-cook like a frightened rabbit. He had never seen a white establishment until a month ago and the pains he has to take to set a table correctly are almost equivalent to our remembering a set of Chinese syllables.

Furthermore, there is Harry, a happy, humorous fool, who runs errands and fetches things from the bush. And a dour shoot-boy, Yabinigi, who is here because he is fed up with his two wives, and Gerud, a *monkey* who can't talk Pidgin, but who is handsome and obedient. Verily a houseful and all obsessed by food. Quarrels over the best part of the cockatoo are the only storms which disturb their rather noisy unanimity.

It's going to be an excellent place to study the genesis of "gender consciousness" (a phrase coined by a lady reporter in Sydney), for the emphasis upon sex difference begins in the cradle —baby girls are decked out in earrings and necklaces, while boys wear no ornaments until almost grown. Little girls of four and five strut and flirt. The women do all the carrying, the weeding, the cooking and have to all appearances a hard life, but they are attractive, valued and conscious of being valued. Shut out from the religion, from magic and from the social life of the men, they nevertheless seem to maintain a firm sense of importance, and it is a sight to see a young woman swish her way across a village square where all the elders have been orating vigorously upon some affair of state. There is menstrual and birth segregation, also. But although the women are formally excluded from the House Tambaran and such, a man spends about two-thirds of his time alone on his farm with his wife or wives and their children, so family life is well developed. Husbands and wives talk pleasantly together in the sight of the village. One man was so pleased when his wife came back that he embraced her in public. The people commented and laughed; that was all. The most frequent cause of women running away is if one wife is offended with another or doubts her welcome; the husband doesn't figure largely.

Alitoa
February 12, 1932

It's pleasant being in the midst of the "big bush," which comes right up to our back door and in its insect form flies in the door. Butterflies and dragonflies drift in and out of the house and occasionally a bird gets ambushed in the rafters. The birds call rather than sing, a long series of plaintive, inquiring notes which begin before dawn and always after a rain. During the day the raucous-voiced parrots and parakeets have the air. The natives have conventionalizations of each bird's call which differ from ours and they laugh at ours and refuse to recognize them. The bush itself is a tangled mass of tall, very thin trees. One hardly ever sees a tree with a large trunk, but slender, four-inch-in-diameter trunks rise and rise towards the sky. The occasional flowers are high up, almost always solitaires and always unexpected. Our shoot-boy shot a *kapul* the other day, a little furry, red-brown marsupial with the most poignantly human hands. The feather duster, which Billy insists upon wielding, is made of cassowary feathers and we mix our photographic chemicals with a cassowary bone dagger.

Some government officer in a burst of agricultural enthusiasm went about distributing seeds here. Most natives would have refused to plant them or at least refused to eat the crops. But these people are epicureans and are delighted with every new taste. So they planted the string beans, the pumpkins, the maize, the cucumbers, the Chinese mustard lettuce, the tomatoes and the watermelons, and we almost always have fresh vegetables of some kind. And yet, who would expect to meet a stark naked *man-o-bush*, very dignified in his shell necklace, walking in one's door with a banana leaf full of tomatoes? Our shoot-boys keep us supplied with pigeons, so that we fare very well. It is easily the most pleasant place to work that I've struck. Cooler than Samoa. Cooler and nicer people than Manus and ditto for Omaha. Our lamps arrived with parts missing so we have only lanterns. But we breakfast at six and take no nap, so we are ready for bed by nine.

The people are very ethnologically unobtrusive. They like to have us here as a neighborhood store, as it were. It is convenient to be able to get salt and matches and knives and pipes and beads whenever they wish. They are quite willing to talk to us to keep us amused, as talk seems to be what we want. The children like to sit and play with my hair or stroke my hands or listen to the clink of the typewriter. They never go beyond sensation—the five senses, with sight and hearing only lightly exercised, and the brain never. Though they know that they think with the brain, with the cerebral hemispheres, in fact. But they forget with the heart, and it is the heart which goes away when people sleep and feeds on the red berries of a special tree, and so growth comes in the night. Sorcery is by getting hold of a bit of an enemy's body-leavings and passing it on into the *man-o-bush* country, where a sorcerer smokes it. If you

Ilautoa, Kule and their daughter, Mausi, in the doorway of their house.

know someone is trying to kill you, you spend your life taking a cathartic, the red sap of a tree which, when it is cut across, looks like a wounded piece of flesh, and so you wear yourself down to an apprehensive shadow. The idea seems to be to cut your connections with your previous excreta as frequently as possible, so that the connection with the bit the sorcerer has will be severed.

The secret of the House Tambaran and the sacred flutes (who knows, the Catholic fathers ask, what the flutes really mean?) resolves itself into the way the men keep meat away from the women by saying that the monster eats it and then secretly consuming it themselves. The flutes the men blow to scare the women away while they hide the meat. So much for one of the great secrets of the New Guinea mainland.

They never tire of exclaiming how weak my hair is and how clean my hands. The very small children's response to a white skin was to ask if they might wash their hands clean. Although these are supposed to be primitive Papuans, they have a fair number of our institutions—the family, the brain, the kiss, the chain. Love to all.

> From a letter to William Fielding Ogburn
> Alitoa
> March 7, 1932

They are almost pure sensationalists, these natives. There is an enormous development of oral eroticism in children, due I believe to long suckling combined with a willingness to separate older suckling children from their mothers for a couple of days at a time. Food and women are the chief values in the culture—women as wives, not as liaisons or violent seizures, as in Dobu and Manus, respectively. Patriliny is put over very strongly and there are definite moves to separate mother and daughter. For example, weaning proceeds by the mother smearing her nipples with mud, which she tells the child is excrement. A mother cannot be present when her daughter bears a child or she, the mother, will go blind.

There is a strong father-daughter attachment which appears—I can of course only speak provisionally as yet—to be translated easily into a dependent wifely relationship, as wives are bought as small children and go to live with the husband's family—the husband is usually only a youth—and are fed and cherished by their future husbands and their fathers-in-law.

There is a great emphasis upon physical contact. Everyone is eternally hugging or patting everyone else, and if a human being is lacking, a dog or a pig will do. Pigs are so petted and cosseted that they assume all the characteristics of dogs—hang their heads under rebuke, snuggle up to regain favor, and so on. . . .

It is a remarkably coherent culture with simple metaphors and fairly obvious mechanisms. The language, on the other hand, is exceedingly complex and rich; learning to speak with 24 third-person pronouns is also a little wearing, considering the simplicity of the results obtained, rather like opening a tin of cigarettes with a blow torch. There is a beach, mountain and plains variety of the one linguistic group. At present we are in the mountains with four boys from the beach, and we shall presently proceed to the unlovely plains, which are filled with blowflies. . . .

Alitoa
March 15, 1932

We have just been through the most ethnologically fruitful and generally wearing week we have had. Balidu, who is the "father of all," a tall, lean old man with a close and grasping nature, a broad and falsely amiable smile and the judicial manner of an important colonial governor, was giving a big feast to celebrate the earlier initiation of his son, Badui, a well-turned-out youth of about eighteen, who has two little wives of ten and twelve, respectively, and who, as the eldest son of Balidu, is already on his way to being an important person. As the big feast meant bringing the Tambaran into the House Tambaran and a huge gathering of people here, other people planned to transact their various small businesses, too. So there were also a series of smaller feasts, quarrels, recriminations, marriage payments, divinations and what not.

To appreciate what it means to have over 200 people gathered here, it is necessary to realize that the village is only a little over a chain (66 feet) wide and about a New York avenue block long. It is just a little level piece chipped off the top of a razor-back ridge with the clay worn hard by years of use. On each side the bush slopes steeply down several hundred feet. There are about 30 houses in the village, some of them only little boxes on stilts, 8 by 10 or 12 feet, others only rough shelters on the ground. As even the village site is not level but a series of little shelves and undulations, the place is flooded when it rains. Every bit of food, every stick of firewood, leaves for cooking and serving food, etc.—all have to be carried in a net suspended from the woman's forehead up the impossibly steep slippery paths.

So to entertain the expected crowd everyone had to work for several weeks beforehand bringing up supplies. They went away in small groups to work sago and came back from sleeping in the swamps with their eyes bleary and some pounds thinner. The yams are small this year because of an evangelistic cult, which promised that the white men would be driven out, a flood would wash the natives white in boiling water, their ancestors would return, and Burns Philp would continue to send them plenty of food, while the German priests would be returned to work as cook-boys and to fill up the shower baths which every native would have. So they built new houses and waited for the revealed time; meanwhile their

Climbing the steep, slippery paths, a woman carries every kind of heavy load in the net suspended from her forehead.

yams sprouted and went bad. Everyone is a little sad over the harvest, but not very sad because no one here, except very small children, ever maintains a mood of any depth or duration. One party was out hunting for weeks, getting tree possums, wallabies and tree-climbing kangaroos with ridiculous little hunting dogs that hardly look big enough to catch rats. This meat was then smoked in the bush and brought in all tied in a bundle decorated with pink and green streamers, very impressive and very high. Although the feast was a family matter, each man piled up his contribution in style and the rest of the family jogged around the pile in line, shouting, in acceptance of the contribution. Every time any member of the clan made his contribution, the family of Balidu, helped by the rest of the clan, cooked a feast of taro croquettes coated with grated coconut and gave it to him. Sometimes 25 men have been busy at once grating coconuts.

Coconuts saved for many months are displayed at a feast.
A Plains sorcerer looks on.

Then they brought the Tambaran into the village and all of us
mere females and children ran away to the end of the village and
repeated solemnly: "If we see it we will die." Meanwhile Reo went
about with the Tambaran, which is really two flutes—a mama and
a papa who very obligingly beget children (the uninitiated are told)
to sell to other villages, which lack flutes, for pigs. When the
Tambaran was safely housed in the village all of us were allowed
to come back again. But later in the evening the Tambaran lost his
temper because, Balidu said, he had not had enough to eat that
day. He started throwing sticks out of the house and we had to
scuttle over the side of the hill and down the slope in the dark.
Children got separated from their mothers and wailed bitterly, and
one kindly little blusterer got up and started beating the outside
of the House Tambaran for its treatment of the women. But everybody made such a fuss over this untraditional behavior that he got
quite sulky and the next day had a fight with one of his wives to
restore his masculine prestige.

I had to pause here while I went to investigate a child's cry, at present a subhead of scientific research. The children have a grand time having fits of hysterics in which they roll on the ground and bite the dust in a very literal fashion.

Once the old Tambaran is safely housed, all the young men in the village attend upon him, beating hand drums which have a deep, pleasant throbbing sound, like very soft drums, keeping the flutes wailing, a pleasant enough sound though quavery and un-patterned like an orchestra tuning its wind instruments, and pounding the big wooden drums which just make nasty noises. They also sing, at first sweetly but more and more raucously as the hours wear on and they become hoarser and hoarser.

After this has gone on for several days the continual noise, combined with children crying, people shouting, dogs barking and the general clatter and litter and confusion of a picnic ground, with people cooking and eating all over the place and a badly regulated orchestra in the background, is overwhelming. People are weary from overeating, if they are guests, and from under-eating, if they

Children gathered for a feast play at imitating possums.

Arapesh men play the sacred flutes, and women and children must hide.

are hosts, weary from the discomforts of travel and too close quarters, from sleeping on the ground or pushed off into some house corner far from the fire, weary of hearing accusations of sorcery. Everyone is cross and ready for quarrels. There was one set-to with clubs and staves and a spear or two which probably would have blown up into a nice little war if we hadn't been here.

Right after that was over, a party of six men wearing black paint on their foreheads and carrying green nettles, a sign that they had come to inquire about sorcery, stalked into the village. Then Gerud, our assistant cook-boy, was requisitioned to have a fit of possession and he dashed about digging in all the nearby mud and producing bits of rotting bamboo, which he alleged contained body-leavings of people from other places, and storing up a fine lot of trouble for everyone. One poor accused man turned up the next day to protest his innocence and finally burst into tears, whereat his accusers gave him some tobacco and that was over. Finally, the Tambaran was supposed to walk about and taboo all the coconut trees, and we all ran away. But unfortunately our shoot-boy caught a pig, which we distributed to our friends, and the Tambaran decided to stay and eat the pig, too, so it's still here, kept alive by the few men who remain in the place.

This great burst of activity came at just the right time, after I'd had time to work up a lot of preliminary detail and knew everyone, so I could make the best of it. But things happened so fast that I fairly raced from wedding presents to sorcery quarrels, scribbling as I went.

We've had a rather stormy month, altogether. Jack ran away because it was rumored he was trying to marry one of the already engaged girls. We had an anxious week before we got him back, for he was afraid of sorcery here, and we can't do without him; at least Reo's work on the language would suffer badly. Intelligence is such a rare quality here. Then Chinnery came up and spent three days with us talking over future places of work. That disorganized the boys somewhat, and then we ran out of sago to feed our boys here. In order to get rice up here, two boys would have to be on the road all the time, as a two-man load only lasts five days. So we've had to think up endless stratagems to get sago, which the people loathe working.

Still, it's such a delightful climate that all these difficulties are compensated for by a temperature which has never touched 80° since we've been here. I'm in better health than I've been since before I went to Manus. In the long intervals of peace when there are only a few people in the village, we even have quiet days, ending up with a game of deck tennis before dinner. . . .

Alitoa
April 20, 1932

We still have not decided what to call this mountain people for they have no name for themselves, just friendly little nicknames or names for sections of a community, like *man-o-bush* or "poisonous snakes." The weather has continued glorious, although now that the northwest monsoon is dying there are bad storms which make the thatch stand up like fur on the back of an angry cat and knock down the more superannuated houses of the village.

All wind and rain come from supernatural creatures called *walin*, who inflict storms on the entire community whenever unwanted people of another clan invade their domain or when members of the proper clan come and do not speak politely, reminding them of the relationship. . . . These people have made the *man-o-bush* into the devil, the man who traffics in the temporary angers of his nice neighbors, the professional sorcerer. The ghosts they have localized under the care of the *walin* of each clan and you do not have to encounter them if you go hunting elsewhere and are careful where you get your firewood.

So in the village you are free to have a good time—to smoke and chew and yawn and hum little songs under your breath and repeat the name of the nicest baby over and over or sing the baby to sleep by reciting the names of your favorite pig—or if you haven't any baby, a puppy or better still a little pig will do. If you are feeling gay, you can put flowers in your hair and red and white paint on your face; or if you like, you can put the paint on the baby or the pig. If you are feeling cross, you put the black paint of war on the forehead of the ten-year-old. If you have a headache, you tie a piece of bark around your head and go and sit in the *place clear* so that everyone will know how miserable you feel. If your mind runs on feasts, you can get out the hand drum and thump it happily all by yourself. If your pig dies, you can fasten a set of spears in a piece of bark and tie a yam to the bundle and set it in front of your wife's doorway, just to show her what you think of the way she looks after the pigs, and then *she* can take a long bright leaf and tie it into a knot and hang it over the door, just to say that she won't cook any more food for the people whose jealous talk made her pig die until they give her something nice for a present. If you have something important to say, you stalk through the village and everybody knows by your shoulders that something is up and trails along to see what it is.

For all that, life is complicated at times. It is dusk. We have not yet lighted our big lamp (which arrived two weeks ago) so dusk means the cessation of work on paper and we sit down for a breathing space before dinner. The village is dark, only an occasional flicker of fire shows through the eyelets in the bark walls of the houses. A tense nervous boy appears by the entry to the house-cook and stands there staring. We know that he has something important to say and wait. Is the sago bad, or has there been a fight, or has someone run away? He explains: "Gerud would like to work tonight after dinner. Myelahai has lost a big knife and he wants Gerud to tell him where it is." Gerud is assistant cook-boy and the only diviner in the village. We assent. Gerud's divining always brings us a fine lot of ethnological detail.

He eats a little bone-scraping from the skull of an ancestor mixed with a little ginger. Then he dashes madly about in the dark, plunging up and down the steep slopes at either end of the village until he unearths a bit of bamboo filled with rubbish, which he can allege is a bit of the physical essence of someone which has been placed in a wild taro root to cause a sore. Then he falls flat on the ground, arms outflung in a crucified position, and answers questions and also makes startling remarks about usually unmentionable things and throws in a few dark hints about future disasters.

Yes, we welcomed Gerud's divining. We comment on that fact and another face looms up in the half-lit doorway. Tommy. Tommy is worried and slightly truculent. He has come to say that he means to ask Gerud whether the brother of Yabinigi, our shoot-boy, hid that piece of possum bone which everyone saw him slip into his basket or whether he threw it away. Now we do *not* welcome Gerud's divining, for Yabinigi is a dead shot and the support of the household for meat. If his brother, who is an aged and faded moron, did hide that piece of possum bone, he means to damage one of our boys. This would mean a feud and the departure of Yabinigi, and with him all prospect of fresh meat. There remains the dinner hour.

Gerud is in the house-cook, just one thin wall and half a dozen feet away. We know from experience that his madness permits him the use of his five senses, tuned more acutely than ever. So during dinner we chatter to the table-boy (in Pidgin, not English) to explain that of course Yabinigi's brother did not want to sorcerize the boys. "How could he? He has no rings to pay the *man-o-bush*, a fine figure of a sorcerer he is!" And furthermore, of course, if it is true, Yabinigi will have to leave as he could not stay where his brother is accused and there is no one to take his place, so, of course, there will be no more wild pigs, no more possums, no more birds whose feathers make such wonderful headdresses. Then, too, we wonder whether it really is worthwhile giving Gerud permission to divine if it is likely to produce trouble.

Dinner is over. Gerud dashes about and falls flat in his trance. Tommy, kneeling and anxious, asks: "What did Yabinigi's brother do with that bone?" Gerud answers: "He threw it away down below because possums are his taboo, so he hid it first to save the boys' feelings." We sigh. The meat supply is safe for the next week, but only for the next week.

Then Reo goes into the interior and in one village Yabinigi shoots two pigeons and Reo keeps them for his carriers and boys. Later Yabinigi shoots a pig and an old man who was angry about the pigeons takes a bit of bone of the pig and fastens it up. Gerud reports this in a trance, which we anticipated, and Yabinigi, who is very temperamental, shoots nothing for a week. Thereupon we give out tripe instead of regular boys' meat and gradually Yabinigi's skill returns. You can never quite tell about Yabinigi. He used to run amuck quite frequently, but people got tired of it and fed him soup made of dog's dung. Afterwards they told him what the soup contained and that he would be fed it again unbeknownst to him unless his mad fits were cured. That was a year ago and he has not run amuck since. Still, we do not let him have a gun at night except when he borrows it to take to some relative who has been annoyed over not receiving some part of the kill, to get him to take away the angry talk which he made about future hunting.

Collecting, too, has its difficulties. In the House Tambaran— the sacred men's house—are carved figures which are named and charmed into a high state of dangerousness. When Reo went into the interior he marked some for purchase. Their owners carried them here, done up like little pigs in pieces of stiff bark. They came by the little side roads which are taken by women who are taboo, by hunters who wish to get home secretly with their kill and by people who want to buy pigs and who fear if others see them go they may say: "I hope he doesn't find a pig to buy." They arrived in the village. Reo put them in the storeroom. Immediately came a storm of protest from our boys. If they ate any food from that room, they would waste away and die. The place where our house ·stood was hot enough because a big House Tambaran had stood there, and these carvings were awfully hot and everyone would be ill. Then came a delegation from the village saying it was not safe to keep those carvings in a house where there were women and children, they must be placed in the village House Tambaran. Very well, we were only too willing, for I had been forbidden to go into the storeroom lest I see these mysterious images. But who was to carry them? The *man-o-bush* were still here, but they were tired and sulky because they had been paid only twice what they had been promised. No one in the place would touch the dangerous things, so Reo had to carry them himself up and down the village from which the women had all been barred within their houses. Then the secret of the exorcising leaf was bought dearly from the *man-o-bush,* and the store and house was carefully broomed. The worst is yet to come, for we have no idea how we are going to get the incubuses to the coast or whether all the Cobb boys will run away if they are brought to the plantation. While they were being carried, I hid in a native house with a woman who spent her time showing me an abortive drug and commenting sharply that men could not see the drug, that they could not even hear the name of it. Thus feminine self-esteem was avenged.

And so it goes. A mad world where little bits of taro and little bits of yam are each bought separately for a separately served spoonful of beads or matches, where every misfortune is magically determined and where one sits ready to pounce on the significance of a plate of croquettes being carried by the door. It is grand to have the lamp working; flickering, smoking lanterns have been a trial. While Reo was away something went wrong with the lamp and I could not light it, due of course to a party of *man-o-bush* who came to sell tobacco, which I refused, and gave them matches for vocabulary instead. When they met Reo in the bush they told him I had crossed them and so they had sold me nothing; this was tactful, for they thought Reo would be angry if he knew I had given them matches for nothing but a little *talk-talk.*

Then there was the night last week when Amito'a and I dyed skirts. This is one of the occasions when the women get back at the men. No men or children can come near, no smell of meat cooking, no knife which has ever touched meat, no feather headdresses can come near. The very sound of men's voices will spoil the dye, just as the sound of women's voices will anger the Tambaran and as the touch of a woman's hand may spoil hunting gear. We squatted in a windswept little leaf shelter and watched the great pot, its top covered with pads of big green leaves, boil over with a bubbling fluid which gradually turned blood red. And once some boys talked, and the skein of sago threads which was being put into the pot caught fire. And Amito'a's husband stayed with Reo until midnight and just to reassert his masculine superiority told Reo all about the nice brain soup which the warriors used to drink, brewed from the scooped-out brains of the enemy, although up to now they had been denying any touch of cannibalism. So Baimal danced about the room, illustrating the savage delight of war, for Baimal is always light and airy even when his talk is of death. And Amito'a and her sister-in-law, Ilautoa, squatted by the watched pot and said: "We feed pigs, we make grass skirts, we dance, two by two we go for firewood, two by two we bring up water, two by two we dye our grass skirts." The wind howled and ruffled the thatch, and I enjoyed it in spite of the smoke in my eyes.

Sorcery delegations, looking for the bits of the physical nature of their relatives, come into the village and talk menacingly to one another of what they will do to other people (not present), people who, when they do find them, they will pat. Then someone asks me to bring out the doll, the snake or the little toy dog. The dour atmosphere vanishes before enthusiastic old men who dance about with the doll, shouting: "Granddaughter! Granddaughter!" and little boys who hold the doll reverently and whisper: "Grandmother." The newcomers, who have not seen the snake before, scuttle up the house ladders.

I show the doll to Nemausi, about 3 years old, and her mother, Whasimai.

When they first saw the doll, they thought it was a dead child and were horrified by it. It took them a long time to get over their horror. Then they asked: "Will it grow?" and "Does it drink milk?" and "Why doesn't it cry?" And even though they have been told over and over again that it is an image, an *aboril*, the women still shout with disapproval if I lay it down with its head lower than its heels. And the bright little boys ask: "Why haven't you a pig, too?" And Reo scolds because of all the confusion which is created by the snake, the doll, the rat and the dog when he wants to get off quietly in a corner with an informant and find out whether a word has a whispered terminal /h/ or not and learn charms which will later make us all sick.

Our knowledge of the outside world is fragmentary. We know that America has done something which is like going off the gold standard only not exactly that. We know that Lindbergh's baby was kidnapped, but not whether it was found. We know that Edgar Wallace and Edison are dead, and that probably Japan is fighting China. Ruth sent some *New Yorkers* and *Times* and they were manna in the wilderness. . . .

On the veranda Reo is doing legend texts and the old men passing by ask: "What are you doing?" "Legends." "Child's play," they snort and pass by. Legends are only for children, you tell them to your children and then heave a sigh of relief and forget the nonsense so that you are free to concentrate on important things like charms, which are just (as it were) "Tweedledum and Tweedledee, Rumpty-dum and Rumpty-dee," male and female. Of one thing these people are very sure and that is "Male and female created he them." But at that, even those who are sophisticated about white people sometimes slip up in talking to me.

Alitoa
July 12, 1932

When I last wrote, I expected that we would be leaving on the June *Mirani*. The possibilities of this neighborhood seemed about exhausted. The next tribe on one side is badly missionized; on the other, an oil company is roving about with 100 boys. Beyond that the area is declared not under control because of a fight with a patrol, and then comes Aitape with a mountain wall behind it that has to be scaled with ropes. On the east is the Sepik River, but no way of getting there. There is said to be one pinnace in 300 miles here and its owner and his wife (departed for Hongkong), leaving a newly come and very green young cousin of Bernard Shaw in charge, with the munificent sum of two shillings . . . and no idea when the owners would be back. So there seemed no way of getting anywhere and we planned to go to Rabaul and leave from there for an island.

Then at the end of May Reo went down to Karawop and found that the government pinnace was going up the Sepik empty to pick up a party which was going to make a patrol overland from Aitape, and he arranged for us to go up in that about mid-August. So we sat down and quickly ordered six months' supplies. The order reads very oddly: item, 1,200 lbs. of rice; item, 1 packet of needles; item, 1 mosquito room; item, 1 tea kettle; item, 24 dozen tins of meat, and so on.

After that was sent off, the news came through that there is a dysentery epidemic in Aitape and a quarantine which may last for months and spoil the trip. But with unexpected good luck for this country, the owner of the pinnace returned from Hongkong with two suitcases, one case of whiskey and one of gin, so we will be able to get up the Sepik next month. We'll stay up there six months or perhaps more. The blessed thing about it is that we can go straight there without an interval of putting on white clothes and talking politely to all the other people who feel that the natives should be reserved for their special varieties of exploitation.

Reo has been away a good deal of the time these last two months and most of the local population have been walking about the country "finding rings," i.e., trading tobacco and feathers for baskets and rings. Most of the time the village has been quite empty, just a deserted, swept space filled with closed houses set on top of the mountain where I lived and typed back notes or painted copies of bark paintings which were too damaged to take home or explored the psychology of stray children. Sometimes a rumor would come through that the government was coming and *garamuts* —slit gongs—would be beaten and people would rush into the village to sit about without occupation and often without food for a couple of days until the rumor proved to be, like most news here, the work of someone's imagination. News here is shouted from mountain top to mountain top in a long-drawn howl which resembles dogs baying at the moon. The high mountains take the sounds and toss them back and forth until they become almost unintelligible. Then one hears people saying: "Oh, the *Kiap* [the government officer] is coming," and "A police-boy has come to Liwo," and "All the men of Liwo have gone to war," and "I think a man in Liwo has killed a pig," and "Now do you suppose the wife of that old man in Liwo has run away?" Any one of these speculations may crystallize into a statement of absolute fact at any moment.

The first time Reo went into the interior they shouted from the next mountain that he had been attacked and wounded and that a runner was coming through with a note. I sent a boy flying to meet the runner, and the two came up fifteen minutes later—while the local population stood about bewailing Reo as they do the dead—saying that he had been attacked with a tomahawk in the shoulder and arm. Then I opened the note and it said: "Please send more tea to keep the exposed negatives in, there isn't enough."

Someone had seen the note passing from village to village. And there had been a murder of a native the day before. The people further down below had lured him out hunting and had killed him and cut his body into bits and buried them in a mud hen's nest. The two bits of news—that Reo had gone into the *next talk down below more* and that a native had been murdered there—just got glued together.

It's curious, these people are not liars in the ordinary sense of the word. We've had one theft and that just a box of matches by an ex-work-boy from another place. But I discovered it and marched up to the end of the village and demanded from a seated group: "Who has those matches?" They are trade matches and we use them as currency, so there are literally hundreds of boxes about. I couldn't possibly have proved a thing. But the silly boy immediately took them out of his ditty bag, looking sheepish, and said feebly that he hadn't stolen them, he had just put them into his bag.

But what they don't do in intentional lying, they make up for unintentionally. The other day I heard a great lot of talk at the other end of the village and turning to a native nearby I said: "What's that row about?" "Oh," said he, "that's Whoiban. He has come over to see Balidu and he's telling him that if he, Balidu, doesn't stop sorcerizing Aden, he, Whoiban, won't help Balidu take pigs to the Kobelin feast." I then walked up to the other end of the village. Balidu was sitting down peacefully under his house.

"Where is Whoiban?" "Whoiban isn't here. He's in Liwo." "Was he here?" "No." I returned to Wabe and confronted him with the fact. He shrugged his shoulders. Someone had said that Whoiban was coming today, and if he had come that is what he would have said.

Sometimes parties of *man-o-bush*, naked except for necklaces and bones through their noses, pass through. They march into the village as bold as brass, demanding food from the few women who are here. If they don't get it, later someone will die, they hint delicately. There was one *man-o-bush* who walked up and down in the middle of a feasting crowd at Kobelin, and remarked loudly: "I am tired of being a sorcerer. I am sick of it. Continually people ask me to kill people. I am weary. Of course, when a man in Dakua died, I revenged his death. Still, I am tired of sorcery. Of course, this is my road. I always go this way to the beach. I never go down the dugong road, only on the road of the death adder. I would have liked the head of a pig. You haven't given me the head of a pig. You have eaten all your pigs. Well, some sago will do."

A Plains sorcerer.

And no one of the fifty men who listened answered a word, but quickly some went and got him some sago. For in his house and in the houses of his friends, tied up in small pieces of leaf, is the *dirt* of the men of the beach and the men of the mountains—a piece of headband, a bit of old bark cloth, a handful of grass skirt on which the personality of the wearer still rests. When the *man-o-bush* cooks this *dirt,* the spirit of the victim leaves the body and crawls towards the interior in the guise of an insect or a snake, until finally the *man-o-bush* traps it in a bamboo and chokes it to death.

Nearly every grown man this side of the grass plains has *dirt* outstanding in the plains villages. The anger of the neighbor who stole it and sent it off to an inland sorcerer has long since evaporated. The quarrel because of which it was stolen is almost forgotten, but the *dirt* remains and the unhappy victim is subjected to systematic blackmail by the sorcerer. Knives, rings, tomahawks pass in an endless stream into the plains where ugly old men, covered with ringworm and unwashed—for a sorcerer may not wash while he works—sit and cook the *dirt* and take it off the fire again when the pay is enough. And small parties of two or three *man-o-bush* walk safely through a population of many hundreds, for the means to avenge their death is safe in the interior.

Meanwhile the beach villages exercise another sort of blackmail on the unfortunate men of the mountains. For from the beach come all the new fashions—armbands and headbands, the newest way of fastening possum fur on the end of a basketry headband instead of around it, an armlet with a pendant of shells, new-style earrings made of grass tassels—trifles and trash, mostly, but immensely valued. All these vanities come from Murik Village, near the mouth of the Sepik. Murik is the Paris of the coast and the Murik people sell their styles dearly, for many pigs, rings or perhaps the prostitution of the buyers' women. One village pays for each new set of vanities and each is a job lot which may include big masks, death-dealing charms, dance steps, sets of ordinary ornaments and a new style of dress. To get the package, each village up the mountain road must pay pigs and rings. Thus the custom of wearing a G-string has gradually penetrated the interior as each village has paid for the right.

So these poor people live between two drains. For all that they enjoy in life—feathers and finery, dances and new songs—they must pay pigs and rings to the beach; and for the preservation of their health and their very lives, which the jealousy, malice and outrage of their neighbors have placed in jeopardy, they must pay and pay to the hated *man-o-bush*.

And even we, although we buy their food and their services, must go into the interior to collect the really good things, as La'abe remarked after he had carried a package of £40 in shillings from Karawop and nearly drowned in the rivers along the coast: "It was hard work for me to bring this money just for the *man-o-bush!*" And now Reo has gone away again into the interior, carrying tomahawks and long knives—for which these people have nothing to exchange—to purchase carvings and paintings from the *man-o-bush*.

We are becoming steadily more disassociated from the outside world. We had stopped Rabaul's forwarding our mail because we thought we were leaving, so we have had no mail for two months nor will we get any for another month. The mainspring of my watch is broken. The only radio news we have seen refers to events which we don't understand for the most part. It is like being on board a ship, condemned to a few hundred feet of moving about and knowing that practically nothing can possibly happen. Recently the District Officer and the Medical Assistant passed through and were hung up here for two days. After they left we were both ill; the impact of white people, sitting about, more food than we usually eat and possibly onions, which we hadn't tasted for six months, was too much for us. I am more convinced than ever that the way to do field work is never to come up for air until it is all over, but of course it is luck to have a spot healthful enough to make it possible.

I repeat my cry for reading matter, old magazines preferably. Novels aren't good, for one is tempted to finish them, which is bad. With a magazine one can ration oneself to one article or story a day.

I even begin to wonder what the date is. These people have names for moons, like "the moon when we get bananas from a deserted yam garden," but as everybody plants at a different time, no two families' moons are alike. As they say: "You count the moons but we just know their names," and all they really know are names which can be applied when appropriate to the moon which is up at present, and no two families have the same calendar. They think it's very odd that we think a moon would have only one fixed name.

The three boys left behind by Reo—who, together with three children, make up the population of the village—are all painting themselves and giving a concert in the hope that I will buy a new flute one of them has made, for the whole sum of a razor blade. Which I have said I would.

From a letter to William Fielding Ogburn
Alitoa
August 10, 1932

We are hoping to wind up our eight months in this culture within a few weeks and go up the Sepik and attack the contiguous inland culture from the river, instead of going three days further over mountains. But there is a dysentery epidemic creeping along the coast which may shut us in—make it impossible to take native carriers through or have them bring us up any further supplies. In that case, we'll probably have to take what supplies we have and lots of ammunition and go further inland and trust to living on the country. It's very poor game country, quickly played out. After the Sepik we shall probably do an Australian tribe if our funds hold out. We are spreading them as thin as possible.

We have been able to get excellent material on cultural change here. This is a flexible, receptive culture, continually importing new ideas, a process which has been considerably accelerated by the opening up of the King's Highway, so that "walking about to find things," once a very circumscribed vested interest, is now open to all. It is also a culture with very transparent social processes. The theory of incest which Reo put into his *Encyclopedia of the Social Sciences* article is here demonstrated most explicitly. There is the tendency for the small group to try to keep its daughters at home or to intermarry continually with one other small group, which soon comes to the same thing—and the counter-tendency to form alliances for cooperative work with other groups. People who refuse to marry their daughters off are regarded as socially criminal and other groups come and abduct them. The only sanction against incest is "if you marry your sister, what will you do for brothers-in-law? Who will help you to find meat and sago? Who will fasten pigs?" Keeping your women to yourself is strictly parallel to keeping your surplus yams to yourself or your pigs.

The saying goes: "Other women, other pigs, other yams you can eat. [This is literal.] Your own sister, your own mother, your own pigs, your own yams which you have piled up [indicating a surplus], these you cannot eat." Seen in this light, incest prohibitions can be understood not as some obscure psychological process in the mind of the individual, but as necessary to social cooperation in societies which operate at the kinship level of integration.

Kenakatem, Yuat River
September 1932

In the mind of the most suburban Rabaulite and in the mind of the wildest bush native, the Sepik stands for mosquitoes, crocodiles, cannibals and floating corpses—and I can assure you we have seen them all. We are not on the Sepik itself—that is Bateson's stamping ground—but on a tributary eighty-seven miles from the mouth of the Sepik which runs east into the Madang area. This river is called the Yuat. It is parallel to the Keram River, where Thurnwald worked, and about a day further up.

The mosquitoes have not been exaggerated; they are the most amazing, determined, starving crew imaginable. The natives can tell at a glance whether they have had a full meal and are likely to make a nasty bloodstain on one's clothes—but most of them never have had a full meal and are fighting for just one before they die. It took us about a week to study out the various ramifications of the mosquito problem: it has a clothing, an architecture, a closet economy all its own. For instance, you can't keep anything in suitcases, for the mosquitoes get in the cracks and when you go to find something attack by the thousand. Air-proof boxes, if you swish the air all about while opening them, will do. But the best plan is to spread one's possessions thin over endless shelves, so that everything can be found and grabbed before more than a hundred wounds are sustained. Bathing except at midday has to be done with a whisk in one hand. Reo has of course discarded shorts, and I have evolved a costume which looks like a beach parade but serves very well, an ordinary dress and pajama legs—fortunately Reo had a lot of old ones in pastel shades, so I can even evolve color schemes. This with a large straw hat—for short strolls a helmet isn't necessary—makes me feel slightly ridiculous but protected. The too-long pajamas bell over one's shoe tops.

Then one can't sleep in a room, for all the mosquitoes will go and hide in the corners during the day, having been disappointed of the feast which they glimpsed through the net. Even two boxes placed near each other give them somewhere to hide. So we have a huge veranda, with the mosquito room standing in the middle of it, and our bed at one side. Away at the back is a dressing room; one side is a store, but most of it is just great open spaces, for air and safety. The mosquito room is a box, nine by ten by ten feet, made of copper wire and uprights which bolt together. The door closes with a pulley made of a box of cartridges. There is a box with two drop-hinged ends, thrust through the wire, and one boy cautiously inserts a dish and drops his trap door, then the inside boy opens his side and whisks out the dish. The floor is made of a ground sheet, and one has to use ash trays inside and not pour the tea grounds through the floor, which seems ridiculous faddishness in New Guinea. Inside there is just room for a table, two straight chairs, and two easy—our old ones—chairs, a box for papers, a tiny bookcase for glasses, my workbasket, etc., and at all four corners hang native net bags containing our slender supply of reading matter, mending, etc. For once you go in, you don't want to open the door if you can possibly help it. It means living in horribly small quarters and climbing over each other all the time, and clearing away work so that the table can be laid, but it represents heaven none the less.

We have another room for working in, as the mosquito room would not be safe with swarming crowds about. The other house has nothing in it and there are usually plenty of onlookers to discourage the mosquitoes.

So the mosquitoes deserve their reputation; as for the rest, the crocodiles do eat people quite often, they make drawing water from the river at night a dangerous matter, they provide the art motif and a great model crocodile actually swallows the initiates, and most important of all, one can cook with the whites of crocodile eggs. "Making corn fritters with crocodile eggs among the cannibals." They were all cannibals until about four years ago; boys of twelve have eaten human flesh and they show merely a mischievous and merry glee in describing their previous diet, but the idea of eating rats fills them with shuddering nausea. And we've had one corpse float by, a newborn infant; they are always throwing away infants here, as the fathers object to observing the taboos associated with their survival.

It's a pretty enough place, a swift-flowing river about two blocks wide with high, grassy banks and a few palms. It looks like a river flowing through any flat country anywhere. In this it differs from the "Big Sepik," which does have a stronger resemblance to the "great grey-green, greasy Limpopo River, all set about with fevertrees" and is full of floating islands and things "too horrible to describe"—according to the narrators.

We got here in a tiny pinnace which had to make two trips to

In Kenakatem, effigy of a man erected for a death ceremony.

get our stores up. There is no anchorage between a point near Boram (Wewak) and the mouth of the Sepik fifty miles away, and the soi-disant nephew of George Bernard Shaw, who is the engineer (Harris says Shaw has no brothers), was scared stiff, so we made a couple of false starts before setting out and in the end he and Reo had a rather anxious night of it. It has to be done at night because one has to get into the mouth of the Sepik at dawn. Boram has an ice machine with 72 chambers and kills a bullock a day, so we fared royally there. We had a day in Marienberg, too, with an anxious young patrol officer who began talking about how expensive visitors were and how he preferred tins to money, as soon as we arrived, and concealed his relief when we only stayed overnight and provided half the food. A glance at maps, etc., decided us on the Mundugumor people up this river, as the nearest large group off the Sepik and out of the mission's clutches. And here we have been for three weeks. It was much easier settling in with all our equipment available and then there were two partly completed houses which we simply altered.

The natives are superficially agreeable, but . . . they go in for cannibalism, headhunting, infanticide, incest, avoidance and joking relationships, and biting lice in half with their teeth. Also their language is simply ridiculously easy—has hardly any grammar at all. I've hardly had to learn it, it's so simple. But the women's grass skirts are quite gorgeous, and at dusk and dawn when there are deep shadows on the water and everyone comes out for a stroll, I like them very much. The village extends along the edge of the river and is under water in the wet season. At one end of the village is the chief man with ten wives, while his rival at the other end has nine. These harems are not primarily designed to minister to a Turklike lust, but rather are up-and-coming tobacco-growing concerns, work all done by the women. None of the women has ever seen a white woman before and I am sure I shall start a suffrage movement among the more distant villages who find me *talking place*—speaking the native language—an accomplishment of which the first white man certainly did not boast.

We brought our two best boys with us—Jack, who is now radiant, obstreperous, swift and forgetful, as cook, and Billy, who is growing more important and bossy every day but is still a jewel. We are also saddled with a child whom Jack calls "grandfather" and who is no use at all, but was brought along as a companion

Dancers wear cassowary feather headdresses; one carries a hand drum.

Kwenda and her son, about 6 years old, lead a dancing party.

to Billy and was finally the cause of Jack's coming, because he was *sorry long two-fela monkey*—worried about the two little boys—he said. They simply can't believe that these friendly people who give them so much betel nut were really cannibals and they come and ask me every other day if it is true.

The longer one stays in New Guinea the more amenities accumulate; at present we have glass glasses, an oven for baking bread and a grater made out of a butter tin. Also our stores allow us two tins of asparagus a month, two tins of cauliflower and two tins of crackers. . . . A local fact which is not a compensation is that, being a river and easy to get about on, there are far too many white people about and the *kiap* has been here once and calaboosed half the male population over a stick fight, and a pinnace passing today reports that he will be up again next week—to get the other half, I suppose. Where one can afford to transport even two tins of asparagus, the *kiap* is bound to be interfering around.

Kenakatem
December 2, 1932

It has been a long, grimy day. I am so sticky I loathe myself, but there is no bathing for another hour or it will all have to be done over again. I have worked on fishing, sago working and hunting methods, which mean diagrams galore, and Reo has been working on various odd kinds of tambarans, which has meant crowds of natives trooping into the inner room to open little baskets and display various esoteric bits of wood.

These people have been charming in many ways; they are even postponing their quarrels until we leave, a point which we—scientifically, of course—do not appreciate. It takes adepts in hypocrisy to be sufficiently self-conscious to think of what a front they present to a white man. The Samoans would do it, but not the Manus, who are too sincere, or the Arapesh, who were too simple-minded, or the Dobuans, who could have thought of it but were too nasty.

Haven't we a fine lot of different peoples to ring the changes on? And in two weeks we will leave these and find some others. It is really much more startling than knowing personalities to know a lot of different cultures. The impact is so much more definite and compelling.

From these people we have wanted very little in the way of food and service and it has been very pleasant. Also, Reo has had a marvelous informant, a man with so good an analytical mind that one feels it is a tragedy that he should have been born in a primitive society where all his powers of detachment, logical reasoning and attention are wasted. . . .

December 3, 1932

I shall be 31 next week. I am not dispirited by the fact as I have gotten in quite a lot so far and I do not seem to be looking any older, although this climate is hard on the skin. I am a little thinner and I play quite a decent game of deck tennis. Think of my playing any kind of athletic thing fairly well!

Initiation ceremony at the "birth" of a flute.

The flute named Kenakatem.

Tchambuli
February 1, 1933

We are now embarked on our third New Guinea culture, although all actual activity is at present suspended in the interests of getting a house built. We finished up Mundugumor quite happily and left them with gayer words and friendlier adieus than we have ever had from any primitive people. We had troubled them so little and they had all behaved so well—even to making us a special sacred flute with a heavily ornamented carving on top, which was named Kenakatem (our village) and presented to us with enormous style. The sacred flute is a baby crocodile, its mother is a water drum, and they took the water drum down to the water where it bore the sacred flute, which cried at first with a weak little newborn voice and then more full-throatedly as it emerged, was carried up the river bank and finally was lodged in state in our

house, where someone came to feed it every day. Our boys ate its
sacred food and were very happy. And the river obligingly rose just
before we left so that there was no labor carrying our boxes down
the river bank and they all smiled at us sweetly out of their so
well-behaved presences. They had even solemnly decided to have
no quarrels while we were there. . . .

All our possessions, still very numerous because we started out
with between six and eight months' supplies, were stowed away on
a slow and lumbering pinnace and we waited at Yuaramo, the
village at the juncture of the Yuat and the Sepik, for the government pinnace. We spent a day in Yuaramo, sitting on the edges of
our windblown mosquito net, and then the *Osprey*, with the young,
very earnest and incredibly and awfully loquacious patrol officer,
named Thomas, came along. Fortunately he likes bridge and we
played three-handed bridge with a grim-death determination not
to change the subject all that day. It is confined and wearing, this
pinnace traveling in the full tropic heat, shut up inescapably in a
three-by-four-foot cabin.

That night we slept in a middle Sepik village—the part of the
Sepik which is by common agreement called Big Sepik by all the
surrounding peoples. It was like stepping into a new native world
to see the great well-built houses with their enormous house posts,
the imposing horned roofs of the men's houses with giant gaping
faces worked in rattan at each gable and the ceremonial roads
threading their way between huge artificial mounds. But Mr.
Thomas had brought two kittens with him and one of them got
shut up in the House Tambaran and one got lost in the grass and
they mewed at each other all night except in the intervals when
squads of angry police-boys were sent searching for them in the
rain. He was very gay about it and kept suggesting captions like
"Cat Catching in the Cannibal Camp," but it was a rather trivially
sleepless night.

At dawn we caught the cat and rubbing our eyes and attended
by clouds of mosquitoes climbed onto the pinnace and made a
duck-shooting detour to see the spot Mr. Thomas dreams of making into a personally conducted tourist resort. And because of it
we forgave him the cats and the compulsory bridge and also his
having put half the big men of Mundugumor in calaboose right
after we got there. For he took us to our first "black water," which
is the loveliest thing the Sepik has to offer. The Sepik itself is a

wide, monotonous and rather dirty yellow river, remarkable only for its varying load of drifting islands which have detached themselves from the half-submerged fen lands and have drifted out through some waterway and finally will float out to sea. But into these fens lead what the natives call *barets*—and you must all learn this word because I know of no English one to describe them. They are like canals. Often the natives either have cut them entirely or widened or changed them. They flow from inland lakes into the Sepik, when the Sepik is low, and sometimes when the Sepik is in flood from its mountain sources hundreds of miles higher up, the *barets* flow backward into the inland lakes. The water in them, unless too much of the Sepik has gotten in, is black, coal black and shining with a dull lustre, and tasting like lily stems and sun-heated oil. And the lake to which we came, through a *baret*, was all black, polished like a mirror, with faraway mountains ringing it all about and on its shining surface floated pink and white lotuses, lying in patches of thousands, their pads still and fixed on the black water, while among them stood, as if posed for a portrait, white ospreys and blue herons. It is all as ordered, as simple in its few contrasting themes, as a Japanese print, and the lack of miscellaneous, only half-congruent notes makes it seem unreal. It was before sunrise when we slid into the center of the lake and the black irregular arms of water stretched away among further and further patches of lotuses, seeming almost to meet the mountains, and there was no human thing there except ourselves. It is the best this country has to offer and very, very good.

But the *baret* which should have taken us out to the Sepik again was choked by an island which had started towards the sea and had gotten no farther than the *baret*'s mouth, so we retraced our path across the lake, out again to the Sepik, and after another broiling day we picked Gregory Bateson up in the afternoon and slept that night in his village. Or rather, I slept and he and Reo talked, after I had finally cozened Mr. Thomas away from them. Gregory was at Cambridge with Reo and has been working in the middle Sepik for almost a year this trip and he was here before. Afterwards the battle raged in the pinnace cabin as to whether we three were to talk anthropology or whether Mr. Thomas, fortified with a year of Radcliffe-Brown's lectures as a cadet, was to talk it. Reo and Gregory took to the baking roof in despair, while I listened sympathetically to Mr. Thomas and steadily made vows about teaching anthropology to otherwise reasonably harmless people.

At Ambunti we stayed with the wholly adorable District Officer, Robbie, who is loved by and loves everyone. He had as a guest, chance-sent on a recruiter's pinnace, a most ambiguous female with a rattrap mouth, mascara eyes and a wholly suspicious and deadly restraint of manner, who was, I think, pretending to pretend that she wasn't a reporter or a spy from the League of Nations. Sometimes she added to the comedy of life, but not thoroughly enough. I only properly enjoyed her the day we drank champagne before breakfast, certainly the only alcoholic drink in the world which can be appreciated at dawn. The fact that it wasn't our champagne, but belonged to some prospectors who were 300 miles further up the Sepik and counted on having it when they emerged with their pockets full of nuggets, didn't spoil its charm.

Then there were recruiters and pinnace owners and a ship's captain who could talk our Arapesh language, having blown up all the drums in one of their villages years ago as a government officer. There was a mad, proud recruiter and a slightly truculent little one and government officers—some good boy scouts and some not. Altogether it made quite an odd party. We played bridge, Reo and Gregory played chess, in between we discussed the functional method in anthropology or some such remote topic and at intervals Robbie interjected: "Stop it, I say, stop it!"

Finally, Gregory took us in his canoe with an outboard motor —we have ordered one, too, and when it comes we will be free citizens of the Sepik world, at least to the extent of two canoe loads of supplies—exploring on the upper Sepik to find a new tribe. Robbie had persuaded us to have our stores brought to Ambunti because he wanted us to do the Washkuk, a mountain people who live on the site of the finest view in this part of New Guinea. They have had a pretty nasty time from government because they murdered a couple of police-boys who had been interfering with their women. Robbie wanted us to go and make it all up to them with loving kindness and beads and knives. So we went to see them.

We had to stay in a Sepik village, Jambon, overnight, where the people are sulky and seemed quite mad, for they kept us awake all night with ridiculous precautions against some kind of attack, which they said was supernatural. We thought it might be natural, but it was only a disordered figment of their own minds—a sort of group anxiety because a police-boy had once been killed there by a neighboring headhunter. They were so sulky that I decided not to entrust myself to their carrying and walked up the Washkuk hills barefoot and without mishap. So now I am emancipated; I can walk everywhere and get brown and freckled in the sun, and I feel as if I had been let out of jail.

The Washkuks are sweet and gentle and proud and so simple as to be a little silly; they speak a gender language and live scattered in a hopeless fashion all about their nice mountain. We decided it was too much like Alitoa and bid them goodbye—to their great relief for they wanted to go hunting for weeks and weeks and were afraid we would be a great nuisance. So we made a good collection and then came down to Kankanamun, Gregory's village, on the *Osprey*. We stayed there through a *singsing,* and then Gregory brought us to Tchambuli in his canoe. All our stores came last week.

Here we are on a lovely lake, not quite black but crowded with lotuses. The people are gentle and polite and slip between one's fingers. They have some of the complexity of the Big Sepik, but they speak a gender language again and it is probably all a veneer. There are about 400 of them within an hour's walk of each other, they have some thirteen House Tambarans and we've already seen a big feast.

Tchambuli women fish on the lake near beds of lotuses and water lilies.

Tchambuli men go to a ceremony in canoes; Reo Fortune in the middle.

The three localities are so jealous of each other that the only way to get a house built was to have two built, and so now we have two houses which they are completing in their own good time, but strictly in step. And the next dilemma is which one to live in. One has the better view, but the other more adjacent usable buildings; one has the higher roof, the other the straighter floor. And we have told them that when there is a big feast in one half we will live there, and vice versa. Meanwhile each hamlet sends spies to the other so that the work will keep abreast, and I fret and fret over the delay at really getting organized and settled.

But it is really a beautiful place, by far the most beautiful in which we have ever been. We can go swimming in the lake or canoeing on the lake; the roads are not so rough but that I can walk over them easily even at night; the people are in many ways like the Samoans, and therefore most intelligible to me and very attractive. It's fun being able to compare our material with Gregory's as we go along and to check up on the probable meanings of things. Our boys are hard at work fencing a vegetable garden and tomorrow I shall have my seeds all planted and some day not so far distant we will have lettuces and radishes. We have fresh fish every day and a constant supply of cold duck for quick meals during intervals in ceremonies. Altogether it is an excellent spot and we think we will like it very well.

From a letter to William Fielding Ogburn
Tchambuli
February 27, 1933

I can't find any carbon, so I don't know whether I told you that the Mundugumor proved a most perfect study in the pathology of incest: a people with an exceedingly elaborate and unstable class system, which had broken down in different ways in different villages. The theory that the only way to get a wife was to trade an own sister for a wife produced the situation between brothers and between father and son which would obtain in the case of true incest if there were an uneven number of brothers and sisters in the family or if the father entered the arena for the daughters.

Reo has been very much interested in the sociology of incest for some time and this was heaven-sent material ready to his hand. Freud's great emphasis upon the son's love for his mother is, I think, the wrong taking-off point for an understanding of society, as it belongs primarily to a period when the son is socially weak and non-significant. But the father's desire for his daughter and the brother's for his sister can be very powerful social factors as the men are old enough to enforce their demands. When the old man of a household in Mundugumor is planning to rob his son—that is, by trading a daughter for a young wife for himself, instead of letting his son exchange his sister for a wife—the father picks a quarrel with his son and ejects him from the household if possible. The psychology of fighting for one's sister, as a way of assuring oneself a wife, is engendered very young. One sees the spectacle of seven-year-old boys standing up and bitterly demanding that the *back* for their fifteen-year-old sisters be given to them, not taken by a father or a half-brother.

All this is played into by a fantastic system of descent according to which the boy belongs to the line of his mother, mother's father, mother's father's mother, etc., and the girl to her father, father's mother, father's mother's father's line—straight alternating sex descent lines, which have totems of their own. All the girls in a polygamous family belong to their father, take his kinship terms, etc., while the sons are split off both from the father and from their half-brothers, who belong to different lines. It was all very good stuff.

Now in Tchambuli we have the opposite kind of society, one which knows all about euphoria and all the rules for avoiding

Mother and child.

conflict. Dual organization and cross-cousin marriage, and the two wives of a man always come from the same clan, if possible, which means there are not two opposed kin groups back of half-brothers. I am beginning to think that something interesting may come up in the way of a correlation between a sense of distance towards affinal relatives, with its accompanying avoidance and jesting relationships, and a sense of respect towards blood relatives, which goes with only diffuse, happy jesting and no strains which provoke jesting relationships. But this is only a hunch at present. These Tchambuli people belong to the simpler New Guinea stratum again, the more Australoid type, with another gender language. They are primarily too happy to let themselves be dragooned by their culture into heavy tragedy attitudes.

We are in a lovely place here, on a big lake sprinkled with pink and white lotuses. A lovely little island has just blown across the horizon and paused in front of our house in the space of time it took to write this letter. The Tchambuli are a people who have been harried for half a century or more by the more warlike Sepiks. Now with government control, they are back enjoying their ancestral lands and working like bees to build up their damaged culture.

It's a hint that the underdog in primitive times is the one to study once government control comes in. These people have been under control for about five years. Mundugumor were hurling spears at every passing pinnace three years ago, but as they were top dog on the Yuat River, they are now so bored with peace that they do nothing at all but enjoy their ill-gotten wives.

> From a letter to Clark Wissler
> Tchambuli
> March 26, 1933

We have settled in one of the lake cultures on Tchambuli lake, adjacent to the middle Sepik culture (Iatmul). This Tchambuli culture presents a complex picture as a gender language is again spoken and many traits distinguish the people from the middle Sepik culture at present, but there are also many traits in common. In some respects they line up with the Mundugumor people, of whom we made a survey study last autumn, who in turn have some traits in common with Thurnwald's Banaro. This whole south bank of the Sepik has a definitely different cultural emphasis from that of the north bank, of which the Arapesh were representative.

We are working here in close touch with Mr. Bateson, who has already spent a year and a half in the middle Sepik. This makes accurate comparative work possible, and it looks as if the Sepik valley would become one of those areas in which delicate cultural comparisons can be made because a number of adjacent tribes have been studied thoroughly. The kinship systems, the personification of supernaturals, which inhabit water holes and are embodied in flutes, and many aspects of material culture show important similarities throughout this whole area. Its genius may be characterized as a fundamental inability to stick to fixed forms, a continual tendency to humanize rather drastic cultural relations, sometimes to humanize them so far that all form is lost and chaos results. The south bank has tended to develop fixed marriage forms and tentative class systems, which have in turn been rather knocked about by human motivations. In contrast, the north bank, as represented by the Arapesh and their border peoples, have relied upon developing temperamental attitudes rather than cultural forms; these temperamental attitudes have successfully resisted and revamped the less agreeable aspects of culture imported from the south bank. This is, you will understand, a schematic statement of a very complicated state of affairs, many details of which have yet to be worked out, but it will give you some idea of the type of problem which faces us.

The Sepik valley is perhaps the richest in material culture in New Guinea proper. I have already completed a collection from the Yuat tributary (Mundugumor) and the grass country between the Yuat and the Keram. The Yuat art is individualized strongly, although it was probably only made possible by the complex and definite stylistic development of the whole Sepik valley.

Tchambuli lake is another important center of Sepik art.

The collections labeled "Sepik River" in the collection of the Museum come from some seven or eight local centers; only a small part of them, the conspicuous wood work, comes from the middle Sepik itself, which is primarily an important trading culture enforcing its economic needs by superior numbers and fighting ability. So I shall be in a position to make a collection and record techniques and art conventions from one of the exporting and manufacturing centers.

The Tchambuli tribe is what Rivers described as a "closed group"—some 550 people speaking a language which is not understood elsewhere and leading a self-sufficient social life. For their trade connections they depend upon the medium of the middle Sepik trade jargon. Fifteen men's houses, each the center of a local patrilineal group, are scattered in a continuous line along the foot of a mountain. The gardens—in the wet season—and the dwelling houses are located back of the men's houses on the mountainside. For large ceremonies the whole group acts as a unit; for smaller ceremonies there are three hamlets which keep their more private affairs within their own limits. Although they are a fishing, canoe people, they were inferior in fighting force to the middle Sepik, and about ten years ago were so badly worsted in raids that they scattered into the more distant mountain regions. With the coming of government control and the prohibition of headhunting, the Tchambuli came back to their old village site, evicted the middle Sepik squatters and began rebuilding their culture. Everything that they possessed had been destroyed or rifled—their ceremonial stools, their big slit gongs, and so on, had been carried off to the middle Sepik. (For old Tchambuli things I am fortunate in

Dancing women honor male masked figures.

having Bateson's cooperation as he is gradually buying these up from the looting villages, which value them but slightly.)

For these special reasons Tchambuli presents a particularly interesting culture. While the prohibition on headhunting discouraged and depressed the conquering peoples like the Iatmul and the Mundugumor, it has given a new lease on life to the harried victims of the more warlike tribes. While this particular new stimulus to Tchambuli life occurred under white control, it is, I think, quite reasonable to suppose that similar conditions occurred in aboriginal days, when the attention of the conquering peoples was temporarily diverted by enemies on another border. In any event, the culture is in a fine state of activity—the Tchambuli are building elaborate men's houses, dwelling houses, working and validating canoes, initiating children and manufacturing ceremonial and useful objects with which to replace the theft and destruction wrought by the enemy.

As the hamlets extend quite a distance—it takes about an hour to walk from one end to the other—we have an organized scout system of selected youths from each men's house who come and report on all events of interest, receiving a safety razor blade for each report. Work is further complicated at present by high water, so that all the better roads are under water and canoe transport is necessary. We expect an outboard motor—to be fitted to a large canoe—at any moment, which will make it more practicable to follow the people on trading expeditions, pig hunts, and so on, and also to arrive promptly on the scene when an event occurs.

Accompanying masked dancers to *mwai* ceremony.

When our outboard motor arrives we shall be able to make collecting expeditions to neighboring cultures, also. At present with the river rising steadily, the mosquitoes are very bad and traveling about is highly undesirable. All sedentary work, either writing up or with informants, has to be done inside a net or in the mosquito room. It is necessary to postpone any work with the children until the mosquitoes are less numerous, as work with a group of active children is practically impossible inside a fragile net on a canvas floor.

As you will judge from this account, I am very well satisfied with this location and, indeed, regard the working conditions as the most favorable we have encountered since Manus. The size and relative compactness of the group, the easy water transportation, the absence of a boys' food problem, our housing conditions and the number of available informants are all excellent. Events move at such a pace that even two of us are sometimes unequal to coping with all of it and there are many days when we have to snatch meals at the most unlikely hours. Fresh fish forms a very welcome diet change after many months of birds and tins.

Like most of New Guinea, the men's houses and the religious cults make for a sharp division between men and women, and it is therefore ideal for a man and a woman to work together in this culture. The language is the most difficult one we have struck; it is also quite interesting as its multiple genders are in the process of breaking down in favor of a simpler, two-gender classification with living and non-living things as its basic categories.

This whole area, as I mentioned to you in letters last year, presents some striking likenesses to the Plains. In Tchambuli one of the conspicuous parallels is the cross-cutting of blood groups by other types of social groups, either matrilineally or arbitrarily constituted. Although the Tchambuli are not as explicit as the Omaha in recognizing the way in which this variety of cross-cutting organizations makes for cementing social ties in a large group, the similarity in actual functioning is obvious.

V.

BALI
IATMUL, NEWGUINEA
1936–1939

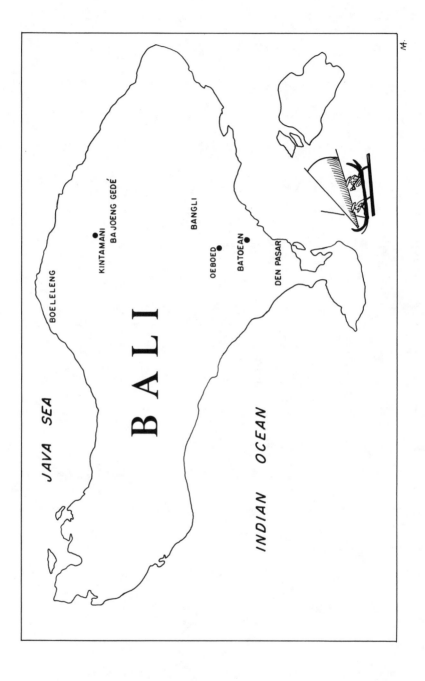

The Bali-Iatmul field trip was very different from any I had so far undertaken. It was the longest and in many ways the most complexly organized of all my field trips. It was planned around the marriage of two anthropologists—Gregory Bateson and myself. Once more I traveled alone on the long sea voyage across the Pacific. We had arranged to meet in Java, but had to fly on to Singapore to get married. From there we traveled on a slow boat moving through the islands toward Bali.

The choice of problem and of Bali as the site of our research was made in response to an inquiry by the director of the newly organized Committee for Research in Dementia Praecox, who asked psychologists, psychiatrists and anthropologists how they would go about studying dementia praecox (today called schizophrenia) in terms of their own discipline if they had a hundred thousand dollars to carry out a research program.

I had some fragmentary knowledge of Balinese culture. Many years before I had seen some films of trance dancing. And in 1934 Jane Belo, whom I had known since she was a student at Barnard, brought me some very interesting materials from Bali, where she had been living. It now appeared to me that Balinese culture had many elements that suggested it would be a suitable one in which to explore the presence—or absence—of schizophrenic behavior. Gregory visited the United States and together we developed a research plan for work in Bali that would also involve Jane Belo and her musician husband, Colin McPhee, who was studying Balinese music. When the Committee for Research in Dementia Praecox rejected our fairly elaborate plan, we decided to pool whatever funds our respective institutions could muster and try to execute as much of our plan as we could in Bali.

In Bali we worked in cooperation with Jane Belo and Colin McPhee, Walter Spies, the German painter, Beryl de Zoete, and Katharane Mershon, a former dancer. We found a gifted Balinese boy, I Madé Kaler, who became our invaluable secretary, and

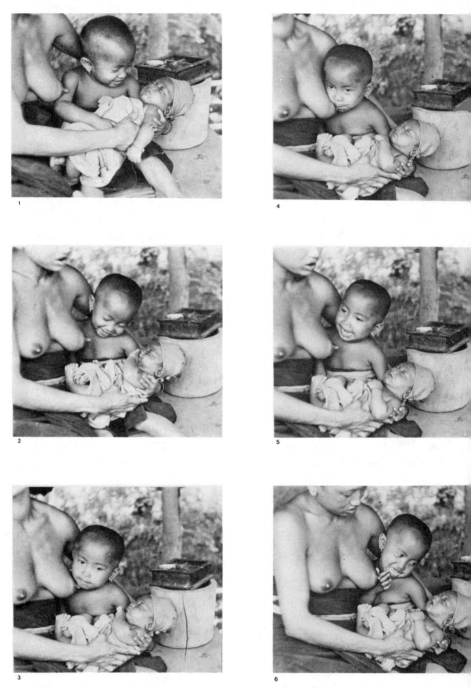

Sibling rivalry. Men Njawi with I Njawa and I Koewat, Plate 72, *Balinese Character.*

trained two other young Balinese, Goesti Madé Soemoeng and I Moerdah, as secretaries for Jane Belo and Katharane Mershon. The seventy-five rolls of Leica film which Gregory had brought were clearly insufficient and we soon sent for a rapid winder and hundred-foot rolls of 35-mm film and embarked on a massive program of cutting and developing our own film.

By the end of two years we had developed such a completely new style of recording with stills, film and Balinese text accounts that we found we had no comparative material. To provide for this we went to the Iatmul on the Sepik River, where Gregory had worked earlier.

After eight months in Tambunam, just as we were preparing to leave the field, a witch hunt against homosexuals broke out in the Pacific which echoed from Los Angeles to Singapore. Many of our friends and associates in Bali were under attack. We had intended to meet Jane Belo in Sydney only to talk over with her plans for her own further research, but in the unsettled situation it did not seem safe for her to go back to Bali alone, so we returned with her for an additional six weeks' work. This was especially valuable as the children whom we had been studying in detail over time were now almost a year older and were again photographed.

On the ship coming home in the spring of 1939, it was clear that war was imminent. Our British fellow passengers were already discussing their military assignments. Our daughter was born in New York in December 1939. Gregory, who had gone to England to report, found there was no immediate role for an anthropologist and returned to the United States. In the months before wartime activities claimed our whole attention we managed to get done a large amount of cataloguing and analysis of our material and prepared *Balinese Character* for publication.

I have returned to Bali only once, in 1955–1956, when Ken Heyman accompanied me to photograph as adults the children we had known, the artists we had studied and the changes in trance and dance styles. We arrived in a tumultuous political period, during the transition to complete Indonesian control, and it seemed unwise to write a field letter. However, the stills and film will provide background for a later return to Bali, now planned for the summer of 1977, when I expect to work with students and film makers already in Bali.

On board S.S. *Tapanoeli*
February 2, 1936

It is a trim, quiet little ship with a sort of furry, warm precision about it which is Dutch. There is discipline, but it is not too intense; there are very good meals and a French menu and a white steward who, himself as thin as a maypole, hovers solicitously in the background and tries to make the officers fat.

There are some five separate social orders. Very much the first, there is the Captain, the Chief Officer, the Chief Engineer and the Passengers. The passengers are a too pleasant asset because they mean a hot midday meal as well as a hot dinner and the officers get too fat, and when their wives see them in a year and a half, they will scold. Then there is the Officers' Mess for all second and third officers, mop-headed apprentices and wireless officers. Then the crew, who are white. Then the Chinese stokers. And separate from them, the Malay cabin boys. The Chief Officer has a short-wave radio in his cabin just off the salon and there we listened to the news of the King's death, broadcast by short wave to the colonies every hour for 24 hours. The Second Officer—to whom one cannot speak—has a cabin just down the corridor and his radio plays all sorts of things, unofficially, during our meals. . . .

Although I have done this three times now, that is, made the long sea trip to the field among people who knew nothing about me and my work and regarded the whole thing—a woman going off alone to study natives—as fantastic and reprehensible, I had forgotten just how weird and isolating an experience it is. If I had said I was a schoolteacher going out to visit my brother who was a clerk in Singapore that would be all right. They would treat me with the gingerly roguery accorded a spinster in her thirties, but my place in the universe would be otherwise approved of. But this way! They had to know who I am because I wanted a freight rebate from the company for my equipment; that is, they had to know what I do. It is extraordinary how most of one's life is spent either with people who merely know one as Mrs. Jones' niece, and so behave, or else with people who know one has done a certain kind of work which they recognize and understand. The peculiar ambiguity of the traveling professional woman has a quality all its own. Although I never contradict the other passenger's endless misstatements, he suspects that I might be able to do so. And the three officers show me pictures of their plump Dutch wives, who all look old enough to be my mother, and of their half-grown children, and they say that one thing about the sailor's life is that when he comes home it is always a honeymoon. And then I work too much, a sin I have not committed on other trips. . . .

In the evening the four men play bridge in Dutch and talk about the Boer War and I sit at the other salon table and sort notes for the day. It is so windy on deck that a lot of time is wasted keeping papers weighted down and sorting is impossible. I weigh the papers down with two volumes of Swettenham's *Malay Language,* but I have not had much time to work on it. However, I shall get off the ship with enough Malay so that new Malays whom I encounter will think I can speak it and so speak back, and that is all that is needed. It is fantastically easy. . . .

Oeboed, Bali
April 29, 1936

I meant to write a bulletin after Durban, but after that I got so much better lighting arrangements on the ship that I was able to work in the evenings and three bouts of writing a day left me too tired to write letters. And then all the ports came at once, one every day or two, with a rush of new sensations combined with heat and the noise of unloading iron girders. After that there was Batavia and the flight to Singapore and the long boat trip to Bali, any segment of which would have made a letter, but which are all hidden now behind the elaborations of Bali itself. So you will just have to take it that I was in all those places and that I regret I didn't have time to write.

Our first contact with Bali was Madé, whom Gregory found in Batavia, a tiny little shy creature who comes about to my shoulder and who had come to Batavia in the hope of getting work. He had learned English at school in Java, taught by a Javanese in Dutch to a Balinese boy! So it was possible to start working on the language at once.

In order to get to Bali from Batavia it is necessary to go first to Soerabaja, the most eastern city in Java. We went there by boat and then discovered that if we continued straight on to Bali we would arrive on the New Year, *Nyepi,* when no fires can be lit, no food can be cooked and no one can walk about on the roads. So we sent Madé straight over—it's an overnight boat trip from Soerabaja to Boeleleng—and took our boat on around Madura and Lombok as the simplest way of living through the next two days. We then arrived in Bali the day *Nyepi* was supposed to be over, to be met by a very downcast Madé, who had walked miles to meet the boat and say that it was still the New Year and everything was still taboo. However, the Tourist Bureau of the KPM (the steamship line which owns Bali more or less) managed to send us across the island in a bus and we were only stopped once by a patrol armed with drawn krises who looked more ferocious than they were.

As a result we had an experience we will never have again. We drove for three hours straight across Bali, through village after village, without passing a soul on the roads and in some villages without seeing a single face. It was the most extraordinary sensation, like journeying in a dream through the landscape, which bore every sign of recent habitation but from which every soul had vanished. The villages consist of high walls which border the road on both sides, with roofed high-stepped gates at intervals of about ten to twelve yards. Over the gates and beside them hung dried streamers of what only recently had been fantastic streamers and banners of green palm leaf. With no people to distract us, we were able really to see the country itself, as it is hard to do when the road is crowded as far as the eye can reach with picturesque and motley crowds of people and animals.

And a lovely land it is! with some twenty equally beautiful and different scenes which repeat over and over in astonishing and unpredictable rhythms. In this inhabited end of Bali there are very few trees, only coconut palms, bamboo and an occasional enormous tree some four or five yards in diameter when all of its extra roots are considered. One of the lovely views is an almost open plain of rice fields, a few palms and one enormous tree of this sort, squatting in a thoroughly primeval fashion in the midst of the fragile rice and slender palm stems. There are gorges, any one of which would be listed as a "beauty spot" at home, unbelievably rough and jagged but with the rough lines all blurred by a light, coarse grass. There are the rice fields themselves with half a dozen characteristic but different aspects—those which are almost on a level, whose principal charm is the great variation in the same texture and color as one small plot ripens an hour or a day behind the other, but all the varying shades remain within the same narrow range, and the flooded fields, which actually do mirror the sky, and the steep terraces, where the roots of each stalk stand out like sharp patterns along the edge. Up above 2,500 feet the landscape loses almost all tropical feeling. Spare brown fields covered with bracken and edged with scanty windbreaks of very sparsely covered trees make it look more like western park land.

The animals and the people all fit so well into this landscape that after one has once seen them together it is a little hard to think of one without the other. The water buffalos are a beautiful gray, rather like ashes of roses, and the young ones are actually pink when they are scrubbed. The little brown cattle are a neat fawn color and the ducks, which people drive in flocks, are a soft gray-brown. The people working in the fields wear great flat saucer-shaped hats on their heads in their fields and as they come in from the harvest, the men with two fat sheaves suspended on a pole over the shoulder, one at each end, and the women carrying sheaves high on their heads, so that in the dark they seem like prodigious masked figures. Normally the roads are always filled with people —people walking with a long easy stride or running at a trot—men who are carrying rice and women who often have some twenty large pots tied together in a pattern on their heads, or twenty bricks or little tables a yard long and two feet wide covered with dishes of food to be sold at some feast place.

Three hours' driving in the bus brought us to Den Pasar, the second-largest city in Bali and the center of the more artistic, more conservative part of Bali. There at the Bali Hotel we found word waiting for us from Walter Spies that we were to go straight on to Oeboed, another eighteen miles. We had written Walter that we were coming—or I had written him and Gregory had written Beryl de Zoete (an English woman who is writing a book on Balinese dancing with Walter). But we had no idea whether he would have room to take us in or whether he would even be at home. We arrived to be greeted warmly and told that he had a house for us and a full complement of servants, so that five hours after arriving in Bali we had driven some seventy miles, passed through some dozen subcultures and become established in a household of our own.

Walter is a perfectly delightful person, an artist and a musician, who has lived in Bali for some eight years and has welcomed and entertained all the interesting people who have come here. He has done a great deal to stimulate modern Balinese painting and has painted Bali himself and in general has worked out a most perfect relationship between himself, the island, its people and its traditions. We are still living about ten minutes' walk from him. Almost every day he and Beryl take us to some ceremony or Walter finds us a *toekan* (craftsman) to build us a house or solves some other tangle for us. He and Beryl will be our neighbors for another three weeks or so, until our house is finished in our mountain village. Our only other neighbor here is a mild, responsible, only a little twinkling Dutch artist who supplies system and bookkeeping in Walter's attempts to protect and encourage the Balinese artists to resist the tourists and do good work.

Our present house was built by a nobleman for his mother and it has a cement floor, doors that lock, incredible Victorian furniture with Balinese motives worked in among the scrolls and two impressive stone gods on the terrace back of the house. Over the heads of the gods we look out across endless rice fields to mountains some fifty miles away. The domestic staff, which Walter assembled from the local supply, includes a gentle and beautiful girl who looks twenty but must be at least thirty and who has trained all the cooks in Bali (there are only four or five) and always comes to peep over the edge of the veranda when a new dish is served to see how we like it. They all have ideas of their own and the household runs along of its own volition gently, without friction, without a raised voice and with only occasionally a little flutter of conversation like a swirl of dry leaves in the prevailing mellow, effortless tone. Their movements seem to have no beginning and no end, but flow on from any point to any point. When a boy is hanging clothes on a line, he picks up a garment, transfers it to the other hand, pins it to the line and picks up another all as part of one undulating sequence.

I don't know what would be the best way to give you an idea of the contrasts here. It is the most extraordinary combination of a relatively untouched native life going along smoothly and quietly in its old way with a kind of extraneous, external civilization super-imposed like an extra nervous system put on the outside of a body. Motor roads of black loose stones run through villages which are each protected by a magic wall against demons and over the heads of the motorists a screen of pointed bamboos is aimed at the demons. Along some of the roads on which people still carry all their rice—as it is taboo to move it by animal transport, a taboo that is now breaking down—there run telephone wires which con-nect all government offices with each other. From shady corners where a dozen men in sarongs may be comparing the virtues of fighting cocks in wicker cages, police in smart green uniforms and broadbrimmed straw hats may step out to ask your chauffeur for his driver's license. At a temple feast by the sea, where all the gods are brought in magnificent procession, held aloft in little sedan chairs shadowed by ceremonial umbrellas and preceded by women carrying pyramids of food and flowers shaped into offerings, one will see vendors of "ice candles." These are sticks on which ice has been frozen in the shape of candles and the vendors bring them in large thermos bottles strapped to bicycle bars. And at a theatrical performance at night, while some 500-year-old dance form is being executed, half the audience will be carrying flash-lights.

But all this apparent "civilization" is on the surface and Bali seems to have learned through a couple of thousand years of foreign influences just how to use and how to ignore those influ-ences. Accustomed to an alien aristocracy, accustomed to succes-sive waves of Hinduism, Buddhism and so on, they let what is alien flow over their heads. Meanwhile an anthropologist is presented with an unprecedented situation—quick, easy transport between dozens of versions of the culture. A journey that would take three days in New Guinea—and more than that to prepare for and re-cover from—is made here in an hour. Each village may have only one or two periods of feasting a year, but they come at different times and one has only to take a motor car out on the roads to find the palm leaf streamers which, stretched across the road and fas-tened to every gate, proclaim a feast or the little unroofed enclo-sures which announce a theatrical performance. Or one may glimpse over the walls of some temple the bright colors of fresh offerings or perhaps meet a Barong, the great supernatural beast

Procession to the sea.

whose mask and body are worn by two men. All this means that in a month we have seen almost all the important types of ceremonial—though we haven't yet seen a cremation—and so will be able to approach the study of one village with a real understanding of what will happen in the future. When people mention a ceremony we will know what they are talking about, instead of substituting inaccurate imaginary pictures for months and months until the particular ceremony occurs in our own village.

We have chosen our village, way up in the mountains, a lovely self-contained square village. And next week they will start to build the house, a horribly elaborate matter in this country of skilled craftsmen who would rather build no roof at all than build a big one badly. . . .

Bajoeng Gedé
June 21, 1936

After solemnly resolving that Sundays were to be occasions on which we did something different, however virtuous and necessary it might also be, we found today that we have too much to do and decided that Sunday will have to be like any other day. However, the unexpected descent of the assistant chief priest cut me off from all my notes and so I shall try to fit in a bit of a bulletin.

The visit of the assistant chief priest is by way of capitalizing on defeat. Yesterday he arrived in style to announce that we would have to pay a fine because in an initial walk about the village I had visited the cemetery, which in this village and in this region alone is taboo to women. Everywhere else we have been in Bali the Temple of Death is filled with statues of female witches biting children in half and Derga, the goddess of Death, is also the queen of the witches. But Bajoeng specializes in being different from other villages. We are filled with prohibitions: A man with curly hair or whose wife has curly hair can't belong to the village council, nor can a man with two wives or a widower. No Brahman priest can come to the village. A Barong can come here and dance, but the men who wear this mask cannot sleep here. People cannot have mattresses. The priests and their wives cannot wear silk, etc. Thus we maintain our identity. When the delegation arrived, by the grace of God Gregory had been to an all-night men's meeting (show) in a cemetery in the next village the night before and had learned that the fine for a woman's going to the cemetery was 5,000 kapengs. So he did not ask what the fine was but pleaded ignorance and it was finally agreed that we will pay for half the sacrificial cow which will wipe out the ceremonial defilement. But now we are trying to double the priest's five clubs by demanding that they teach us all the law at once or else we shall refuse to entertain any more communal responsibility.

We have been here over a week now, feeling our way—and that not cannily enough, as the tale of the cemetery shows. Before anything is done, one must work out points like this: Anyone who visits a house where there is a new baby under 12 days old (if a later child) or under 42 days (if a first child) becomes ceremonially unclean for a day. What is a day? The rest of the time after seeing the child until one has slept a full night in one's own house. (*Note:* Visit a new baby near the end of the day.) Can one go from one taboo house to another? Yes. (*Note:* Visit new babies in bunches.) Fortunately, there is no birth due for a month or so.

Building this house and moving in have all been like a miracle in New Guinea terms. All our gear had to be carried in from the road, a good twenty minutes' walk with three steep dips in it. Peloedoe, the village on the road, was to have done the job, but they asked seven and a half guilders, whereupon the two coolies on the lorry took the contract themselves, hired six other men and carried everything themselves. They would arrive with two tables and four chairs or three huge boxes on a pole and literally run back for more, quite matter of factly and without any enthusiasm. In the same way, this house has been built merely by finding a chief carpenter and paying him money. He has paid other people money, paid for buckets of sand, paid for every scrap of bamboo, bit by bit, and the house has gone up.

The combination of such primitive conditions and the power of money is fantastic. These people think in kapengs, and one kapeng is a Chinese coin with a hole in the middle equal to one-seventh of a Dutch cent. The kitchen bookkeeping goes something like this. Madé comes in: "I have given Nang Oera five guilders to take to Kintamani [the market] and Meregeg has given him fifty cents. The clothes for the boys were exactly 2.20. This is the change for the chickens and the vegetables. He could not get nails, so this guilder comes back. There was last night fifty cents in the kitchen and from that I have paid thirty-five cents for firewood. I need fifty cents to give to Meregeg." On the table lies a guilder, twenty cents and some forty kapengs, and from Madé's statement I have to figure out whether they are ahead or behind on their guilder a day allowance. I was proud when I finally discovered that they had spent three cents of the next day's money. And with all this they can't count. They get into endless muddles—they are always forming clubs with a common treasury which becomes so involved that the club has to dissolve.

The house is quite an establishment. The Balinese are so short of building materials that any very large house terrifies the builders, so this had to be planned as a set of houses—one of their compounds usually contains more houses than people. First there is Gregory's house with a veranda almost on the road, so that we can overlook the village, and a room in which we receive special informants and where we work in the evenings. It contains a high built-in couch, bookcases and endless other shelves, the dictaphone, dry boxes, etc. Then there is a little cement path, covered with a bamboo roof, a gate and the diningroom, which is a square veranda, just closed in with shutters at night. This is the one spot we reserve entirely for ourselves. It has pretty bamboo furniture and a pleasant view of the village over the tangle of little gray roofs to the temple gates and the great dark trees which stand behind the temple. There are three gates from the diningroom; the second leads out to the kitchen and the boys' rooms and the third into my house. Here there is a large workaday veranda with a big table which has two sets of legs, so that it can be lowered to the level of children sitting upon the floor. Here I keep a pile of mats for visitors, boxes for the more daring to sit upon and shelves of medicine. At one side is the bedroom in which shelves filled with square baskets do the duty of bureau drawers. The kitchens are very imposing. There is an ironing veranda, but there is to be no ironing as we cannot get either charcoal or coconut shells up here, so it only contains a drying rack for pots and pans which wandering dogs come and knock over at night. Then comes the bathroom, which contains a huge cement tank for storing water, then a storeroom, then the actual kitchen with a Balinese clay stove perched on a bamboo and cement table. Then the boys' room and then Madé's room, which contains a table and chair and is an endless

Our house temple is consecrated.

source of curiosity to everyone. And finally another sunny veranda on which the boys do their bargaining and where people wait about early in the morning. Although there are tiny glass lamps or lanterns hung about at intervals, finding one's way at night, after all the sets of shutters are up, is rather difficult. . . .

(The conference is over and the high priest, worn out, has vowed that the list of taboos is complete.) Now a whole week has gone by, but I have not had another chance to add to this. We seem to spend our days covering unlimited numbers of sheets of paper with typing; even keeping track of them is a part-time job.

About the village itself. It is about a twenty-minute walk from a tolerable motor road, which, however, afterwards becomes so steep that no motor car ever comes up it, as there is a more direct route to Kintamani. The walk is a path which winds up and down and over two dry river beds and finally reaches the wall of the village and the West Gate. There are three of these gates, guarded at night by two men from the one of the three divisions of the village to which the gate belongs. The whole village is surrounded by a hedge. It is said by local ethnologists that this is a wall to keep evil spirits out; to date, the people of Bajoeng insist that it is a wall to keep thieves and robbers out.

The village is a stepped triangle about 350 yards long and 250 yards wide with the temple at the elbow. Our house, which takes up about ten house sites, is also along the elbow so that we are almost at mid-distance from the two ends, north and south, of the village. The village is laid out in streets and the house sites are neat little rectangles, about ten-by-twenty meters, which contain a half-dozen buildings: a house with a raised earth floor and a bamboo platform, perhaps another of these, a rice barn (shaped like a corncrib), two or three open sheds, perhaps a special one put up for a feast, and a little fenced enclosure full of planted flowers

Bajoeng Gedé, looking south from the crossroads at dawn.

where the family shrine stands. The roofs are either of bamboo tiles or of bamboo placed alternately face up and face down after being split. The roofs are all rather sharp. The unusual ugly one widens out to an angle of 80 or 90 degrees. The village lies on a slope that is not steep enough to let one house overlook the other but that makes it possible to look upward to the temple, which rises through a series of walled courts to an inner court at the high, sacred end nearest the center of the island.

The village is filled with pigs and chickens and cows and there is always a pleasant barnyard murmur about and a touch of barnyard in the air. The cows wear wooden bells which clatter softly in the night. And all of the village sounds have as an almost constant undertone the deep resonance of some woman beating rice. This begins before dawn and sometimes lasts well into the night. Occasionally there is a snatch of song on the road but on the whole they are a silent people, in contrast to the people down below who sing stentoriously in their bathing places. But then there is no bathing place within three miles. And if the people are silent, their dogs make up for it. We once asked Madé whether the Balinese dogs ever did anything, for they are not used for hunting or herding. He answered: "They work at night." We thought that was a jest, but it is not. Every flicker of light, every footstep on the path, every bamboo cracking in the fire sets the dogs off, and one dog's cry is like a stone dropped in a pond of widening sound. It is best to creep from one house to another and risk stubbing a toe rather than flaunt a Tilly lamp and unleash the tongues of all the dogs of Bajoeng. It reminds me of the summer on the farm when we had a bull who objected to conversation and we used to sit on the porch and whisper for fear of rousing him. Every one of our houses is fitted out with a plaited bamboo dog switch and periodically a horrible yelp announces that some dog has caught the irritation which our boys never display in any other way. There is a peculiar slinking, creeping walk which one adopts as one approaches a dog, the switch held ready, hidden behind one's back.

The people— Well, some of them are very beautiful, especially the old ones. They are variously dressed in dull, dirty, colorless pieces of cloth which function as a skirt one day, a head cloth the next and to wrap a baby in on the following. Old Balinese cloth was as strong as canvas and could withstand the wear and tear of life lived in the mud. But the cheap Japanese cloth they buy today won't stand up against such usage, and the result is horribly depressing. Our best informant begged a piece of heavy sacking that Gregory's table came out in and had a coat made of it. Now he walks about with Gregory's full name and the name of the ship in huge black letters on his back. It is beautifully tailored and the material is quite appropriate, but we do not know what to do about the name.

The people come wrapped in their dim rags and stand about the veranda and stare. If one smiles at a stranger there is never an answering smile, just a blank, rather hostile stare. Then some event makes it possible to identify some of the bystanders and call them by name. Immediately the whole atmosphere changes. They smile and when they go away say they are going and when they come again, they say "It's me," quite politely. No caricature of an Englishman who has not been introduced can equal their behavior beforehand.

They are essentially peasants, afraid of anything they do not understand, a striking contrast to the New Guinea natives, who will tackle anything. They go from their walled village to their fields, driving their cows before them, and come home again, ignorant of the very names of the bushes and trees they have passed on the way. Here in the mountains, in a self-contained village of 500 people, very few of them ever marry out or leave Bajoeng except to go to market at Kintamani. Yet we lead a curiously town life. There has even been a gang here—three adolescent boys who got together to steal a box of money from the house of the high priestess, who is also a moneylender. One of them went to the house and lured the watching child away with a fake message and the others broke in. We have town criers who go about at night announcing meetings, corvée work on the roads for the Dutch government, feasts in the temple and so on. The criers are appointed monthly and if they make mistakes, they are fined.

Every sanction in the society is negative. You never praise anyone or thank anyone or compliment anyone. If you like an artist's work, you pay well for it. If your boys do well, you pay them their wages. If they do not, you cut their wages. At first we were at a loss how to apply negative sanctions to the village, but now Gregory has worked it out. We contribute a *ringet* a month (about $2.00) to the village and from that *ringet* we "cut away" (a) the cost of any small objects stolen from the house and (b) any money begged from us. The village heads thought it would be much better to refuse the beggars, but Gregory said "No," firmly; he would give anyone who came begging money and subtract it from the village money. Since this announcement we have had no beggars and no thefts. For temple feasts we pay one florin (that is, one guilder), for large house feasts a florin and a half and for small ones half a florin. It is quite the oddest way of doing ethnology we have ever tried but it seems to work.

Today we have had another illustration of the power of money. About two months ago (before we came up here) a slender charming boy brought us for sale two incredibly bad objects made for the tourist trade. They were so bad and he was so charming and something about the pity of it caught us; we refused to buy, but we contributed a florin to the club of three people which he said he belongs to, people who have just begun to carve. Since then he has returned again and again. We have criticized his work, shown him the few lovely things we have collected and bought his steadily improving work. And now he has twice walked up here, 25 miles, to see us and bring his most recent work. And this time, knowing that we can get no duck eggs up here, he and his uncle carried up eight ducks and many eggs. He was very embarrassed, though, by the noise that the ducks made along the road. If we asked him to walk 100 miles, he would probably walk it. He is thoroughly fixated —not as a shopkeeper might be on a "good" customer, but like a child on an adult who feeds and shelters him.

These people have never seen any sort of medical work before. The Dutch government does practically nothing with medicine. The nearest clinic is eight miles away, once every two weeks with a Javanese doctor, and the patients have to pay for the dressing, so of course people do not go. So it is all like a miracle to them. Have we medicine to make the deaf hear, the old and halt walk quickly, the blind see and the decrepit lust for life again? When I dress a sore a whole circle gathers around to watch. It is an extraordinary comment on colonial policy that the Dutch, who do little medical work and tax the people to the bone, get a contented people with a rising birthrate, while in the Mandated Territory of New Guinea much better medicine and much lower taxation have produced a falling birthrate. The difference I cannot help suspecting lies in the absence of missions here. But the Dutch have been given more credit than they deserve for keeping missions out. The truth of the matter is merely that the bulk of the Dutch territory is Muslim and so not amenable to missionizing. The Balinese have so far resisted missions, but now there is a Christian village where they all address each other as *toean*. But there is not much hope for Bali ultimately because their social system is founded on religion and that is bound to crack before the Muslims, the Christians or the modern sceptics who worship industrialism.

I realize there is a kind of hiatus between the earlier bulletin and this one. We spent our time while the house was being built creaming the culture. Especially seeing all sorts of ceremonies: temple ceremonies in which the Witch is battled by the Barong, assisted by kris dancers who go into trance and stab themselves without injury; modern novelistic light operas which burlesque all the points of strain in the society; cockfights at which these slender, undistinguishably masculine men sit and stroke their fighting cocks and feed them spices to ginger them; trance dances in which a man in a trance rides a hobby horse with fiery eyes and scampers back and forth over flames; long processions in which fifty women wearing long black skirts and golden bodices with golden flowers in their hair walk for miles kicking their flowered trains behind them with a faultless gesture; cremations in which towers, gaudy with gold paper and colored cloth and higher than the tallest trees, with a corpse guarded by a relative or two at the very top, are carried by panting, sweating, mud-splashed crowds of men.

We also went to photograph especially important pieces of wood carving in the big collection of the new artists' guild just before the collection was sent to Java for sale. And every morning we had painters on our doorstep from the village of Batoean and we have a very good collection of work from there, including sketches, half-finished pictures, early work of artists who are now very good, and so on.

All of these high spots together form a sort of pattern of the potentialities of Balinese culture; the whole island is a ferment out of which a series of apparently different but internally related manifestations come bubbling up. And with that much in our heads, we have now buried ourselves very firmly in the lowest, dourest stratum of Balinese culture. Once we have understood that, we can begin to work our way up again.

It is 8.30. We have finished dinner, a specially good one because the cook was showing off to our artist visitors. There remains the diary to be brought up to date, the medical record to be filled in fully, five tropical ulcers to dress on one of the boys and an interview with our visiting artists.

Tiang pamit—May I leave you.

Visiting carver, I Wajan Keleopoes of Bedoeloe, works on the veranda while villagers look on.

Bajoeng Gedé
August 28, 1936

My last letter ended on the evening our artists from Bedoeloe arrived. We decided to do a really thorough piece of work, comparing their techniques as they worked side by side on carvings on the same theme. On the third day the third member of the club turned up and he was included and we had ten days of meticulous recording of any tool change, sneeze, spit, wriggle, or exclamation by any one of the three. Of making reflectors out of silver paper to make the best of the most erratic light—you can hardly ever take pictures here after two o'clock—and of improving our techniques as we went along. When they finally went home we breathed a huge sigh of relief, but we have had their ghosts with us practically ever since as batches of the Leica prints or the Ciné films have come back from Batavia or as Madé has turned in another page of text of their conversation or I have finished up another page of three columns of synchronized accounts. But at last they are finished and I feel I am entitled to the dissipation of another bulletin.

It is just the wrong time of the moon for anything to happen, but it is the calm before the storm. In another three days a thin, miserable, scrawny little old man is going to be advanced one step more toward sanctity and it will take four days to do it. Four days during which the orchestra players will have to sleep in the temple and everyone will powder their face in yellow. He cut his hand about a week ago, most fortunately, for it has cured up beautifully and landed us right in the middle of the family circle. He has borrowed two of our tanks to store water for the feast and I am at present resisting the importunities of his wife's sister, who wants to borrow one of my Balinese cloths—which I use as a table cover —to be his wife's second petticoat. If she were going to flaunt the lovely pattern, I might have yielded but I draw the line at the petticoat.

These feasts are the way in which the community strips the rich man of his surplus, but they have got a little mixed and put everyone through the mill. For now the village has to lend this man, who is poor, enough rice so he can feast them all as if he were rich. It is an astonishing system. The chief priest is simply the oldest man who is still a temple member or rather the man among the temple members who was one first. But if your wife dies, your youngest child marries, you have a sore for more than a year, you lose a fingernail or you have a great-grandchild, you have to stop. Otherwise you go on and up. And it makes no difference how stupid you are. The system is sufficiently watertight and controlled so that it runs itself. Our present chief priest is a little old man whose only son died as an infant. As a result, he can't be a man whose youngest child has married and he can't become a great-grandfather. His wife is a husky lady with a goiter the size of a basketball, two teeth and a general air of Red Ridinghood's grandmother after the wolf got into bed. He, far from lacking a finger, has an extra one.

The assistant chief priest is a tall piratical creature with a hawk nose, a sinister smile and a heavily sanctimonious manner. He never prays when the other priests are praying but always chooses an empty space to let the torn flower petals dribble pontifically through his fingers. Soon after my last letter he tried a new move. He announced that we had to pay a cow to the village because everyone who married here had to pay one. After a little scrabbling about, we collected the facts, namely that only those who live in Bajoeng and *then* marry have to pay a fine to the village. Meanwhile they had never asked us to pay for the famous cow which was the fine for my going to the cemetery, although once when Gregory went with them to hunt for the village herd (for these cows are not eaten, they become village property), "our" cow was pointed out to him. And last week we discovered that it is not forbidden for a woman to go to the cemetery except during a funeral. So that was a bit of blackmail too.

But the gods remember and punish, for village law is a sacred thing. Our assistant chief priest now has terrible boils and he came twice to ask for medicine and then came no more and his boils got worse. We met him outside the gate of a temple which we can't enter because we haven't paid the proper cow for that and he said that other people get well quickly when we doctor them, but not he. The next day the wife of the chief priest, who doesn't like him, came and told me that priests cannot ask for medicine from any-one. They can only pick herbs in the woods and doctor themselves in their home temples. So now *we* know why he is getting worse and we take care to tell people, too, how shocked we are that he ever came and asked for medicine.

* * *

We are all gathered—that is, the medium, the priests and their wives, all the little girls and a scattering of mere adults—by a temple which is three streams away from Bajoeng. The temple is a small wooden shrine set in a fenced enclosure in the fields. The little girls with tall offerings on their heads slipped and hurried down the steep ravines and up again, stopping now and then to lay a few little palm-leaf baskets on specially sacred spots. But now we have all arrived and the offerings are set out in front of the shrine. The medium has offered them and now the offering of the Trance Dancer Club is to be made.

Low wooden pedestals are set up about ten feet apart. A young

I Misi (back) and I Renoe (facing camera) dancing in trance.

Jane Belo waits to photograph I Misi, whose costume is being repaired.

man looking rather taut takes his place at each of the four of these. From long wooden boxes are taken the two pairs of sacred puppets, dolls with huge headdresses and clusters of little bells on their feet. They are fastened on a long string attached to sticks with bells on top. The sticks are stepped into holes in the pedestals and are firmly grasped by the young men, who make the sticks vibrate but forget that they have done so. On the principle of the old game with the Bible and the key, each one knows he is not moving the stick. And the dolls dance faster and more furiously, approaching each other, separating, approaching. They are no longer dolls but gods.

Meanwhile our two little trance dancers are brought forward— Renoe pert, self-possessed, enjoying herself, and Misi dark, stiff, dutiful and unhappy. Renoe always peeks and never falls down or gets hurt; Misi believes it all and is always tripping over things or falling off someone's shoulders. They are about nine years old. Each kneels by a pedestal and grasps the stick with both hands. As the rhythm invades their bodies, they begin to sway faster and faster to the music. The song changes and the stick is made to stamp; they fall back limp, in trance. Now they must be dressed, gold brocaded bibs hung around their necks and fantastic golden crowns placed on their heads. Sometimes the singers start singing before they are dressed and the little dancers begin to dance in their dressers' arms.

Once in trance they are possessed by gods and their wilfulness is sacred. But wilfulness can be very inconvenient. It has often happened that it has been rainy or cold or late at night and the priest has said: "Ascend into heaven, my lord," and Renoe has merely stamped her foot or gone and bedeviled some small child in the crowd. So our old medium is providing against spending the night three streams away from the village. As the little dancers bend and sway to the music, we hear a moan and a groan from the medium. She puts her hands into the lit brazier, she writhes, tears run down her face, which is contracted in a kind of ecstatic agony, and she cries in the childish voice used by gods to the mortals whom they call their parents: "Mother! Father . . ." and speaking as a god she says that we must all move to the Temple Doekoeh, halfway home. We gather ourselves up. The little trance dancers both insist upon being carried by one man. We set out across the fields. Renoe decides later to stand on the shoulders of another man and dances in the middle of the ploughed field. As she shifts her weight, he has to shift his and she keeps him skipping, a fantastic sight on that high and very rural upland to see a child in a golden headdress standing on a man's shoulders and elegantly posturing with a fan.

We had never seen the Doekoeh. Its god is said to ride on a tiger which is neither yellow nor green. The temple itself is set in the deep woods, a tiny enclosure entirely carpeted with green moss. Monkeys run about on the branches of the trees and divert the smaller children from their devotions, but not the little dancers who solemnly sway and bend not even opening their eyes when firecrackers are set off in the corners of the temple. But afterward Renoe peeps just to be sure they have all gone off and little boys dash to the exploded clusters looking for unexploded ones. If you are a clever little boy you get the job of lighting the firecrackers and can wet the fuses of a fair number so that later you can take them home.

It begins to rain and again we start for home—for the home temple where the little dancers will dance for another hour. By this time they are wide awake but it takes a long time for them to come out of trance—which is done by their alternately clapping their hands and pressing them on hot coals. Perhaps they had to go in and come out again. And in the home temple one of our patients, a priest from another village who cut his toe cutting wood in the cemetery, is asking for medicine from the trance club. When his cut heals, which will he say cured him? But he has gone back to his own village, so we will never know.

* * *

A hot wind is blowing over the village. From our neatly rolled and scraped home temple ground where the dances that we pay for are given, clouds of dust blow up into the house. People go about with cloths wound about their heads to protect their eyes. I fill my boric acid bottle again and again. The kitchen fire leaps and wavers; the primus, which is used for emergencies, won't light at all. We barricade the doors of the house, which face east from which direction the wind is coming, and climb in and out the windows. Meanwhile the bamboos of which our house are built pop with a horrid loud sound. It's like building your house of unpopped pop-corn and then turning on the fire. From node to node the long cracks spread. Crack, bang! they are like explosions. Will the house fall down? Nang Oera, who is our best friend in the village, says when ten or so have completely cracked he'll come and fasten new bamboos beside them. No, says Madé, the house will not fall down. The posts will merely get weak. And this, says everyone, is not a bad wind. Wait for the wind six months from now! But now the bamboos have stopped cracking, the weather is cooler, we have got used to the dust and at last we believe in the dry season.

* * *

A frail middle-aged woman with exquisitely delicate features squats beside my veranda. "Djero Baoe [the title of assistant priests] is very ill. He is in his house and cannot come. He asks for medicine." I go in a great hurry. Djero Baoe Tekek, who is no longer a priest because his only son is married, is the most intelligent man in the village, the calendrical expert and the one man who really thinks about ritual. If he should die the village would be an intellectual wilderness. He is a frail gentle man, proud of his erudition, not above a little gambling, always smiling and gay. I find him lying moaning on the dark platform bed which practically fills the dark little house. A terrible pain that comes and goes, that shoots into his leg. We fear kidney trouble of some sort but we have no medicine. I give him salts and rhubarb and soda and make a hot-water bottle out of a clay Dutch gin bottle, and he gets better. Three days later he is sitting all alone in the road in front of our house singing sacred songs because he is well again.

* * *

Moederi, the houseboy, is merry and looselimbed and casual, more like a Papuan than a Balinese, but then one of his toenails is missing and he can never be a member of the temple. He puts his head in at the window and in a low mysterious voice says: "There is a cockfight just near here! A stolen one." For the government only allows cockfights by license on special occasions. With all the hushed delight of innocent transgressors we hurry down the path to the first stream between here and Peloedoe. The stream is dry now. We turn south along its bed and after a couple of turnings come on an open place beneath deep shade, well hidden by a cliff. But, says Moederi, the policeman has already been squared!

Here under the trees there are little knots of men comparing their cocks. Rows and rows of baskets filled with fighting cocks stand about. At square low tables there is gambling going on. Nang Djeben, who only keeps cocks and does no work, walks about looking proud and happy. His anxious, gentle little wife has a stall on the side where she is selling banana fritters; all her takings would not cover one of his bets. I walk about in the crowd noting the Bajoeng people who are present: Djero Baoe Tekek, who can no longer use his erudition in the temple; Belasin Keri, which means Bereaved of a Child, who had only a girl child who died and so he cannot be a temple member; Nang Oera, who has had three wives, among a people who are rigidly monogamous and opposed to divorce; I Sadia, whose dancing annoys his fellow club members because it is so much looser than theirs; and Den Njoe, whose father was Chinese—all the social misfits, the unplaced, the strangers.

Back in Bajoeng the invincibly sure, invincibly dull temple members carry their ploughs in and out of their houses, count their cattle, sit in solemn little groups in the temple on feast days and count out the shares of rice—one for each member, an extra two shares for the head priest, an extra three shares to be divided between the next two priests and an extra share for those who distribute it. They do not go to cockfights.

Only Nang Nami is missing from the cockfight. Nang Nami is our bad man, a tall abrupt pirate who wraps his tattered blanket around him and shouts. But Nang Nami is very poor at the moment. He has just been repairing the results of an excursion down the primrose path. He is a grandfather and he is sixth in line for the priesthood. Dozens of his expensive ceremonies are finished. If he married the girl, he would then have two wives. He would have to go to live in Peloedoe and could no longer belong to the temple. If he didn't marry her, he would have to pay a heavy fine and go down the line and start his ceremonies of purification all over again. So he paid his uncle to marry her, his poor doddering uncle who had never married. He paid for the cow to the village,

Nang Oera and Nang Salib watch a cockfight in the ravine.

Making the cocks angry.

he paid for the pigs for the feast. And, says Madé's text, "It was very easy for Grandfather [by courtesy] Kiter to get married for he didn't have to bring forth anything at all—meaning the expenses." But just at the moment Nang Nami, who loves cockfighting, is too poor to go to one.

Gregory is busy adapting the stenotype to Balinese script and then Madé is to learn to use it for quick text taking. Madé continues to amaze and delight us. He has learned to report on the personnel at a ceremony and if a dog happens to play a social role, Madé's text reads: "And they called the dog. The name of the dog was————." He isn't a bit abashed by the stenotype; in fact, he isn't abashed or excited by anything in the world. He takes synchronized notes on ceremonies, keeps calendrical records of coming events, trims the lamp wicks, tacks black cloth to the shelves, makes Dutch, Malay or Balinese translations of anything he is given, turns his mother into an informant when he goes home for a holiday, takes his bath in an icy stream three miles away at 6 A.M. so as to be always on hand, goes to Den Pasar and brings back 200 guilders, and takes down conversations as ungrammatically and brokenly as they occur. Oh, and as soon as we have learned a word for *than* or *but* or *perhaps,* he remembers to use quite a different one in the next text.

It is said that we belong to the caste of those who make books. My arms are beginning to ache as if that were literally true.

Tiang mepamit.

Bajoeng Gedé
October 28, 1936

People are now hoeing their corn and our friends send us sticky sweet rice with a brown sugar sauce which they have fed to hoeing bees, instead of the same sweet rice which, earlier, they fed to ploughing bees.

We have had the "day for moving houses," and houses were lifted from their beaten earth foundations onto the shoulders of some forty men and were carried riotously around the corner. We have had the "day for roofing houses," and everybody who needed a new roof gathered together all his friends and relatives who weren't doing someone else's roof at the moment and new tiles of

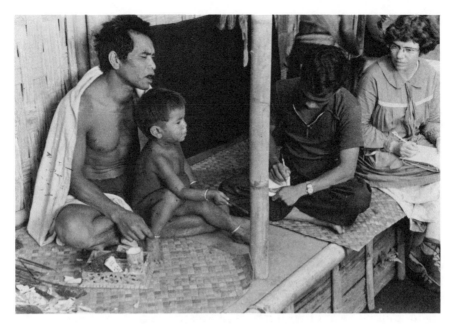

I Madé Kaler takes notes during my talk with Nang Karma and his son, I Gata.

Men Karma with her children, I Gati, I Kenjoen (infant), and I Gata and a cousin, I Karsa (standing).

bamboo have been cut and fastened on, so that here and there a new roof shines out from the constant gray. We have also had the "day for killing," which refers to the butchering of pigs for Galuengan, the Feast of All Souls, but as we had three wounds to treat that day, the boys made a pun of it. One of the victims was the result of a fight with knives about a knife. In Bajoeng you don't fight with knives for some other reason; you have a fight with knives about a knife, with someone with whom you have no other cause for quarreling. There is just an argument about whose knife this is and presto! a ripped-open shoulder and lots of work for the Toean and the Njonjah (Gregory and me).

Then there was the feast of Galuengan, but it was only a little one because we had had a death in the village within 42 days. The day before in every house people were busy cooking, the women making offering foods, the men cooking pigs. People from other villages walked through the streets buying little pigs, and people from Bajoeng went to other villages desperately searching for pigs. They like doing that. The price of pigs was very high. I had to go about to see what was happening, but I left each house with a little less appetite for my dinner, having been forced to eat at least one sticky sweetmeat, and with a pile of gifts which necessitated my going straight home before the next visit. . . .

For Galuengan there should be offerings in one's home temple; it is primarily a feast for the dead. Weeks before, people began asking me: Would I spread out offerings on Galuengan? To which I replied that I didn't know how to make them. And Men Oera, the wife of our best informant, and Men Singin, the mother of my Exhibit A child, and Men Djeben, the wife of the cockfighter, and Men Leket, whom I had just given a course of worm medicine, and Men Njawi, whose household gets iodine in its salt every other week, and Priestess Sani, who draws heavily on our empty butter tins, and ex-priestess Tekek, all of whose family we have saved from what she considered to be imminent death, and Men Karma, whose set of children form our constant stock in trade for studies of sibling jealousy, and Priestess Poepoe, whose husband had again failed to blackmail us out of two cows, all brought towering baskets of offerings. These I had to offer: in our home temple, in the livingroom, in the bedroom, in the kitchen, at the water tank, in Madé's room. I had to kneel and holding a glass of water in my hand—a different glass for each set of offerings—I had to sprinkle the offerings with water, using a flower dipped in the water three times, and I had to pray, letting a broken flower trickle through my fingers. Each woman who brought me an offering had an idea. The home temple ground ought to be swept; I ought to wear a sash even if I was in European dress; I should wash my hands first, and so on. The glasses of water had to be left in the middle of the beds, in imminent danger of drenching them, until sundown when I went about and asked them back from the gods. All except the ones in the kitchen. The boys coveted the cakes and so they asked them back themselves earlier while I was out paying return calls. Meanwhile, to entertain our visitors, we showed them Ciné views of a Barong dancing down below, while I took pictures of their expressions as they sat with one eye glued to the little projector, the muscles of their throats working and their lips moving.

After Galuengan is the time of traveling shows. The Barongs of every village set out accompanied by a priest, an orchestra and some kind of dance or theatrical troupe and they go from village to village. They are lodged in the temple, the Barong mask is solemnly ensconced in the shrine for visiting deities, the local priests bargain over the kapengs that the troupe is to be paid, the wooden gong is beaten to call the people in from their fields and the eldest daughter of each household runs home to make a few offerings. Then the people gather in the temple, the priests bicker

Village street, Bajoeng Gedé, with food sellers.

solemnly on the shrine steps, the little boys play tag in the open square and Gregory who ostensibly photographs the show as a rule photographs the people with a telescopic lens. If it is late, the whole party sleep in the temple and are fed by the village; if it is early afternoon, they start on to the next village, whose streets will soon echo with the children's shouts of "Barong! Barong!" which sounds for all the world like our "Fire!" or the Polynesian "Man-o-War!"

It is an odd scene—the wide gracious temple court, flanked by its roofed platforms, with higher courts rising behind and above all a mass of green trees. The sun beats down on the little group of strangers sitting around their instruments in the middle of the court. In the shade sprawl the villagers in the most everyday attire, dirty, wrapped in rags, poverty-stricken, gaping. The visitors who play the orchestra are hardly less dirty and ragged, though they may make some pretense at a uniform. Then the dancers appear resplendent in cloth-of-gold, in satin and silk embroidered with gold, wearing krises with jeweled hilts and headdresses of gold-plated leather. With infinite elegance they reenact some scene of godlike courtly life and on the sidelines the grim, clay-caked people squat and gape and chew betel and spit and criticize their costumes and their gestures, rating them good or bad with inimitable good taste. The dancing is worthy of a court and the audience, as they pinch the babies' noses dry, appreciate the finesse of the language and feel themselves subtly powerful to have purchased all this display for seventeen and a half cents. If they like, they will order the performance again this evening, but this time they will pay only ten cents. However, these performances can go on only for a month. After that if you catch a Barong in your village, you can imprison and fine it. So say the Dutch, who want people to stay at home and make money to pay taxes.

Last week we went "down below"—our first excursion out of the mountains since we came up here four months ago. We have walked to feasts in nearby villages, but we had not been in a car or a town during that time. We visited the Mershons at Sanoer, filled with misgivings as to how we would stand this touch of civilization. How would cocktails feel? would it be very hot? would clothes be an awful bother? But we had to go down to find a house to use as a base while Gregory's mother and Nora Barlow were here and we did want to see Sanoer, the seaside village where the Mershons live and in which Katharane Mershon has laid the scene of her very good Balinese novel. We had read the manuscript and now we were to be taken over the ground and shown all the characters and have a chance to see how Brahmans live.

And we had a beautiful time. Katharane has lived for five years in Bali and has mastered the fine art of saying no—of driving resolutely by temples which flaunt banners and palm-leaf pennants, whose gods are dressed in checked sarongs and whose gates give forth compelling music. She believes in eating meals at fairly regular hours and she doesn't generalize as the Balinese and most Europeans do—"Barongs never dance at night" or "That feast is always at sundown" and so on—which is the surest way of missing everything. As a result, in six days we saw Mario dance and saw three of his pupils dance and filmed him giving a first lesson—he is the most famous dancer in Bali and a gay, delightful person. We also saw three new kinds of trance and went to a feast on an island, which is the feast at which all the new fashions come out, and passed miniature carts drawn by tiny horses filled with beautiful girls with beaten-gold flowers in their hair and carrying beaten-silver bowls of offerings. We saw the "Fight of the Gods," in which all the gods fight the head god, each in a sedan chair which the bearers use as a battering ram, while extra attendants go into trance and dig krises into themselves. We saw half a dozen other dances, heard the three best orchestras in South Bali, visited all the temples described in Katharane's manuscript and saw weaving, carving and mask-making going on in the Brahman households.

And we got ourselves a house—the palace of the former Rajah of Bangli, who once had a summer palace in Bajoeng Gedé. But I will save a description of the palace for my next letter. It rents for about nine dollars a month and has three gold doors.

Meanwhile, up in the mountains, we've been having a marriage and very complicated it has proved to be. The girl's name is I Sami. She was the least attractive of the three unmarried daughters of Nang Ringin, who is ninth in the local hierarchy, and she is the sister of Renoe, the little trance dancer. But for all that she is rather stout and has coarse features, Sami is a very successful vendor and she was loved by two boys, Wari and Poendoeh. Wari comes from a large and not too prosperous family. Poendoeh is the seventh son of the ex-chief priest, a very rich family indeed. The parents favored Poendoeh. Sami, it is said, had once smiled on Wari, but she had stopped smiling.

Then one morning at dawn when she and her sister went for

water, Wari and his brother-in-law carried Sami off. She held on to the bamboo until it cracked but they got her and carried her off to the garden cottage of Wari's uncle. The two messengers decreed by custom went to her father to tell him that he need not look for his daughter as she was safe and caught. Men Ringin moaned and wrung her hands and said she had no children (she has ten) and alas, Sami was gone, surely against her will. Nang Ringin refused to accept the second set of messengers who went to get his consent to the marriage. Meanwhile all the relatives of Wari said Sami was delighted. All her relatives said she was not. But as no one of them could go near her, no one knew how they knew. Her family were taboo; Renoe could not dance and her father could not serve in the temple.

After about ten days of this our calendrical priest came to borrow a flashlight because he was going down to see Wari. He was related to both sides. And the next day we heard that he had persuaded Wari to go away so that Sami would come to like him better! And then he made Nang Ringin accept the proposal of marriage. But Sami escaped in the night and ran away to Poendoeh, who received her with delight. Since then at least a million paragraphs of ceremonious familiar talk have been wasted on the subject. Nothing like this has ever happened before. (I can't for the life of me guess why not.) Her father now reversed his position and said he wanted her to marry Wari. He demanded her back from the messengers who were legally responsible for her. They, poor men, tried to "borrow" her from Poendoeh's brother, but she refused to be lent. Finally the day came on which the cow for her and the cow for Wari were to be paid to the village and she was summoned to the village. Poendoeh came with her leading two more cows to ratify his marriage to her. She refused to go home to her father and went back to Poendoeh's house.

And then our gentle, gay Djero Baoe Tekek, the calendrical expert, showed his fine Italian hand. He simply announced that somebody had to be enemies over this. It was incredible that all this should have happened and no one be enemies. SOMEBODY HAD TO AGREE TO BE ENEMIES. Either the family of Wari would side with him and be enemies forever with the family of Poendoeh or they would have to be enemies with him and all his family. The poor harassed family of Wari, who had got nothing out of it but a cow to pay and a loss of standing, protested miserably that they didn't want to be enemies. The sister of Poendoeh was married to an uncle of Wari's. Never mind, let them get divorced or make up their minds, said Tekek. And finally, after twenty-four hours of quiet chirping wrangling, it was agreed that the Wari family and the Ringin family would stay friends and both be enemies with the family of Poendoeh. Madé says he thinks that Djero Baoe Tekek is a bad, bad man. Really he is just irresponsible and followed the favorite Balinese vice of arguing from a major premise: in a case like this somebody ought to be enemies.

In two weeks we shall go to Boeleleng to consult with various Dutch authorities on archeology and *adat* (native law), to meet our visitors, Gregory's mother and Nora Barlow, and to witness the ceremony of three months' birthday for Madé's nephew. Madé came in very portentously the other day and said in an accusing tone: "You have as yet made no study of the customs of Boeleleng." Boeleleng is a large and very much culture-contacted city. No, we admitted, we had not. "My nephew will have his three months' birthday on the sixth, and I must be there," said Madé. So as we were going down on the seventh, we are now committed. Then we bring our guests back here for three days to see what this place offers and after that we move into our Bangli palace and associate strictly with high castes for a month.

Tomorrow perhaps Gregory will fight one of his new fighting cocks. We have two, and every day their special toilet is performed. They are bathed in onion water, they have sticks thrust in their eyes and their legs are painted with red pepper. They are here for all unoccupied male guests to play with by the hour. And both are ready to fight and, so everyone testifies, can never be readier.

We wanted a poinsettia hedge for our home temple. We told Madé. He quietly told every petitioner for medicine who came from south of Peloedoe, where the poinsettias grow, to bring a part of the hedge. Now we have the hedge.

And so, since I am practicing my higher manner:

Tiang noenas loegera mepamit (which is much more elegant).
I entreat your kindness to permit me to depart.

Bajoeng Gedé
Christmas Eve 1936

It is two months since my last bulletin and it seems a great deal longer than that. On the 6th of November we went to Boeleleng and stayed in the expensive, austere and remote Dutch government rest house—and found that we might just as well have stayed with Madé as he had fitted up a charming little house for us, but without telling us he had. And there for the beautifully fair, plump baby of his eldest brother we saw a ceremony performed which contained elements with which we were familiar but all raised to the sixtieth power. The baby was wrapped in yards and yards of cloth-of-gold, dozens of gold sovereigns hung from its fat little neck and on its fontanel, where the Bajoeng people would put a daub of red spittle and a lump of yellow powder, a round jeweled disk was fastened. (It did keep falling off, though, which was a familiar Bajoeng touch.) The mother and baby were sprinkled with some sixteen kinds of holy water—and not merely sprinkled but drenched. And then for two successive nights there were shadow plays and at midnight, when the play was over, the *dalang*, the master of the shadow play, solemnly blessed and sprinkled the baby all over again.

These were my first shadow plays (*Wajang Kulit*). I had handled hundreds of the angular, grotesque puppets of painted leather as they lay uncomfortably in Museum boxes. And I had seen a model of a shadow play set up in a German museum with the puppets flat against the other side of a thin screen and the light shining through the ornamental perforations in the figures. I knew that the hands were fastened to sticks so that they could be gestured into all sorts of angular but significant positions. But I really wasn't prepared for a shadow play at all.

The lamp, instead of casting the steady dull glow of the museum model, is a great swinging lamp with a high irregular peak of flame and to add to the uncertainty of its light the *dalang*, who sits behind it, swings it now and then. And the puppets, far from lying flat and clearcut against the screen, move hither and thither, now half-defined, now with one whole edge or only the top of a nose fluttering in the swinging light and changing distance from the screen. Figures swoop down from the top, flutter up from the corners, retreat, advance and behead each other, all in what is really a dream world of half-definition. Meanwhile the *dalang* shouts, screams, expostulates and sings, the little four-piece orchestra tinkles on and the *dalang*'s hammer bangs and bangs against his puppet box.

It's a taste that grows. The first time one thinks a *Wajang* is hard on the eyes, that the hammer is trying, that it is hard to follow, that it is nothing but fighting (for the one requirement of a *Wajang* story is that it must have a war in it), but as one sees more and more *Wajang,* the taste grows. We have just started collecting *Wajangs,* especially weapons, of which there are many varieties, at five Dutch cents per weapon. Gods and heroes are a guilder each and minor characters fifty cents each, so we economize on them. A dangerous taste is for *Babats,* the lovely musical tree which marks the beginning, the end and magic. Each *dalang* has only one or two of these and usually they are enchanted, at least if you want to buy one. The puppets are beautifully painted—for the *dalang,* the orchestra and dozens of onlookers to enjoy, although of course color doesn't affect the shadow image on the screen. Half the audience sits in front and the other half clusters behind the scenes. The Balinese have no sense of a greenroom at all; putting on the make-up of dancers, tying the last flowers of a headdress, tuning a musical instrument, putting up decorations, unpacking the puppet box, all are part of the show to be commented on, criticized and enjoyed.

On the 8th of November our guests arrived and we had a day's driving in North Bali and a special orchestral performance at night by a new kind of orchestra, all girls, mostly around eight to ten, with instruments graded to their height, who bobbed up and down as if they were curtseying while they played. The next day we drove to Bajoeng and got there just as the rainy season decided to start.

We had ordered an opera for the next day. (It gives one a fine feeling of being a patron of the arts and lord of the manor combined to be able to order an opera.) The president of the opera club arrived in the midst of a nasty, cold, rainy morning to discuss possibilities and we paced off our various verandas, considered knocking down balustrades or settling the orchestra, some eight pieces, on a large table. It was finally decided that the opera would be given in the diningroom, which is just a pavilion about six yards square. There is a narrow ledge around the outside on which the crowd could stand three and four deep with the raised shutters half protecting them from the rain. We felt thoroughly beleaguered in our own house as the other two verandas were turned into dressingrooms and the opera went on and on into the night, while we stole away to eat in corners or catch a little sleep. But the people liked it and the next day, when it started to rain in the middle of a trance dance, the goddesses decided that they would like to come and dance in our diningroom, and we said we followed the desires of the gods and they came. When one of the "gods" decided to dance standing on the shoulders of a tall man, we had some anxious moments as the little dancer has been known to fall and our diningroom floor is cement. But the people were stubborn. If the god willed it, she wouldn't fall and if she fell she wouldn't be hurt. Nevertheless everyone held their breath while the stiff dark child in her great gold headdress bent and swayed five feet from that hard floor.

Then we moved to Bangli. In Balinese terms Bangli is a city. It has a regent of its own—that is, a Balinese vice-governor appointed by the Dutch—and no end of palaces and great temples and a huge market, but no shops or Muslims and only a few Chinese—a very comfortable city, in fact, which actually preserves the form of a village. The house we had taken belonged to the last rajah. At the beginning of Dutch contact all the wealthy members of the ruling caste, the Anak Agoeng, built themselves houses more or less after a Dutch model. They were built of cement, contained some glass—usually imitation stained glass—and had tin roofs, but the woodwork was carved and gilded after the older tradition. Our palace—its name was "the palace of beautiful experience"—is one of these. Now the rajah is dead, the rule has passed to a cousin, whose wives and daughters live in an adjacent courtyard and are only too glad to rent the great house.

One leaves a little side road lined with the low stalls of the food sellers and walks up through a long open court walled on both sides and filled with lichee trees to reach our gate, a high narrow oblong in a broad square block with a golden demon's head surmounting it. Inside the gate is the second court with raised platforms in each corner, high stone walls all around, more lichee trees and at the top the palace, its three great doors heavily carved and painted gold and red and blue. The long veranda gives onto all three rooms—a bedroom on each side and the central hall which makes a diningroom and can comfortably house two conversations at once. Katharane Mershon, who has taken the house half-and-half with us for the next months, had hung the edge of the veranda with orchids, which would "bloom tomorrow"—and they did. In this court we gave dances or shadow plays. Or the women servants of our little landlady, a delicate and gentle little aristocrat who has never married because she would lose her Dutch pension if she did, spread out coconut meat or cut up sweet potato to dry there. At night strange lights would come flickering into our eyes. At three-thirty in the morning a band of the palace children had slipped out with a tiny lamp to hunt for the lichee nuts that had fallen during the night. Whenever there was an official hunt for lichees, a silver bowl of nuts was brought to us as a gift.

While we were in Bangli I specialized in being a Balinese lady of Anak Agoeng caste only. With a row of *tchampaka* flowers in my hair and a bunch of praying flowers, which looked for all the world like a Valentine bouquet, I knelt in the elaborate home temple of the family and was doused with holy water, drank the scented holy water and followed as best I could the whispered directions, "red now," and "now a white flower," and "now to the god of the South," that flickered up and down the line of kneeling people— some seventy women and fifteen men, for the Anak Agoeng of Bangli have run to women.

For three days they gave this feast all for themselves—only actors, no audience at all, as if priest and choir performed alone in a cathedral. The great orchestra of the Regent played in a far courtyard all by itself with no one listening. There was a shadow play, but without the screen and the lamp. The *dalang* sat and recited and waved his figures in the dark and no one listened. And finally, late at night, there was an excited hush. The Regent was coming, the Regent came; he said "stop it" to the *dalang* and the shadow play that no one had seen was over and we all prayed and went home. Everywhere else I have been in Bali the audience of common people is an essential part of life. The shyest, the most frightened people walk boldly in when they hear the sounds of singing and dancing. To see the same pattern, the same type of offerings and prayers and entertainment enacted to an empty house in a mutual-admiration family party was very odd.

Then we had a big cremation of a woman of the Brahmana caste, higher in sanctity and lower in wealth and power than the Anak Agoeng. I walked in a procession with some forty Anak Agoeng women, all dressed in silk and brocade, their breasts tightly bound and their shoulders bare, their trains held up elegantly, masses of gold flowers in their hair. We arrived and were all put together on a veranda where we could see practically nothing, while visiting ladies chattered to us in the very highest language. Meanwhile groups of Brahmana ladies sat on other eminences, Brahmana men entertained each other and servants, grubby and badly dressed with heavy rolls of cloth about their waists and disheveled hair, walked about carrying food and offerings. Finally the fifteen-day-old corpse was whisked over the fence into a little private plot and again had a cremation, complete with royal orchestra, to which no common people who were not servants of the house came. Long before the lighting up of the great cremation bull, we ladies rose at a signal and walked home again. Seven hours of sitting on one's feet, smoking cinnamon cigarettes and drinking horseradish-ade—you should try that!

When the Regent came, three servants wriggled over the ground toward him, the first with a silver salver containing two glasses and topped with a little woven hat, the second carried an open coconut, again on a silver salver with a hat and the third carried betel leaves. He washed out the glasses with a bit of coconut juice and then offered me a drink in the indubitably clean glass. Then they started to move the corpse and we all got out our pocket handkerchiefs and waved them and a fat Anak Agoeng lady passed me some essence of a very strong white flower, which it was daring to use because it gives the Regent a headache.

One of our main reasons for going to Bangli was to have access again to motor roads and do some quick survey work in a motor car. Our chauffeur was Bagoes, one of the most beautiful people in Bali and a first-class musician. He owns a house in South Bali and a house in North Bali and keeps a wife in each; additionally, he owns a whole orchestra, in which he plays the leading drum, and two troupes of dancers. He drives his own great seven-passenger car, which never goes wrong, with a fine reckless flair and curses wandering pigs, chickens, dogs and bicyclists in a thoroughly satisfying way. He is so charming that he is used to being the center of the stage with Europeans and life was a little difficult at first because of course Madé, demure, unexhibitionistic, incurably serious and adorable, is the Balinese center of our household and so Bagoes, when he wasn't driving the car, sulked.

It was a complicated household. Nora had just a little less than a month in Bali before she had to fly back to England. We had lots of work to do. The staff consisted of Madé, Bagoes, our two wild mountaineers, Ngemboet and Moederi, little Sambeh, who was charming with a flower behind his ear and nearly got his head turned from being treated like a beautiful little boy of nine instead of a serious and not too adept adult, Meregeg, our beautiful houseboy from Oeboed, who came to make soups and desserts (two of Ngemboet's weaknesses) and a great stupid giant from Bangli who seemed to belong to the house and the stupid giant's wife who made lovely offerings whenever we needed them to take to some temple or dance. Then there were the streams of relations with the Anak Agoeng to keep going, the stream of sellers bringing cloth and carvings to the veranda steps and last but not least, the recurrent contacts with Europeans, always the most trying thing in the tropics. In Bali there is as much gossip as anywhere else, but it is all in artistic terms.

We got a lot done and came back to Bajoeng very sure that we prefer our cool mountain top and no visitors and no motor cars, even if our village people are sulky and frightened and dressed in rags. At least we know them and can work ahead without fever or haste or prima donnas or Medicis.

Boxing Day

About a week ago we discovered that Madé meant to deal with Christmas. He had read about Christmas. The custom here is that strangers give gifts to the Balinese at Galuengan and the Balinese return them on Christmas or the Chinese New Year. We discovered that our staff had ordered an opera. On Christmas Eve they started to make the decorations, great swaying pennants thirty feet high with bell-shaped cutouts hanging from them to stand beside our gate, and every pillar is wrapped with sugar palm and ornamented with ironwood and hibiscus and ti leaves. The boys appeared at breakfast, all in their best, with flowers in their turbans and shining faces, to repeat "Merry Christmas" with varying degrees of assurance and Madé had written a poem in English to Gregory's mother. It has nine verses, of which this is perhaps the best:

> Njonjah Biang we all love you
> But we don't know how we can show that to you.
> Only God knows and he probably will tell you
> If not by day then in a dream of you.

On Christmas morning, after all the decorations were complete, packets of firecrackers had been set off, an incense burner had been put in the temple to keep away the rain and offerings had been made in the home temple, we played the phonograph. We played it for the first time yesterday, set up in the home temple with two umbrellas over it, lovely blue Chinese paper ones, as if it were a god. And silently and instantaneously the crowd gathered to listen, paying attention to the strange records and relaxing and chattering during the Balinese ones.

It did rain, in spite of the incense, and we had the opera in our diningroom. It was a lovely tale. There were three kingdoms. In one there was a princess and the mother of the princess thought she was old enough to marry. So the mother went to the second kingdom and asked the young king to marry her daughter. But the king did not like to do it. (I quote Madé throughout.) It is not usual in Bali that a woman should ask a man to marry her. Then the mother went to another kingdom and that king did like to marry her daughter. So they were married in seven days. And they made a kite and put their pictures on it and on it they wrote: "To the King [the one who refused her]: This is the picture of one who has become the strumpet of King Number Two." Now King Number One was flying his kite and brought down the other. He saw the picture of the girl. She was very beautiful. He said he would not go home until he got her. So he got a love charm and married her and gave his younger sister to King Number Two. That's all.

Bajoeng Gedé
May 2, 1937

A frightful lot of water has run under the bridge since my last bulletin. Most notable events: (1) The village has taken us to its heart (or their hearts?); we now belong and are treated with the gentle, unemotional gaiety which is the norm of those who belong. (2) We have started photographing on a huge scale using uncut film and developing ourselves, so that photography looms much larger and takes up about one-third of our time. (3) Jane and Colin McPhee have come back and are settled at Sajan with constant communication between us, which adds, as it were, another dimension to life. And (4) the rice harvest came and passed and Bajoeng plunged into an orgy of ritual activity; day after day we had feasts here, there and in other hitherto unknown temples until all of us were exhausted.

This headlong festivity was partly owing to a blessed period of 42 days when nothing happened because a boy had had an affair with his titular grandmother, his first cousin twice removed. Both were banished to the "land of punishment" and the village was unclean for 42 days and no offering could be lifted up and no dancer dance or even practice. *We* got a little caught up during that period, but the *village* got behind with the calendar and has been racing after it ever since. The Governor General of the Dutch

Women prepare offerings.

Indies was in Bali two weeks ago and held a reception on a major Balinese holiday. Before we left Bajoeng we attended a ceremony to build a new house, a ceremony for moving a home temple, a ceremony for a child's six-month birthday, a wedding and an ear-piercing ceremony. Then we left to go down to Jane's to hustle into camphorated clothes.

Then the gods from the next village decided to come to visit us. It is quite a new village of immigrants from near Bangli and I am sure the gods are not related at all, but one of the priests went into a trance and was possessed by a goddess there who said that her mother lived here. So all the gods of that village, Katoeng, and all the people and the dancers, and so on, came and spent three days here, and we put on our best clothes and made our tallest offerings and kept our children from playing under the feet of the dancers—as they do when the "war" dancers dance. Our seeress went into a trance and impersonated the goddess's mother and their priest impersonated the goddess daughter and it was all very exciting and crowded.

In the middle of it all, our calendrical expert, Djero Baoe Tekek, decided it would be graceful if Bajoeng and Katoeng shared a temple which had been overgrown with woods—perhaps for centuries, no one knew. Sometimes a boy looking for a runaway cow strayed into the woods and fled because there were stone statues there. Once a year offerings were laid at the edge of the wood. Madé woke us up the morning after Katoeng went home with the news that a new shrine was to be started in this temple. We had not heard about the stone statues. All we knew was that it was a temple where offerings were made by the people who had fields to the west and that once a man digging near there had found one plate of an iron musical instrument. Our plate, numbering 13, had been buried in the big earthquake of 1917, so they carefully put that one plate away in a cave and solemnly bang on it at our most sacred ceremonies.

We walked over to Peloedoe, the little no-count village to the west where people live who cannot come up to Bajoeng standards, and followed the little group of men with bush knives, a priest with a few small offerings and a handful of children, walking warily for the woods are tangled and full of nettles. The priest knelt and laid the little offering on the moss under a tree; the others sat down to share jovially a huge breadfruit-like fruit. After he had prayed, the priest cut the first few vines, then everyone started. I sat with the children, expecting nothing in particular. They were clearing a space in which to build a shrine. Suddenly one of the little girls whispered: "Tigers, tigers? They say the god here rides on them. . . ." This was her quick interpretation of the men's comments as they uncovered the stone statue of a tiger. Then came lifelike stone figures and a stone head, archaic and strange in flat relief.

The men looked at them, these old gods from long ago, indifferent as to whether it was twenty years ago or two thousand. They commented on the strangeness of a head without a body. Someone tried to get the second tiger up but it had no legs. Someone said this must have been the original temple when Peloedoe was a big village long ago. Only Madé was excited. He had been to the movies. He knew about excavations. He whispered excitedly that he thought the head looked Egyptian and went about with a hushed air, recognizing that this was an historical moment. But the Bajoeng people were more interested in a nest of bees inside the stone. They agreed that if they dug in other spots they might find other figures; if God so directed, they would. At the moment this sufficed and they sat in the shade and drank a very peppery drink. Djero Baoe commented that no one would know what day to have a feast there until we found out who the gods were who lived there. Then we came home. Perhaps—no one knows yet—that head is a thousand years old, but it is now just another sacred bit in just another Bajoeng temple.

We have been in this village for almost eleven months and have almost rounded the calendar. Babies I saw at birth are walking; girls married since we came will soon be mothers. New walls have been built, the temple land has been redistributed, the rice is all in rice barns and the maize in corn barns. The Goddess of Rice, Batari Seri, is an old figure but they have split her in two: Batari Seri with one kind of hair for the rice and with a different kind for the newly introduced maize—and no one knows that one goddess is new and the other old.

The only things that have not happened are a birth of twins and the falling down of the roof of the chief priest's house. We need both of these events. The priesthood here is merely the top of a formal citizenship. If one lives long enough and one's wife survives and one's youngest child does not marry and one has not yet become a great-grandfather, one becomes chief priest. Sometime thereabouts one has a big ceremony and invites a god who-is-dangerous to live in a special new house. Later still the god goes away and lives with someone just lower in rank. Then when the roof falls in, one has another ceremony and goes to live in the house oneself, instead of the god; by then one is so holy that one can wear white. (I got well tangled in this paragraph; the problem is that the priests are of both sexes.) At present we have no one so holy in the village and we do not know what it would be like. No schemes avail to rot the sturdy bamboo shingles of the priest's roof.

The house is now as full of children as ever I could wish. I have persuaded the little girls to draw and Sambeh has become an outstanding artist whose drawings adorn the mossy walls, cut out in relief, and practically every house in the village. But this leaves less and less time for writing.

In the Bajoeng vernacular and with no fancy phrases: "Leaving you."

Bangli
July 1, 1937

We are in Bangli which, after the last months in Bajoeng, is almost like a direct move to Heaven. It is of course the Balinese type of heaven for Hell is located in exactly the same locality. So at any time we may have to get into a car and go to fifteen ceremonies at once, encounter shopping in Den Pasar or tourists and the trails left by tourists in the homes and tempers of our friends. But at this moment we are at peace.

Our little princess-landlady is building a house for the only male member of the family, a reedy boy of twelve, and entertaining a Brahmana priestess by playing her Chinese phonograph records which come almost comfortably muted over the wall. The full moon has passed and for a week or so there are to be no feasts—unless, of course, we do go to the witch play tonight at Blahbekioe, where all the stone statues of Rangdas are decked out with nightcaps and aprons, their protruding stony bodies almost smothered under a look of primness. We saw the Rangdas dressed in this way the day before yesterday when we came back from Sajan and there is the witch dance tonight. But maybe we won't be able to get a car.

Here we write up and translate texts with Madé and sort and catalogue pictures to prepare ourselves for the nest of painters into which we are going to move in about three weeks. And occasionally we even play the phonograph to ourselves. You have no idea what fun that is. Fifteen seconds after the needle hits the disk in Bajoeng the crowd begins to gather with that firm look of "ours by divine right" which is such a beautiful part of the Balinese attitude toward the arts and is capable of filling one's house to overflowing.

But here no one comes so casually into palaces. The Anak Agoeng have never appreciated the claims of the common man and here we hide behind their habits of exclusiveness. And in this peace one realizes what a strain conscientious anthropological residence in a native village of 500 people is—people whose every word, grunt, scratch, stomach-ache, change of wearing apparel, snatch of song sung on the road or jest flung over someone else's wall is *relevant*. There is no event about which one can say: "Well, I don't have to go to another birth feast" or "I know how that kind of ceremony works." Every one is different in terms of behavior.

Sometimes I think it is the known claims of each day that make it most difficult. That is, to know very well that there is that very bad cut to dress, that the old man with dysentery will have to be visited, that Pindet is going to make offerings for her baby early tomorrow morning so one must be up in time, that this is the one dark of the moon which has followed two months without a death and therefore the village council will meet south of the village instead of north—and one must catch the ritual now because it may never happen again—that Gregory will have to cut film today whatever else happens because all the cut film will have been used up by tonight and that new solutions of argyrol and hexylresorcinol will have to be made up.

And sometimes I think it is the *unexpected* things that are the most trying. The bad cut that turns up right after lunch when medicine is otherwise taboo and a siesta is just in sight—for there is only one old woman who, because she is too holy to step on the veranda where there are bamboo gutters which would run over her head, feels entitled to pry open the bedroom shutters with a present of one pineapple or a request for a rubberband for her grandchild. Or the ceremony which no one had warned us of, but which must be attended, or the call of a mother and child who haven't been observed for a month and so must have a half-hour of observation and photography, or the boys who are just beginning to

I Gata.

carve and who are so shy that they come creeping about the house like the first and second murderers, scratching at the door to be let in, until their carvings are accepted, or the woman who comes and leans over my table just as I'm trying to make sense of a set of notes which were written so hastily that they will again get cold —but who is such a good informant that I *can't* neglect her.

At any rate there comes a time in Bajoeng when one postpones getting up in the morning, races to bed after lunch and even is a little apprehensive about the safety of staying up after ten o'clock at night. Bed is the only refuge. And it is a partial one, for they are sternly commanded to waken us for anything important.

July 4, 1937

Bangli continues peaceful.

We went to the witch play and were just assured of a long play which was to end with men in trance attacking Rangda, the masked witch, with krises—when it started to rain. The thinly dressed crowd huddles and shivers through a slight rain, very unwilling to leave any performance. The orchestra can't bear to stop while the crowd is there and as long as the orchestra plays the dancers in all their resplendent finery dance on. Finally the rain becomes a downpour, everyone scurries for cover, the dancers stand under the umbrellas which mark the dancing stage, the orchestra pauses. After three minutes someone cries hopefully: *"Endang!"*—the cleared state after a rain. Then we all go back for fifteen minutes more with a slight drizzle, while the dancing ground gets more and more muddy. Then hard rain, repeat. This goes on for an hour and a half until finally the dancers are seen, their gold headdresses nodding in the bad light, being escorted home under the umbrellas in the rain. Then we all know it is no use and come home too.

I went to call on the Lady Priestess who was visiting next door. She presented me with a piece of dried buffalo meat and asked whether there were any rhinoceroses in my country because she needed a piece rather badly, preferably the meat but a tooth would do. And our little princess asked: "When are you going to Bajoeng again?" And I told her in seven days, and she said: "You can't do that because there is to be a great birthday feast here in the West Palace and there won't be another for a year because there are no more children." And I explained: "But there is a special kind of death feast in Bajoeng which I have never seen," and she looked very firm and said: "Well, you must choose." If you can imagine telling the duke that you prefer to go to the goatherd's party, you can appreciate the situation. So after working over our schedule with appropriate anxiety, we have finally decided that if we send Madé up to an earlier death feast to do a lot of preliminary work, so we will be prepared for everything, and if we send Ngemboet up ahead of us on the lorry to arrange his elopement, which is to come off right after the death feast for his lady's maternal grandmother, and if we go up after dark and sleep in Kintamani (because our road is too dangerous for a car after dark) and get up at dawn the next day, we can please both the princess and ourselves.

When we have three series of events to handle in this way—in Bajoeng, Bangli and Batoean—it is going to be even worse. Of course, we can always separate into three groups, as we had to do the day before we left Bajoeng, when there were three important weddings besides Moederi's, at two of which the bride was weeping and at the third, the groom. But the general theory is that one event observed by three persons simultaneously is better than three events each observed by one person. For a ceremony in South Bali which you have never seen, even if you know all the people there—or at least someone does—the minimum to cover it all is about five persons, as there is one little rite going on outside the gate while another goes on under the bed and another in the house temple, and so on.

But we have now finished the ceremonial year in Bajoeng. This death feast is one we saw the day after we reached Bajoeng before we knew anybody. Now we plan to go back at intervals to keep track of growing babies, new births and marriages, to develop our pictures in the cool water and to connect up odds and ends which are hanging loose. With Bangli as a base where clothes can be washed and peace attained, we will go back and forth to Batoean, where our new house is located plumb in the middle of a walled courtyard inhabited by a Brahmana family. Batoean is a big town, 3,000 people, although they are all distributed along little lanes with neither the impressive great market place nor the regal palaces, the dancing hall or the cockfight places of Bangli. There we shall work primarily with the dozen or so artists whose work we have been collecting.

Batoean
September 1, 1937

We now live in three places and everything in the way of carbons, memoranda, and so on is always in one of the other places or else we have only super-sensitive film when we need another kind or the salicylate powder is all in Bajoeng. It is a complex and perplexing and perhaps an overexciting existence. The only thing that makes it possible is that some of the things we ought to do or go to in one of the other places don't come off.

In Bajoeng the house is faithfully guarded by a queer introvert high caste who has left his village and come to live with us. He keeps a horse for company. We suddenly noticed it in our front yard after we had been back in Bajoeng for several hours—there was the horse next to the shed where the bamboo xylophones are kept. We can now move in or out of Bajoeng in half an hour, and in a three-day visit there we took some 600 photographs, developed 1,500 photographs, covered three major ceremonies, photographed fifteen babies to record their present state and cured most of the same babies of bad eye trouble, scabies or dysentery. Then we came to Batoean.

Bangli—the palace, you remember—provides a retreat from Batoean for jobs that require space and quiet, like cataloguing and photographing a large number of paintings or spreading out 100 puppets to look at. It is also a comfortable place when one is sick. And one of the boys goes there to do the washing and ironing as Batoean living conditions hardly provide the necessary space. Moving to Bajoeng from Batoean takes about two hours and to Bangli about an hour. We send most of the boys on by bus and take the essentials in a motor car. Without moving any supplies or spare clothes, we fill a car with what we have to take—three typewriters, three lamps, a dry box with all the photographic gear, a tripod, coats and raincoats, a small medicine box and a filter. Then I have to keep track of the market days or else we arrive in the new place without food. Sometimes it is necessary to take ducks and chickens and vegetables with us from one place to the other. Also bus communications between the various places is only possible on certain days, and I have to keep track of that. One slip in dates and your boys do not turn up or there is no food or you have to spend two or three dollars on an extra motor car trip.

Now for Batoean. Our house is a pavilion with a set of woven hanging shutters which make it possible to shut out sun or wind from any or all points and provide a fair degree of visual privacy. Open all around, the Balinese can approach from any side and may be correspondingly ignored. The house stands a very high step off the ground and is high and roomy inside. Inside we have one huge high table on the edge of which I type and Sambeh puts his serving things for meals. Then there is a lower table which during the day serves as a combination table, settee and place where the children sit in a row and draw. At night the boys bring a mattress out from the storeroom and this lower table becomes a bed. Between the bed and the big table stands a very tall metal box of portfolios containing the collection of Balinese paintings, which it taxes all of Gregory's length of arm to handle. They are always being taken in and out to check over the pictures by some artist, to enter a new picture or to compare a new picture with previous work by an alleged or suspected artist, and so on. Then there are five boxes on which people sit and two straight chairs and two canvas easy chairs; on these we sit, a little lower and more comfortable than our high-caste guests.

At the moment—the middle of the morning—Gregory is taking dictation from a very elegant and languishing member of the Kesatrya caste who has just brought a series of pictures in various stages of completion to be photographed and a picture to sell, of which Gregory is taking down the story on the typewriter. He is sitting on a camp stool as befits his rank. At his feet are three younger boys and our Sambeh listening to the story. On the "bed" are ranged six small boys, my children's drawing club, with a piece of plywood in front of them to draw on—a little low caste, a Brahmana, a Kesatrya, two more Brahmana and a Kesatrya all seated in a row because where art is involved, all work is on a level. About seven more boys, mixed in caste and age, are sitting on the opposite side watching the children from a distance because they have been forbidden to come up and interfere with them.

Over at our other house, which is a combined darkroom-storeroom, Madé is sitting on the little veranda at a big table typing with about five people sitting on the table, as befits high castes, while he is seated on a stool and bullies the high castes into telling him what he needs to know for a text he is writing. Over in the corner, with the Big House on one side of them and the family kitchen on

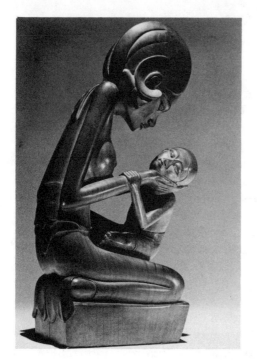

Mother and child, a contemporary carving.

Reproduction of a painting of the witch in Batoean style.

the other, our boys have an open shed about six by eight feet. There the cook cooks, Madé types when we are asleep and some twenty people hang about without anyone getting in anyone else's way and without the tea tasting of onions, the soup of kerosene or the gravy of machine oil. How this is accomplished I do not know.

The family in whose courtyard we live consists of a father, about fifty, a Brahman, with a low-caste wife who goes out harvesting every day and brings home a sheaf of rice. (Very useful, a low-caste wife.) They have five children. The eldest is planning to become a *Pidanda* (a Brahman priest) and has accordingly married a Brahman wife; they have one small boy about five. Then there are the younger children—a son of about twenty and one of about fourteen who paint, a daughter of about sixteen whose main business is to make offerings and a small boy of six, who is the president of my little boys' drawing club. Father is the head of the Classical Dance Club, which will begin to practice here soon. The eldest son, whose name is Dice and who is restless and intelligent, a less happy equivalent of Nang Oera, our most trusted informant at Bajoeng, is secretary to the *Proebakel,* the head of the village, and so people come and go all day long on village business.

In three weeks we are to have a cremation here and already the home temple court is piled with firewood and the women sit up at nights under little lamps making all kinds of cutouts of stiff palm leaves. There is a pile of 500 coconuts in the middle of the yard. And beyond our bathroom is a wall and then another court where the pigs are kept. They were all sprinkled with two kinds of holy water on the feast day for pigs. The courtyard also is studded with points at which offerings are always being made. After every meal little squares of banana leaf with bits of rice on them are taken about and laid on these points—at the gate, beside the house where the afterbirths of the children are buried, at the entrance of the home temple, beside both kitchens. These are propitiatory offerings to the bad spirits.

Looking straight across from our house to the Big House, I can see Father, sitting on his haunches, writing with a pointed iron tool on a thin piece of palm leaf which he holds in his hand. He is making a list of fines for the rice club to which his wife belongs. Such are the services rendered by the educated and erudite Brahmans to the boastful ruling caste, the Kesatryas, and the humble and self-deprecatory low castes.

This family belongs to a strange and anomalous group, the Brahmana Boda (Buddha). There was once Buddhism in Bali and a few of its tenets—bits of prayer—have survived in certain families of the priestly caste, a most contradictory state of affairs in terms of the Hindu caste system. There are 18 households of the Brahmana Boda in Batoean and they form our little community which we follow as if they were a small village. It is not, of course, as self-contained as a village. They marry the regular Brahmana—Brahmana Shiva—and also the other castes, and all their relatives and friends flow in and out of the yard. But it gives us a nucleus of people we know.

Next door live two more artists, one of them the man whose work we have studied most intensively, Ida Bagoes Togog (Ida Bagoes is the term of address for Brahmana males) and next door to them three more painters, brothers. One can see their work in all stages, follow their fits of petulance or inspiration, photograph

Watching a Batoean painter at work.

their first drafts, snatch away a sketch which has particularly good lines which are bound to vanish under the meticulous inking in the finishing technique. They tend to work in little groups and the beginners get a better artist to make a sketch and they fill it in. The one who finishes the picture sells it as his own and it is necessary to know who made the sketch in order to follow the development, first of the sketcher, who may sketch for half a dozen beginners, and second for the style of the learner. We have been collecting pictures for 18 months, so that we have a fair sample of the development of Batoean painting and a selection of paintings by individuals over that period.

We have just had a big cremation, in which all castes participate. Of course we had seen cremations; they are one of the spectacles of Bali and on the whole a most trying kind of spectacle. One arrives in a strange village about noon in a motor car. The roads are already choked with crowds of onlookers, who also help to churn the roads to mud. Some ten or twelve different kinds of specially archaic and noisy orchestras are playing. And finally, along the road to the cemetery, the high towers and big animal coffins are carried by crowds of shouting, sweating, over-excited men who stop at stream crossings to splash each other and the onlookers and who delight in dangerously tipping the 20-foot towers on which ride the corpse or the bones and some unfortunate relative of the dead. These are all taken to the cemetery, from which usually rises a stench of mud, people, decayed meat offerings and sometimes new corpses, and are burned up in a series of bonfires. The offerings all look faded and decayed for they were made days ago. Beggars with baskets cluster around trying to steal what they can of the money which is being used in the offerings. Each family manages its own obsequies and it is impossible to find out what is happening. One comes away with a special stench in one's nostrils, very tired, and swears that one will never go to another cremation.

But to be on the inside of a cremation is a very different thing. Then the burning is a mere episode and a relatively unimportant one. Most of the time is spent on endlessly repetitious little rituals of blessing and dressing the bones and later the ashes, and putting the bones or ashes in lovely dolls with big fanshaped headdresses and carrying the dolls around like babies in white slings—because

Procession with a cremation tower.

the gods are really the children of the living and ancestors and offspring are one—and combing the doll's hair and feeding it and making it pray and putting a flower in its hair to show that it has prayed. This goes on and on in some dozen forms. We spread a whole set of clothes on the grave, then open it and put the bones in a package while the doll goes home for a call. Then the doll comes back and is undressed and put in with the bones. Then it is put in a little chair and covered with the set of bones again. Later we carry the dolls to a little imitation house in an imitation village in the middle of the cemetery and later still we take them out again and wash them with all the ceremony accorded to the newly dead. Then they are packed up again, put on chairs and basket-shaped covers are put over them so that the whole is just the size of the grave and these again are covered with clothes. Endlessly taking the body apart, resolving it into spirit and matter and then recombining the elements. The last day the ashes are once again in the set of dolls—and the bones which have been finally pounded to ashes. Then the dolls, dressed up with clothes, are carried to the sea in little brightly decorated chairs and the carriers, arriving at moonrise, dash down the beach and throw them into the sea.

Later. It is night and there are only four people here and our chief artist is dictating dreams at the other end of the house, dreams of which he has already drawn us fascinating pictures.

We spend our little spare time wondering if we made a mistake to go up into the mountains where the people are hypothyroid, sulky and frightened, and the culture so simple and inarticulate. Yet the year in the mountains has given us a ground plan from which to work and a knowledge of the language and health instead of languor, which would have come from a year down here. It has also given us a background against which we find these people charming and intelligent and welcome the warmth and assurance of the high castes. It has given Madé an invaluable training. A year ago he could never have tackled a ceremony of which his written account runs to 50 pages. He is so shy and gentle that it took a year of dealing with the mountain people to put him on his feet. But when I think of the work of the mountains—the endless pushing against distrust and fear, tempting each child bit by bit (whereas here they come in such droves that eventually one's impulse is to scatter them)—it sometimes seems a hard fate.

But we would never have devised any new techniques down

here. The culture is too rich and varied. And we would have got intellectual indigestion from too much cake. Speaking of cake, for the cremation we made 600 each of 75 kinds of cake, mostly representations in colored paste of faces, hands, feet, flowers, onions, navel cords, torches, brooms, horses, crabs, dogs, leaves, weapons, and so on, and these were placed, some 20 to 50 mixed, in different offerings, looking like random handfuls of color. But the kind and number of every bunch of assorted inedibleness was fixed.

And so *Titiang mepamit..*

From a letter to Franz Boas
On board M.V. *Maatsuycker*
Passing through Torres Strait
March 29, 1938

When I said I was going to Bali, you said: "If I were going to Bali, I would study gesture." And that is one of the things we have tried to do. We have accumulated a mass of photographic material, stills and Ciné, on everyday activities and on the more stylized ones, such as dancing, cockfighting, prayer and trance gestures, and so on. We have about 1,000 little grotesque carvings which are full of points about posture and balance. We have children and adolescents and adults doing the same kinds of things. It is the sort of problem that needs fine analysis at home, especially time to project and study the Ciné film. Jane Belo McPhee and Mrs. Mershon (who has lived here for eight years) have done a lot of work on special projects for us also. With three native secretaries, that has meant seven persons' careful records on selected events. I am still not perfectly clear in my mind about the problem of tackling these complex cultures and the legitimacy of different types of cross-sectioning. But we have tried to assemble as many types of cross-sectioning as possible, so that we have material for studying the same ceremony in different areas, the complete set of ceremonies for one area, and studies of topics like trance, theatricals and painting which crosscut areas altogether. All the materials, films, paintings, carvings and notes have been sent to the Museum. . . .

I know you think I go into the field too much in proportion to writing up, but the Arapesh material is all written and at the rate the Museum is going now won't be published before 1950. . . .

Meanwhile we have been able to use so much finer techniques in Bali than any I have ever used before that I feel very definitely at sea in interpreting the results without some comparative material collected with the same care. I never realized as vividly how very dependent I am in my thinking upon having good comparative material always present in my mind. And I can't compare 40 observations on a Manus baby, all merely recorded in words, with 400 observations on a Balinese baby, a good part of which are photographic and combined photographic and verbal records. The levels are so very different. Where before I occasionally made a sample of behavior over time which would run to two typewritten pages for an hour, we now have records of 15 typewritten pages and 200 feet of Ciné and a couple of hundred Leica stills for the same period. The recording is so much finer that I feel as if I were working at different levels from any work I've done previously. And every time I tried to think comparatively about Balinese materials I was stuck.

We haven't the funds or the energy or the time really to tackle an entirely new culture. But by going to the Iatmul, we are going to get our comparative material in much less time than a new culture would take. I already know the area and a great deal about the culture. Gregory is teaching me the language on the boat and of course there is Pidgin English ready to hand. The material will all tie in closely with Tchambuli and Mundugumor. . . .

I remember asking you once whether you thought it would be possible to work in Indonesia without an extensive knowledge of Indian religions, the high ones, and you said yes. It certainly provides an entirely different approach from that of scholars who approach everything in Bali from the standpoint of a knowledge of Hinduism and Buddhism and see every Balinese form as a degradation and very often miss the essence of it altogether.

It has been customary to say that the mountain villages of Bali are almost completely different from the higher culture of the Plains, and yet on analysis the basic patterns turn out to be almost identical. Records of conversations between a Brahman priest and a man who wants to marry his daughter are almost verbatim the same as conversations between two mountain peasants. The princely uncles and aunts say the same things to the child of a rajah as do the peasants to their babies. So one of the things we hope to do is to lay down the pattern of Balinese culture, in skeleton, in such a way that the differential flesh of the different caste and economic and locality variations may be put in relevantly.

We barely touched the literature, which is for the most part in old Javanese that is only partially comprehended by Balinese scholars. But we have come right up to the edge of it, in work with the absolutely illiterate, with the partially literate and with the aspiring scholar who can tell what a sentence in the old palm leaf books means, but cannot translate literally more than half the words in that sentence. I think it will prove useful to have material like this on the edges of a very old and partial literacy, to help to define more clearly the borderline between really literate and absolutely non-literate peoples. It seems very clear that in Bali literature has served primarily to paralyze thought and to give everyone a sense of intellectual inferiority.

We have accumulated sets of materials with which to examine the relative usefulness of using traditional artistic materials and modern, semi-stylized artistic materials as cultural data. For the first we have a large collection of shadow-play puppets, subdivided into the standard figures, which have been faithfully copied for centuries almost without a dot changed, and the comedy characters, which are much freer and more passing compositions. Then we have a large collection of modern paintings all done within the last two years in a definite modern local style, within which however the individuality of the artist still has considerable play. Besides this, we will be able to make a study of the cloth paintings —Jane Belo has a big collection and so have the Dutch museums —which were almost, but not quite, as stylized as the shadow-play puppets. Then I have children's drawings from the mountains, where there is no art, from the Plains, where there is no modern art, and from our artists' community, where there is a flourishing school of modern art. With this material we hope to be able to tackle the relationship between artistic symbols and the most basic cultural emphases. . . .

I hope this hasn't been too long a letter. At least I feel as if I had given some partial account of myself.

Tambunam Village
May 13, 1938

We are back in New Guinea and very glad indeed to be here.

Leaving Bali went off with all the smoothness and protocol that is Balinese. Madé had a Batoean artist paint us a farewell picture: Above, the shores of Bali with the Balinese showing theatrical grief and the Balinese volcano belching forth "Goodbye and Good Luck" in an elegant scroll design—and in English! In the middle of the picture a tiny ship with us in it, done correctly to scale as to our relative heights (which, when extended to our relative breadths, made me look like a kind of wooden toy), with me looking back towards Bali and Gregory waving excitedly to the Papuans in the lower front of the picture, who greeted us with waving bows and arrows and spears and proclaimed their savagery by wearing only G-strings and towering hair arrangements. In the lower corner was the Rabaul volcano, belching forth "Welcome." Goesti Madé, Jane's secretary, had his father do us a series of pictures designed to contain the principal trance dancers Jane and we ourselves had studied together, but he explained sadly that they all looked too young. They did, in fact, look like all the other faces that his very gifted father, Goesti Njoman Lempad, had ever drawn.

In Bajoeng the chief priestess made a series of farewell offerings and we went about to every temple, and in our names the chief village priest asked permission from the village gods for us to depart, ending finally in our own little home temple, where we asked permission also from our own ancestors. (As they were said to be in our country anyhow, this was a little obscure.) At the end of this little ceremony, I said to Madé: "What will become of this shrine, will it just rot away?" He answered: "Nang Oera [our best friend in Bajoeng] says he is going to take it out to his farm" (and added, as I was looking properly touched) "he says he is going to make a dovecote out of it."

All the things we were going to leave behind us were sorted out into grades of desirability, and we made lists of deservingness among the Bajoengese. The morning we were to leave, all those who had been notified that they should come—and many onlookers and prospective carriers—gathered in the yard and I spread out all the middle-rate things in the diningroom and permitted the mothers of much-photographed children to make first choice in order of the amount of photography to which they had been subjected rather than the number of children. Each one went in and hesitated among the pillows, lamps, clothes, glass jars, etc., while a good-natured crowd shouted advice from around the railing. None of the chief women of the village who had been busy shooing me out of this and that sacred place for two years were allowed in; this was for the unclean, younger married women. They grinned a little sourly, but I was very firm. Then the large and important gifts—the four big water drums, the two mattresses, the larger lamps, etc.—were given to high officials who had been helpful. And last of all came the matter of the house, which had been agitating everyone for days. We made a club of our three chief informants, each to have a quarter-share, and our boys, all to share a quarter-share, and gave the house to them to rent to some artist, if they can find one, or to pull down and divide among themselves. From some people at least I expected murmurs, pleas, recriminations over help they had given and for which they had never been properly rewarded, but there was not a word either of envious or invidious comment or of reproach to us. The bearers lifted me up in my carrying chair, for I was still lame from my malaria injection; the people stood about, smiling gaily, not angry or deprived or deeply regretful, but standing there in the clear mountain air as a group of slight acquaintances might who had had a good time at a picnic and were now scattering far apart. Nang Oera said: "If Karba were only a little bigger I would let you take him to your country, Njonjah, but he is so small. Remember he is the child who has always dared to come to you and the Toean—he is unique in Bali!" And we went out of the village gaily, without tears but also without thanksgiving for leaving it, although it had been such a sombre, unresponsive, stubborn village to ever become a part of.

In Bangli the palace floors were littered with carvings and paintings to be counted and packed away—and in the midst of it two Swiss, who spoke only French, came to ask us about our three houses and to discuss—in French—the finances of living in Bali. And Gregory, from whose tongue Balinese had at last driven his French, addressed them with innocent fluency in a language which had French verbs and nouns and all the morphemes were Balinese. It left the Swiss very puzzled and unsure how much they ought to pay for a motor car or which of our three houses they ought to plan to rent.

Our little princess-landlady brought me a splendid piece of

cloth, woven in gold thread within the palace precincts, and a bottle of distilled flower essence which I gave to Madé's wife, because no one could venture to use it outside of Bali. In Batoean they built a decorated dancing place in front of the house where we had lived and the Barong danced for us, and Ida Bagoes Teroewi gave us a piece of the very rare "Balinese batik" which was once made in Batoean village. . . .

In Boeleleng we stayed with Madé's family, and so did all our boys and a number of our informants from Bajoeng and Batoean, all of whom Madé had to entertain. He put on a special shadow play of a style which was in vogue ten years ago, so that we should have seen all the stages from the South Balinese conservative style to the North Balinese modern style. Goris, the Dutch linguistic scholar in charge of the Balinese archives of local literature, gave us a massive lunch, with pinks arranged in garlands on the white tablecloth, like a birthday card, and song doves, one each, as the main course. The next morning everyone came on board in a long stiff line to say goodbye, and as these were almost like members of a family they were a little more intense and uncomfortable than the village people had been. And then, as the ship sailed, Gregory dived into a box and got out a Iatmul notebook and we started Iatmul.

Madé, who was, when we got him, profoundly uninterested in everything Balinese and had just one ambition—to be a small clerk in Java—had decided to stay in Bali and had married a Balinese wife, a mountain girl whom he met in Bajoeng, who was very pretty but who could not read or write and was in no sense a "new Balinese." At Christmas he wrote us a letter saying that he had grown up while he was working for us and that he had come to appreciate the customs and religion of his own people. This was far more than we had hoped for; we thought the Dutch schooling had done its work too well. He hopes to work for the KPM as a special interpreter for the specialized traveler who is interested in expert interpreting and special investigations.

We had seven days in Soerabaja for the repair of everything from teeth to cameras. It was Javanese New Year in that district, the same old ceremony which gave us our empty roads and closed houses the day we entered Bali, and we were able to see a Javanese shadow play which is only given once a year. I had saved some papers to sign at the American consulate so as to get three American witnesses, but when I went there they all turned out to be Chinese or Armenian, with very distinctive non-American names. So the Consul arranged for me to come around for a cocktail party for Bill Tilden when he could collect some witnesses, one of whom was introduced as the salesman of "the skin you love to touch." All the men stood on one side of the room and all the women on the other and Tilden just stood.

Finally, typewriters rejuvenated, new tripod attachments made, new shoes made, watches cleaned, camera gates clicking, we left Soerabaja on the *Maatsuycker,* looking forward to ten days of Dutch food and hearty English-speaking Dutch officers. But the ship was full of tenth-rate Australian and New Zealand tourists. . . . So I finished revising a section of my Arapesh monograph ready for the press and Gregory gave me lessons in Iatmul.

Rabaul has almost recovered from the effects of the earthquake. There is a great ugly sugarloaf mountain of dead brown in the middle of the harbor which will not be green for many generations. Here and there in the town there are gray piles of volcanic dust; the roads are still very bad because the surface of the ground became coated and resistant to water and the floods from the mountains tore down in great torrents and cut across the roads. But although the lawns are green and the gardens fully planted again, the houses are scrubbed and repainted, the roofs from which the stuff had to be pried off in small flat layers are clean enough to give fresh water again for the tanks, Rabaul itself has not recovered. The slightest earthquake, the least puff of unexplained steam out of an exhaust pipe in someone's backyard, makes them jittery—and everybody has another drink. A sort of wartime atmosphere prevails, no one knows where the capital will be located in another two months, no one likes the sound of his own thoughts. . . .

Meanwhile we looked for ships. Our old and piratical friend, Bill Mason, met us at the *Maatsuycker* with the news that he had a small boat which would take us straight from Rabaul up the Sepik, she just needed a few days' work on her keel. Before that work was done, she was moved off the slips so that a barge behind her could be slipped into the harbor, and she very quietly sank at once. That ended the first hope. Then there was the *Gnair,* a tiny craft, really just a big motor boat, but with a fast engine which would have made good time up the Sepik—if it had ever got that far. But the owner had a contract hauling lumber and he couldn't make up his mind whether he wanted to leave Rabaul before Easter or stay to take a cargo of vacationing natives to New Ireland, where all the Europeans go also, for a cricket match. Then there was talk of a schooner which was to bring new houses for the government station on the river, but upon investigation it wasn't leaving until May or June. Meanwhile we waited for the BPs (Burns Philp) boat and sent radios to the two ports near the Sepik mouth and finally heard that the Chinese trader, Tcheu Leong, would probably be going up from Madang and also that a schooner named *Manuan* would be willing to take us. So we radioed to the *Manuan* and took the *Montoro* to Madang. . . . Fairly settled in our minds, expecting the *Manuan* to meet us in Madang, we had five days on the *Montoro* and our first touch of out-station life again. Rabaul is very civilized and full of cocktails these days. On the *Montoro* there were two sisters come to inspect their order, two Methodist missionaries who didn't drink anything, a huge Australian priest who looked like his German brethren and whose Queensland accent was like a blow in the face, so unexpected it was, a mob of miners who told one the names of imaginary public schools they had once attended and how their fathers refused to let them go out to Africa with Cecil Rhodes because it was "like going into trade" and who solemnly discussed the charms, probably never seen, of Budapest, and an earnest-faced boy coming up to do two years at a lonely trading station in Papua. (The Arapesh country has been devastated by an earthquake which tipped whole mountains on their sides. Gold has been found all through there and there is an airdrome at Butte, on the beach, which was just a small mission station five years ago.) At Salamaua we met Father Kirschbaum, the priest who has spent 20 years here on the river, and he suggested that probably we would find Tambunam the best village. We had also heard from Bill Mason that Tambunam had resisted the mission and it is the only Iatmul village without a catechist and that some of them have priests or brothers. It is also the largest village, about 900 people.

When we reached Madang there was no sign of the *Manuan* and a recuiter from the river told us that the District Officer (the very same one who cost me £60 back in 1933 by a broken promise about transport) had said that we were coming in May—although there was no *Montoro* in May! But we could go with Tcheu Leong. Of course it would be pretty crowded—there was himself and his stores and Fred Eichhorn and his father and the patrol officer and his police-boys and his gear and a lot of *finished-times*—returning work-boys—but we could probably all get on. Meanwhile Tcheu Leong wasn't there either, he was working copra somewhere. The next morning the *Manuan* turned up, delayed by an accident when its engine was being built up again after cleaning. But Gregory had talked with Tcheu Leong by then, so he decided to toss between their claims, without having seen the *Manuan.* And the coin decided for the *Manuan.* It turned out that Tcheu Leong was full up without us and our six tons. His is only a motor boat, and we had a delightful trip on a trim little two-masted schooner with her sails up most of the way. True, she drew a lot of water for the Sepik and we stuck on a couple of sandbanks, and while we were on one had an earthquake, but not a strong enough one to dislodge us. But the captain was charming, very like a Balinese, and the trip was a pleasure rather than the ordeal which I had expected and which it would have been on Tcheu Leong's crowded little pinnace.

When we reached the river we found more good luck—no high water this year. If it had been high water, we might have had to wait two months or more to build with all the interruption of work that comes with late building. As it is, we are building two houses on the ground, with cement floors, as we don't expect to be here next high water. We decided on the house on the ground after two days of life in this government rest house where we are now camped. The floor of this house is made of loose pieces of beaten-down palm bark, laid on irregularly and not fastened down. Chairs go through the cracks, edges break off, tables dance every time anyone walks about, flashlights and glasses clatter to the floor at one end if a pig rubs against a house post at the other. The consumption of time and energy in adapting to such a floor is enormous.

Meanwhile we are perforce living on it and will be for the next two weeks at least. There is a big mosquito net set up in the middle, inside of which are kept most of the necessities of life—milk and sugar and mustard, the camera box, the paste and ink and paper clips, ammunition, a bowl of razor blades, fishhooks, matches and beads for small trade in pawpaws, bananas and fish; also my sewing box, a large Dutch cheese, the Flit squirt, a row of notebooks lined along the floor, a box of money, goldlip shells and the revolver, etc. The floor is covered with a heavy canvas which wrinkles into the cracks of the floor. For a bed we brought a big kapok mattress from Bali and this is set up in one corner with a separate net, and inside that is a square Balinese covered basket containing all the things one can't bear to climb out of a net for at night—spare handkerchiefs, aspirin, quinine, drinking water, a book to read, etc. In another corner is a *house-washwash*, walled in by our spare canvas ground sheet and three mats. All around the edges, three and four layers deep, are boxes of cargo, most of which have been opened and checked, the tall and very modernistic fan which runs with a little kerosene lamp, the new outboard engine, bags of rice and salt, and along the rafters are stuck books. Among all these things the mosquitoes find good harborage, but they are not as bad as I had remembered them; they buzz and one notices them as they bite, but the bites aren't very poisonous.

This Sepik country is more lovely than I had remembered it. I have always tended to assign all the beauty to the *round-waters*—the lakes like the Tchambuli lake—and the ugliness of the Yuat River, on which the Mundugumor live, to the Sepik itself. But the truth is that the Sepik below the Yuat—we are about 20 miles above its mouth here—is rather dull. But it gets steadily more beautiful up towards Tchambuli. The wide, wide open landscape with a half-sphere of sky overhead and the tossing white plumes of the elephant grass floating in the high grass plains, matching the clouds overhead, is entrancing. One feels that one is really out of doors. Against this background the narrow canoes with their paddles arranged single file are etched very sharp and small. The village itself stands on a high bank and the houses stand in little shallow ravines between artificial mounds on which are planted coconut palms, and the roads of the village are deep passages between these high mounds. At this time of year the people live under their houses and one sees them most often in silhouette, part of the design made by the house posts, the platforms, the fishtraps and fish spears outlined against the Sepik which can be seen down each deep road—as one can see the Hudson through the crosstown streets in New York, only without any enclosing other bank behind to spoil the background. The people are enormously friendly and merry and I can already walk through the village and answer simple questions which are shouted at me as I pass. A pack of small naked boys attend my steps and correct my grammar.

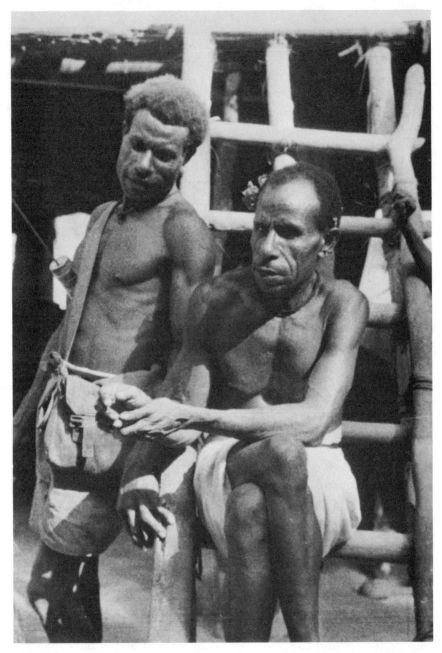

In Tambunam Village, the *tultul*, Ndjutndimi—known to Europeans as Tomi—with Washoe.

The *tultul* here, known to Europeans as Tomi, is the man from whom Gregory got his big genealogy when he visited this village for five days in 1929. The people can still tell him what birds he shot and who cooked for him, and Tomi points out the small boy of ten, who was a baby then, upon whose relationships Gregory worked out the *iai* marriage system. It is going to be a big help in dating people's ages because they usually know relative ages. Tomi was trained by Mrs. Parkinson—he was Paul Parkinson's nurse-boy —and he is marvelously good. He is supervising the building of our house, shooting for us, and he acted as substitute cook-boy till we got one and as informant in between times. We have a full household. Washoe, tall, proud, assured and a little intimidating to me because I have never before had a boy who knew anything I didn't teach him. Washoe was cook to young Macdonald, who was District Officer at Wewak while I was in Arapesh and who was later shot by one of his police-boys. Washoe is the cook, and an offsider of his, whose name is also the name for the small fish which are the staple diet here, Mangen, is the wash-boy. For the table I have a brand-new, extremely bright *monkey* named Mbetnda, all eyes and ears and intensity and eagerness, a delight after Balinese apathy before anything new.

We have been having a perfect plague of white men since we got here eleven days ago—seven separate pinnaces or schooners and seven evenings wrecked by Europeans to feed and talk to. But it's an accident and soon we will be lucky if there is a pinnace once a month which can bring stores. The reason you are getting this long letter is mainly because the descent of five government officials, including the Administrator, and three ships has left both us and the village too depleted in spirit to settle down to work.

It is a new experience, this coming into a village where I am virtually a beginner with someone who speaks the language and knows the culture. I had seen Iatmul villages before and a couple of Iatmul ceremonies and, of course, Tchambuli is a related culture and I have read all Gregory's stuff. But I have the language to learn and I can do that and organize the household and store up the first impressions from eyes alone with no desperate urgency to find out whether the people have clans or not or to get down the words for father and mother. It's very pleasant. On our first walk through the village I managed to say: "No, I won't go into the House Tambaran. That is the men's house. I am a woman." And that pleased the old men so much that they shouted it up and down.

Tambunam
June 24, 1938

We are installed in our new home, very oddly assembled but quite comfortable. . . . The house is rather like a series of booths at a fair, with a fine open appearance calculated to display all the wares and exhibits inside. In the center of Gregory's house is the big mosquito room, twelve by ten feet, which holds a big table and a small one, a bookcase, a little wooden tool chest we brought from Bali, two chairs, two stools and two dry boxes, and it isn't crowded except when we add four or five informants and boxes for them to sit on. Inside the *room-wire* is kept small trade—a bowl of matches, fishhooks, razor blades, beads, and so on—the ammunition which has to be doled out to two shoot-boys, large Dutch glass candy jars containing drying chemicals, cameras, lenses, film, the cut Dutch cheese, small supplies of medicine, milk and sugar. . . . From the side posts of the house hang maps, sausages, spare tripods, nail pullers, saws, opera glasses, etc. There is a fine high shelf that runs the length of one side and holds books and a variety of tins now used for the wrong purposes—a peach tin full of nails, a Camel cigarette tin full of cotton wool, a cookie tin full of empty film containers, sometimes a few eggs which are a present from a passing pinnace, methylated spirits for lighting the lamps, the spray for the Shelltox, thread which the boys borrow to sew up their *laplaps.* There is a batik headcloth on the table—because the mission varnished it—and a bright red and green trade mat on the floor, a combination which gives a slightly half-caste wife of wealthy planter air to the scene and is a sad comedown after the pleasant mats and lovely cloth available in Bali. When the lamps are lit inside our cage, we can't see out and forget that we ourselves are simply washed in light.

The baseboards of the mosquito room did not fit perfectly on the slightly uneven cement floor and the interstices are filled in with clay from the banks of the falling river, a fine gray flaky substance. Tomi started to pack the clay along the outside crevice, but soon he had ten women and girls at work and he then stopped doing it; they were working far more evenly and efficiently than he

Our main house in Tambunam, built on the ground.

Gregory and I work together in the mosquito room.

was, and he modeled a charming little crocodile on the outside, one paw up and one paw down, on the cement edge. That little scene about sums up the position of the sexes in this culture: the men lead and decorate; the women do the steady work on which living depends. . . .

This building a house in the field is such a funny business; one is limited by time, by the materials available, by the skill of the natives, by the size and layout and condition of the site. One wants to build a place in which to live with a maximum of comfort and a minimum of effort. The comfort is all a matter of few steps, having everything inside the mosquito room which may be needed inside and everything outside which will be needed outside—for every slip-up means opening the screen door and letting in mosquitoes. . . .

There are five islands under the roof: the big mosquito room; the small mosquito room, in which I receive women and children and in which Gregory works with single informants occasionally; the bed, which is an eight-foot-square platform, on which a six-foot mattress is set, entirely surrounded by a big net, always tucked in, with a white canopy over it to keep out some of the dust and some of the insects (at that one spends five minutes picking up caterpillars, small spiders, swallow-tailed nits, mosquitoes, flies, borers, etc., which are always to be found speckling the bed when one climbs in); the storeroom, in which Tomi has lined all of the tinned goods, as to whether they are singletons or have a large number of *one-talks* (members of the same group, one kind); and the bathroom, which is our pride and joy, with its cement floor that drains and a broad shelf made of real planks (tops of kerosene cases) on which bottles will stand up, and a water tank, Dutch style, made of an oil tin, begged from a schooner and chopped in half with an axe.

But aside from the question of comfort and expedition in matters of bathing, dressing and eating, the house has to be primarily considered as a combination laboratory, observation post, fort, outpost, dispensary and gathering place. There must be room for people to gather without breaking or spoiling or pilfering anything. There must be a place in which to do medicine which has a wall dividing the audience from the operating theater; there must be blank surfaces on which children can put their papers to draw, and a shelf on which their clay modeling can be displayed; there must be from all points a view of a road or a bit of beach or another house, which can be utilized with the long lens; there must be ways of dividing visitors into informants and mere *looklooks,* seats for the real visitors to sit upon, newspaper and tobacco for them to smoke. There must be small trade ready at any moment to buy a fish or a coconut brought by a daring three-year-old. It's all a little like planning how to live comfortably in a show window and at the same time keep up continuous observations of the crowd that gathers outside.

But we are excellently placed; our veranda stands where the main road ran, and the main road now curves around it, and everyone stops to look over the fence. This is the main women's road; the men's road goes by on the beach side of the house, and important processions of self-conscious males carrying shell valuables or shamans in trance, hunting for suspicious-looking shadows of sin, stand out in conspicuous silhouette. Baangwin's house is about four feet from the edge of our house, and his brother's house stands at the end of the little dip of land in which we live. Here there is a wide cleared space where the children play games and make drawings in the dust. The kitchen also stands on the main road, and from its flimsy shelter I can watch events outside, and have a boy dictate the abuse which is raging outside, without the boy's being too embarrassed. Baangwin is our landlord and nearest neighbor; he is a charming person, graceful, high-spirited, decorative, with an endless range of styles of doing his hair, and a fine angry oratory at five-thirty in the morning, when he discovers that someone has robbed his fowl's nest. He believes in his culture, accepts its bombast as real and its rules, which are only meant to insult other people, as applicable to himself, and so he plays his roles with a conviction that most Iatmuls lack. . . .

We now have five boys and Tomi, who is shoot-boy and informant. The three big boys take turns, turning up or going to their own work; the two little boys, Mbetnda and Ashavi, are always present and the only ones who have no alibis. Under these conditions of too many cooks not stirring the broth it took a long time to work out a procedure which would make bread rise, bacon not too salt, tea brewed with anything like consistency, clothes put anywhere near their destination. But order is descending upon us, rather in spite of them.

I am writing this while Gregory cuts film in a black calico net hung up inside the other mosquito room. All lights are out except two small standing flashlights, which stand at my elbow but outside the net, hidden in a kerosene box, and give just enough light to illuminate the keys of the typewriter. I had them inside but I found I was getting too many mouthfuls of small insects.

And I haven't told you about our substitute for a motor car— a small canoe with an outboard motor in the back, in which we can chug rapidly up and down this mile-long water front with no worry as to who will carry the various cameras and tripods. While we were still living in the government rest house we had a ceremony every day for ten days at the extreme other end of the village. The river was a bright horrid glare when we would go up at four, but lovely for the ride home into the sunset. To transport our things up to the completed house, we had two big canoes made into a raft and Gregory nosed into the stern of one of them with his canoe and pushed the whole raft up with three tons on board each trip. All went well until the last trip when one of the boys complained broken-heartedly that we had not brought the island of river "spinach" which he had towed ashore to give us a supply. So that was added to the canoes laden with the big mosquito room and proved to be a horrid weight. There was more ground than there seemed to be under the sprouting "spinach"!

These Iatmul are a gay, irresponsible, vigorous people, always either laughing or screaming with rage. The two types of behavior are more or less alternating and seem to give them about equal satisfaction. Children learn to yell for every satisfaction, and later they decide it was the yelling they enjoyed. When anyone loses his or her temper, the bystanders stand about, grinning from ear to ear, feeling reassured that this is a world in which people can lose their tempers HARD. They enjoy anger more than any people I have ever seen. For they are not cruel or stingy or greedy. They have no infanticide, they look after their poor and orphaned, they share food and betel and tobacco with a lavishness which the state of their food supply hardly justifies and they lose their tempers all over the place, without guilt or shame. It's a world in which one has to keep raising one's voice in order to be heard at all.

Tambunam
August 12, 1938

For the first time in two months I am almost up to date in writing up notes, which is the nearest I can ever come to affluence. It's impossible ever to get on the credit side of the matter, but just

Kavwaishaun paints a portrait skull of the dead.

Avangaindo, his face painted for a trance performance.

to be free of the knowledge that there are pages and pages of faintly scratched, rapidly cooling notes waiting for me is almost affluence—an affluence which may be celebrated with a bulletin.

The whole rhythm of our lives, of the lives of everyone in the village, including the ghosts and the shamanic spirits, is at present dependent upon the slight variations in the height of the river which mean it is or is not possible to shoot crocodiles. This is the lowest water in five years, the first time that the people have been sufficiently in the good books of their capricious shamanic spirits to be allowed to find an abundance of meat for the death feasts which will be made at high water. For hundreds of square miles land that is usually dotted with lakes, cross-cut with *barets*, and itself a mere squashy quagmire, has dried up, and the people go and burn it off in great patches, laying bare the remaining sorry little puddles in which the crocodiles and turtles and fish are plunging about. Then the whole hunting group takes part in the actual crocodile hunt. They go and camp for days while this is going on and only return to the village when there is a death or a quarrel or when their supplies of worked sago run out.

The village is almost empty. Women with small babies and the rest of their brood, old people, the sick and the lame and an occasional malcontent are the only people about sometimes for a week at a time. Then the water rises a couple of feet, the grass becomes a quagmire again, and they come home, to go out again when it falls.

Last month we joined one of these camping parties. We fastened another little canoe—about fifteen feet long—beside our canoe which carries the outboard engine, and with three boys and four days' supplies we started on the three-hour trip downstream which ultimately, after going up a long *baret,* brings us to a place which, seen from the village, is up-river.

This was my first sight of the black water this trip, and although there is something very fine about the expanse of the Sepik landscape, the unlimited sky and water on which people are the merest black specks, the black water has a different and a more intimate charm. To turn suddenly from the quite unbelievable proportions of the Sepik into a narrow stream which flows between high banks, on which thinly leafed trees are set like worn-out sketches against the sky, where the lotus leaves are green when they lie flat and pink when the wind catches them, ruffling them up off the water which

itself has a changeable pink and green powder on its darkness—
this is to find oneself in a land to which one might conceivably
belong.

As soon as we turned into the *baret,* we began to meet canoes;
the *baret* was a busy little village street, where the Sepik is a great
lonely empty track, which a whole fleet of canoes could never
crowd—first a canoe with men armed with hunting spears and
containing nothing except lumps of firewood, then canoes of children out gathering lotus flowers, and merrily chewing on lotus
rhizomes, while some of the girls had braided the long white rhizomes into belts from which they chewed bits at intervals. . . .

We found our party camped on a little ledge of dry ground
about six yards wide, about twelve feet above the stream, and
sloping off into some of the newly dried grass country, over which
one could look for miles. The people had built no shelters at all
but merely stood their huge cylindrical basketwork mosquito bags
—in which they sleep—up along the bank and used the trees on
which to hang up baskets of food, rain capes, and other bits of
personal gear. There were seventeen men, about ten of them with
wives and children, encamped together on a ridge about forty
yards long, so close together that one man's fire was practically in
another man's bed. They had brought with them tough pieces of
sago bark which could be used to cover up their most precious
possessions, like their lumps of sago, but they had made no attempt to build shelters. It had not rained the five nights they had
been there. The air was thick with smoke, for everywhere fish and
the meat of crocodiles which had been so exasperating as to die
were being smoked. Almost my first job was to bathe a couple of
dozen sore eyes; every child's eyes were red and swollen from the
smoke. We spent the first afternoon taking photographs on the
edge of a little lake, a lake which had become little more than a
series of mud pools in which the fishers wallowed up to their
waists, first stabbing at random in the mud in the hope of hitting
a fish and afterwards feeling about up to their armpits in mud to
find their victims. The fish were then tossed ashore where children,
up to their necks in mud, caught them and strung them on string.

Our own camp was simply a large piece of canvas set up like
a tent on a few pieces of light elephant grass, with a mosquito net
under it. But no sooner had we got comfortably inside it in the
evening than a strange shouting and bellowing began, men of

importance standing up and ordering the moon to come out, so
that there would be no rain. Then our two shamans went into
trance and began stamping and gesticulating up and down, among
the fires and the smoke frame, the pitched mosquito bags, the little
wooden stools and the women who were just finishing cooking, or
trying to turn or stow away their fish. The shamans have to pretend
to be reasonably *non compos mentis* and so they pitched about,
knocking their heads against hanging baskets occasionally, but
doing much less damage than I did, embarrassed by an electric
torch, a notebook, ignorance of the ground, and a strange interpreter just roped in at a moment's notice to dictate the shamans'
shouted incomprehensibilities. The smoke stung one's eyes, the
mosquitoes bit and bit, the interpreter wearied, one stumbled over
crocodile tails and put one's foot into the sides of baskets—all with
the assurance that the written record would certainly turn out to
be illegible. Finally, after an hour of this we went to bed, and then
in the night it poured.

Next morning it was a shivering disgruntled company which
listlessly gathered up its wet belongings and prepared to move
camp to another spot. The next day they were to go to an appointed market where their smoked fish and turtles would have got
them enough carbohydrate food and betel nut for ten days. But
just as the camp was finally breaking up, an old man and an old
woman, both of whom were planning to make death feasts for
which their clan was hunting in this communal way, had a quarrel,
and the old woman threw away the crocodile she had been given.
Someone brought it down the stream and laid it on the bank and
later one of the hunters went and sang mournful totemic songs to
it, as it was his totemic thing, a water thing, thus inappropriately
left on land. And everyone was so dispirited and angry over the
quarrel and the rain that they abandoned next day's market and
any further hunting and went home. And so did we.

It was a beautiful place for photography. No high houses to cast
deep shadows, absolutely no privacy and also men thrown together
with their families as they never are in the village. We planned to
go back and stay a week with them when they went again, but the
wetting damped their spirits and they have never gone back there.
They go instead to people's garden sites and all camp in a couple
of houses, and so our photographic plans were all lost.

Gregory made two trips more before he saw them really kill a crocodile, but I did not go because there was going to be a birth next door at practically any moment. The birth had been so near for so long that the husband even upbraided the wife for her slowness. To which she replied that women were not like pigs and dogs, bearing their offspring quickly, but there was a time for these things. I had studied the family so hard: I knew the other children, the relations between the two wives, the behavior of the expectant mother two months ago when she had false labor pains. It was going to be such an ideal birth to see, right next door, so that if it lasted ten hours one could at least come home for a drink of tea. And then, long after Gregory had made his expeditions and actually seen a crocodile hunt, she had her baby—out fishing. She brought it home to her sister's husband's father's home, instead of coming home, so it is practically as hard to keep track of as any other baby.

We even had a false-alarm rumor that it had had its first real bath without our being told. To this news we responded in proper Iatmul fashion. I smashed a glass and Gregory went and smashed a big Ceram shell on the father's house post. Then we found out it was a false alarm and when it does have that bath we will probably be told. But I was so relieved when I found it wasn't true and we could laugh instead of having a real quarrel! I find I don't enjoy displays of anger as much as the Iatmul do. But it is the only language they understand. Every statement of good behavior is explicitly motivated "for fear So-and-so may be angry." Never for fear that property may be destroyed or morals shattered or hearts broken.

We have had three deaths since we moved to this house—the death of a newborn baby which never learned to suck, the death of a little boy of two and the death of a mature man who was bitten by a death adder while crocodile hunting. The people treat death with great simplicity and such genuineness of feeling that even the small children are impressed into voluntary quiet and good behavior. There is not the slightest sense of horror or revulsion towards the dead body. A mother holds her dead baby in her arms, strokes it and fondles it as she would in life, and a widow leans over the body of her dead husband fondly, tenderly.

Mourning is almost entirely women's business. The father of a child may sit and mourn a little apart; a young mother's brother may come and sit with the women, mourning for his sister's son.

But for the most part it is only women. The main mourning group, the close relatives, sit about the body, weeping loudly if it is their habit to weep loudly, otherwise quietly, while the more distantly connected come in and sit for a while in the shadowy corners of the great house floor from which all the mosquito baskets have been removed. There is a keening tune into which words are fitted, extemporaneous and almost always very simple statements of some past event: "We went together to fish, we were of one mind, we did not disagree saying this was to be given, this was not to be given. We were of one mind, why have you left me?" Or repetitions of the event which led to the death: "I took you to my brother's house. They lied and said you would live, now you have died."

The two-year-old child looked singularly beautiful, his body painted with red clay, his face painted white, with a pubic covering of ti leaves; on his breast, ornamental shells and in one hand a piece of sago cake, in the other a little set of children's panpipes. By the grave the mother whose baby had refused to suck put her breast to its mouth and squeezed a few drops of milk into it.

There is only one harsh note. They have no appreciation of an inability to mourn aloud. The mother of the two-year-old could not cry aloud; slow tears fell from her eyes, the kind that are squeezed painfully out of tense eyes and roll down one's nose unnoticed, but she could not cry aloud. A terrible old woman, her enormous head made more enormous by her long widow's locks covered with yellow clay and her peaked, clay-smeared widow's cape, scolded her unmercifully: "Do you think that he will come back again, that you will see him again, that you do not weep? It is not so, he is gone forever." And the father, who had sat out on the house ladder and mourned aloud for hours, went away with the next recruiter to work for the white man so that he might not have to stay and watch his wife's lack of feeling.

You will notice how often clay comes up in describing this culture. Mud, in fact, is what we are made of. At low water, the sides of the river display great banks of fine river ooze in which the children carve fanciful figures, splashing the smooth, pliant mud into fish and birds and grotesque heads, sometimes sustained on sticks, sometimes sprawling life-size on the river bank. When they are tired of that, they have only to convert the mud into a slide and wallow up and down it happily. Up in the village, we exchange mud for dust, and women and children sit about on the ground aim-

Working with a group of children.

I take notes while Gregory films a children's play group.

lessly drawing line figures in the dust with sticks or fingers. Or they cooperate in groups of five or six to draw ten-foot crocodile figures, into whose coat you put the scales by wiggling your whole body as you draw. Dusting the babies' bottoms after they have been sitting down in the dust is one of the mothers' regular occupations. And then our cosmetics are clay—bright red clay, which looks astonishing on the faces of young children whose bodies have been painted white or yellow. Pink clay is specially used on little babies, so that they look like plump pink roses against the darker skin of their mothers. Children paint themselves for a lark and then trace elaborate geometrical designs on each other's wet body surfaces. When the baby is hot and fretful, one gives it a bath and then covers it with wet paint. For dances, the faces of the chief characters are painted with the lovely curvilinear designs that one sees on Sepik modeled skulls. And with all this happy wallowing about in the mud, playing with mud, dressing with mud, they are exceptionally, nonobsessively clean. The little boys who have just been sliding on their bellies in the mud never fail to go in the river to have a grand wash afterwards. It is all a change from Bali, where people kept their children off the ground but never succeeded in keeping them clean.

The House Tambaran, Kerambit, and dancing ground.

The face on the gable
of the House Tambaran.

The open ground floor
of the House Tambaran with
low stools and hearths.

We are doing very well indeed in every respect. Fresh food most of the time and a kitchen staff well enough organized now so that if one leaves the others can break in his successor. The bread rises regularly and the coffee is reasonably black. As a substitute for Madé, on a humbler scale, I have had great luck in finding Tjavi, a boy who lost one leg while away at work. He is practically desexed, joins a group of women and children without embarrassment and is delighted to have a job for which he can earn money. To follow the quarrels and séances which make up life here one must have someone who can dictate at one's elbow and until I got Tjavi I had to use young boys, fifteen years old or so, just on the edge of being too old for the women's group and all full of prickliness and embarrassment. I have two women I can use in exclusively women's groups, but they are too shy if there are any men in sight. So this boy is a godsend.

Madé's last communication was a gem:

"Anyhow with this letter I do you a request. But when you think it will be bad for your Bali book, I won't do it. Do you think I can write a short article about the cockfight? I should like to put this in the collection the KPM has. As many of the guides have written something, I won't be behind. But I tell you if you think this action will be a bit bad for your book, I won't do it. I don't want to make profit of any of the stuff we have collected. It belongs all to you. My love to both of you. M. Kaler."

Which makes one realize over again that there never will be any substitute for Madé. One of the things that wears me out here is trying to do his work as well as my own, for in Bali we halved recording.

At present we plan to be here until early December. Our route home is still uncertain. We have to wait for the water to rise to get into Tchambuli; the lake is nearly dry. And we have to wait for the water to rise for this village to do any ceremonies. At present it simply eats, drinks, sleeps and has séances about crocodiles.

VI.

RETURN TO MANUS
1953

In 1952 the studies of national character, which had preoccupied us since the beginning of World War II, drew to a close and I began to think about field work again. I made a short lecture trip to Australia to explore new possibilities, and I was persuaded by my Australian colleagues that the most useful thing I could do was a restudy of Manus, where, it was reported, the most extraordinary things were going on.

So I began planning a year ahead for the return to Manus. I circulated departments of anthropology in search of a graduate student who was well qualified in linguistics, theoretical and applied electronics and photography and who was interested in culture and personality studies. Only one qualified student appeared, Ted Schwartz. His artist wife, Lenora, also wanted to do field work. Given a year's lead time, I could help them prepare for the field and Ted could experiment with his cameras and the new kinds of equipment—tape recorders, generators and special lighting. We planned to do the kind of work Gregory Bateson and I had done in Bali, but to add recorded sound.

My problem as stated for the Rockefeller Foundation grant to the American Museum of Natural History Admiralty Island Expedition was a restudy of Manus, which would yield information on change within one generation, in contrast with the kind of second- and third-generation change with which we were more familiar.

I returned to Peré and Ted and Lenora settled in Bunai, in good weather only 45 minutes away, but in bad weather perhaps as much as three days away. I worried about their inexperience; they had never seen an open wound, a birth or a death. But the calm and expert way in which they handled the difficulties brought about by the volcano in their first days in the field laid my anxieties at rest.

I left the field in December 1953. Ted and Lenora stayed on for six months and visited another expedition on New Britain before coming home. Our field material, much of which still has

The field work team, 1953. Lenora and Ted Schwartz visit me in Peré.

not been worked up, is almost inexhaustibly rich and has provided the background for all the later expeditions to Manus in the 1960s and 1970s.

> Peré Village, Manus
> July 2, 1953
> Written at Patusi Patrol Post

    I am writing in a temporary camp on top of a high hill above the old village of Patusi and looking down on the site of the old village of Peré. There the small high islands, on which women once dried their grass skirts and children hung their swings, and the little flat islands, which were once meeting grounds and feasting places, stand empty and flat, defining a vanished way of life. At present I am sharing a deserted and somewhat dilapidated semi-

European house, roof of sago thatch and floor of plywood (left over from the American occupation), with some 70 natives. The rest of the villagers are scattered in a few broken-down houses designed for police-boys and station staff; a few are sleeping in canoes at the foot of the hill and a few of the sick are in the village of Patusi, now on land about two miles away.

We are here because a volcano has suddenly appeared between the islands of Lou and Balowan about twenty miles away, spouting beautiful white smoke, a prelude in this country to ashes and lava, up into an innocently pellucid sky. The smoke goes up in lovely cumulus clouds, sometimes abating, sometimes shifting a little and sometimes, when there is no wind, looking as if it had diminished. This is our third day here.

I had just been settled in Peré a week and was peacefully writing up notes at eleven o'clock at night with the whole village asleep except for those who had lit their great Tilly lamps (salvaged from the army) and set out for all-night fishing, when a police-boy appeared at the door with a letter from the District Commissioner, Malcolm English, who is quite the most enlightened, intellectually curious, morally responsible and delightful district commissioner I have ever had any dealings with. The letter began with a few casual social comments and went on to the desirability of immediate evacuation of those coastal villages which had no high ground, suggesting that they build temporary shelters up in the bush and that I move to Bunai where Ted and Lenora are on a shore edge. However, the Peré natives had another idea—that we of Peré move instead to this deserted patrol post, which has some buildings, is on a good high hill and would not be as crowded as Bunai would be if Peré's some 250 people joined Bunai's 600 in temporary shelters on poor and inadequate ground space.

So I sent the police-boy off to help Ted and Lenora evacuate their village, started packing basic necessities and had all the lamps in the village filled with kerosene. In an hour from the time the police-boy arrived, the big canoe which carried my more valuable equipment—cameras, tape recorder, typewriter, medicine, a few tins, tobacco, money, rice, boys' tinned meat, newspaper for native cigarettes—was poled slowly out of the village. Everyone else, with the exception of Manoi, the head of the Council (of whom more later), and old Pokanau, Reo's chief informant, who is now the most important living man of the old regime, and a few miscellaneous young bachelors and a widower with two children, had left the village earlier in smaller canoes. The big canoe was poled slowly through the low tide on a clear moonlit night, past the site of the old village where the house posts still mark the site of all our former houses. Kilipak, now grown to be a tall, gauntly handsome, but still gay, curious and delightful person, poled from the outrigger side. He had sent his wife and children ahead but stayed to manage my canoe.

The trip took over an hour, while Kilipak told stories of the wartime and people roared with laughter over the way one practical joker succeeded in frightening the just-evacuated people by waving a cartridge case which they were still too ignorant to know was empty. Now the people say: "We know about war, about bombing planes and cartridges and bombs. Suppose war comes, we know what to do. We are not afraid of war. We know how to send the women and children to the bush and we, the big strong men, would go about and fish and look for food, not fearing the war. But this new volcano—of this we know nothing yet. Until we understand it, we are afraid. Some of us were in Rabaul at the time of the earthquake. All of us have heard about Rabaul. We have heard a little about the Mt. Leamington eruption"—when the Europeans underestimated the danger and were gaily taking photographs when the whole side of a mountain blew out, killing many people. "We have never seen such a high-water as that of which you now speak"—that is, a tidal wave, which is actually the only danger for the coastal villages and the reason why we have moved to higher ground. "So we wait. We go about as little as possible; we wait until we understand this new thing."

So I have some 250 people on my hands, a three-day-old baby, two pregnant women who may have a baby at any moment, two cases of pneumonia and so on. The whole group moved together with no shouting or panic and not a child cried, although usually the air is rent with the insistent screams of young children, rhythmic, stylized proclamations of their rights and wishes. But in the moment of action, waked from sleep, bundled into canoes, they were quiet and intent. Now they have made themselves at home in small spaces comparable to the platform of a canoe at sea, with small carefully watched fires on bits of galvanized iron or broken pots, and in small family groups they sit, sleep, cook, smoke, chatter, play with the babies and wait.

Each day I send people to some nearby market and into the bush to buy sago and taro to supplement the food the people have brought and each night now more people will fish and trade for themselves. Meanwhile I explain that I will not lend tobacco or money to any individual who wishes to exploit his trade connections with the land people for his own family alone, but will keep all of it for the group; that I will give no one any rice except the very sick, but hold it all for a real emergency when we might have to feed all the small children. I actually have—in the village, to which people go every day—a six weeks' supply of European food, but tinned peaches or tiny tins of anchovies would mean very little to this group.

Meanwhile we wait for further orders. Messengers go back and forth to Bunai, where Ted and Lenora have got themselves installed on high ground. A native comes from Lorengau, two-thirds of a day's walk away, and reports that the DC (District Commissioner) has gone in the station ship to look at the volcano. A plane goes over from Lorengau to Wewak but takes no apparent interest in the volcano. There is a patrol officer on Balowan running the new native cooperative there, and he has a wireless set. News will go from Balowan to Lorengau by wireless and to us overland presently. There is a cheerful happy-go-lucky Australian plantation manager, named Gus Dodderidge, on Drova, an island four or five miles off Bunai, but the sea is running so high that his pinnace cannot get through the reef. Drova is a flat little atoll with no high ground.

I have not yet decided whether this is a beneficent earthquake nicely timed to my special needs, as all the other earthquakes I have encountered have been. . . . Certainly, if I had not been here the news might not have reached the villages here so promptly, they might have shilly-shallied about evacuation, and if the village were swept by a wave everyone might be drowned, the village be destroyed and no record remain of the people I have come so far to find again. It has enormously speeded up the small babies getting accustomed to me and has given me a chance to observe sleeping behavior, which is always hard to see en masse and may be impossible now that the great wakes during which people slept with the dead have been discontinued. It gives me a chance to see how they respond to an emergency. So on the whole, especially if there is not a tidal wave which destroys the generator (too heavy and established to move) and all the houses which the people have so lovingly built in the "new fashion" with carefully laid out streets and uniform measurements for all the houses, I shall count it as good rather than bad luck.

The hurricane in Samoa, which destroyed the village just a few weeks after I got there, was completely bad luck. But hurricanes and volcanic eruptions can be regarded as in different classifications. I remember Mother wrote me then, very reproachfully, "I suppose you knew there was going to be a hurricane. There is one every ten years, you say, and you chose this year on purpose."

This letter has such a different beginning than if I had written it three days ago. Then it would have begun with the village and the complete social revolution which has taken place. It began in 1946, when Paliau, a native of Balowan, who had been a police-boy in Rabaul under the Japanese, returned to the South Coast, here, and talk began to go about that the natives could build themselves a new way of life, on their own. There are still many obscure elements which have to be cleared up. From the various documents I have seen and from reports by individual government officials, and so on, it seems clear that at some point there were

New Peré Village, built ashore.

elements of what can be classified as a "cargo cult."

Now cargo cults are the New Guinea-Melanesian form of nativistic cult, at the core of which is a promise that the ancestors will return and after throwing out the white men or making them into servants, will bring all the white men's goods, the "cargo." Often these cults contain an apocalyptic element: only if the believers destroy all their present property, kill their pigs and dogs, and so on, can they hope to receive the cargo. Sometimes a sort of quivering hysterical manifestation spreads through the group.

These nativistic cults have been a commonplace in the area for years. There was one among the Arapesh just before we got there, during which the people invented a new form of house to withstand the flood and darkness which were predicted and bought out all the traders' supplies of lanterns. These cults sometimes come to the government's attention, if the excesses result in destroying the people's food, but on the whole they rise and fall without making much difference to anyone. They have even been reported now for the interior of New Guinea, where the bizarre elements born of culture contact are simply treated—by natives who as yet have had no culture contact—as new forms of ritual.

When I was in Australia in 1951, I was told that the Manus had a new cargo cult, which was mixed with a desire to get European machinery, such as they had seen in the war—bulldozers and such —and a desire to learn English, and so on. Somehow the story was hard to believe. I could imagine that the Manus had returned to parts of their old religion of personal dead ghosts of ancestors, but it was hard to construct the conditions under which their very high level of realism would collapse into an immediate expectation of a supernaturally arranged Paradise.

I still don't know enough to be sure of what did happen. In the eyes of the European observers the whole enterprise, unfortunately classified as a cargo cult, which by dint of anthropological sophistication has now become a part of the official apperceptive mass, was the work of a single leader, not a Manus native, regarded as an unscrupulous and subversive character, who used an outbreak of cargo cult to further his own ends—to establish a totalitarian-type little empire with himself as dictator.

Seen only as the people of Peré present it to me, it looks very different. They speak, with rapt looks on their faces, of *"1946"* with the devotion of the true revolutionary. In 1946, the new order began. Where did it come from? It came up like an earthquake, from nowhere. Who started it? No one, we ourselves altogether initiated it. We decided to have a new way of life, to throw away every evil custom of the past and set up our own form of life.

And they did. Out the window went—not the pigs and gardens which are destroyed in mystical cargo cults, but all the trappings of the old culture—the ornaments, all of which were economic counters of some sort, the dog's teeth and shell money, which had continued in spite of the conversion to Christianity, the arranged marriages, the taboo between affinal relatives, the name taboos, the customs surrounding childbirth, puberty, marriage. Some things were sold to the *man-o-bush;* in the end the remaining ones were packed up in a drum and thrown out to sea. All the Manus villages moved on land, new houses were built, designed like European houses with kitchens and windows. With the masses of material salvaged from the war, they set up empty drums as cisterns, galvanized iron to collect water. All native dress, all ornaments vanished.

Now all of this kind of thing has, of course, often been engineered by missions. House Tambarans have been broken and all the trappings of supernaturalism—old style—thrown away to make room for supernaturalism—new style. But the curious thing about what has happened here is that it is not really supernaturalism at all, but rather a sort of collective assertion of the dignity of man. The main tenets are that all customs that interfered with good relationships or individual moral autonomy should vanish. Men and women should choose their own mates. Each man should determine whether he would go away to work for Europeans or not; his elders should have no voice. Expensive affinal exchanges which caused people to slave should be abolished.

At the same time communal organization was stepped up. Each village or section of a large village has a "Council," an elected leader, and a "Committee," who is his assistant. The village has a central square, which is said to combine all the old individual clan speechmaking islets, and a place in the center for meetings. There are gongs to wake people up, a gong for church, a gong for a daily mustering of the population to receive communal assignments. There has been a strict separation between evil *thoughts,* which are a man's moral responsibility and which can lead to death, and evil *acts,* which are an affair for the village government or, if they are too serious, for the government officials.

Magic of the land people can only hurt those who are afraid of it. There is a great calendar of thou-shalts and thou-shalt-nots, rhythmically arranged: "Throw out the custom of taking sides with clan members when they are in the wrong; adopt the custom of not taking sides with anyone who is wrong." It is a kind of manifesto which is quoted with its date, November 6, 1946. Disease is regarded as having natural causes—poor food, lack of work which makes the blood sluggish, etc.—but the wrong thoughts will prevent medicine from working and ultimately may kill a man. However, each man's wrong thoughts are his own business. The sex life of unmarried people is their own business. A father can no longer interfere with the affairs of his daughter. Originally this movement apparently had no anti-mission elements in it, but (so the present account goes, and here native and official reports coincide) the mission opposed the new ideas. So the Manus said, "Never mind, we'll run our own church." Which they have proceeded to do, complete with two daily services, Catholic in origin, Protestant in tone.

The astonishing thing about all this is that it seems to work. In the two weeks I've been here not one quarreling voice has rent the air, and the air used to be blue with fury. During this whole trying time on the mountain there have been no quarrels, no accusations. The meeting to discuss whether people should stay or go back was a model which no enthusiast for a New England town meeting could improve upon. You will remember that in *Growing Up in New Guinea* I described the children as generous, friendly and cooperative, on whom a harsh, coercive adult economic system clamped down. Removal of this system of driving, exploitive, shame-enforced, fear-ridden affinal exchanges seems actually to have permitted this generosity and gentleness to come out.

They are appallingly earnest. The Council of this part of the village often reminds me of a Bolshevik in his singleminded devotion to the Line. The whole thing also is extremely monotonous compared with the complexity of the old culture. There is incipient tragedy because much of the new system depends upon American Army dumping, such as plywood for floors, canvas for awnings, chairs and tables and pressure lamps. Their imaginative grasp of the possibilities of modernity outruns their resources. They understand how to tell time and set a meeting for "one o'clock." But there are only two clocks and one watch in the village and the meeting is less likely to start on time than when meetings were set by the sun. They have learned about dates, but they have no calendars, so what day it is, is a matter for protracted discussion —or was until I arrived. They want good materials and good equipment, but they cannot write to order it nor have they any way of sending money.

Today Manoi, fanatical, stubborn and serious, brought me his work book in which he had laboriously spelled out in Pidgin a new set of rules for child care, based on his personal observation of how Europeans cared for babies, saying the child should have a bed of its own, have its own clothes, be bathed twice a day, never be fed with pre-chewed food, and so on. They have decided that tobacco and betel nut, chewed by the young, keep the brain from being clear, and so have forbidden them to children. The whole thing is fascinating, a little heartbreaking, but also something that makes one proud of the human race. I think I can give an account of it all that will make sense to Americans, give them some new sense of the new things that are stirring in the minds of backward peoples everywhere.

Peré Village
July 6, 1953

On Saturday we received news from the District Commissioner that the volcanologist who had been flown over from Rabaul had examined the situation and pronounced the volcano benign. It seems a contradiction in terms!

We had had a long chatty evening on top of our hill with the 50-odd people who were still left with me in the big house telling stories about the war and the coming of "all America" and about the move from the old place. Finally, Pokanau deigned to remember that his grandfather had told him of a tidal wave in his father's childhood. Then Manuwai, who was one of our first boys—the one who interrupted his activities to have his ears pierced—came to say they had decided to have three weddings the next day! Then Kilipak brought letters from Bunai, from the District Commissioner, saying that the alert was over and we could go back.

All night people kept waking up, lighting lamps, looking for the dawn, and soon after dawn a fleet of canoes took us back to the village which had not, as we all feared, been destroyed. Not a single thing had been stolen. Everything lay as in the buried houses of Pompeii, but not buried, quite safe among this disciplined and careful people. And there were three weddings in the church and now each young couple, free to talk together, eat together, go about together in public, freed of all the old irksome taboos and exploitation, can sit down comfortably in a section of the house which is their very own.

My house is "second from the dock" and looks directly on the ceremonial square, where now a council is being held in something called the "ring," a square of logs on which people sit. From my veranda I have a view of the mountains and it is two minutes' walk to a view of the open sea. There are houses on three sides of me, about six feet away, so people practically look out of their windows into mine. But this is excellent for field work and since my five days on the mountain I am no longer distressed by the children's screams in the night. This is learned behavior, an aggressive asser-tion of their dislike of waking up or of a desire to sleep with a different parent, etc. All day the children play in the white sand of the square, which in the early morning is pockmarked with the holes of giant crabs.

Although the houses lack the style of the old village, on the whole it all seems more beautiful. There were lovely sunsets and fair moonlight nights in the old Peré, but the angry voices, the strident drums, the shouting and the turmoil somehow spoiled the tropical landscape. Now the air is filled on a Sunday afternoon with the sounds of ukeleles strummed very softly and of children play-ing singing games. Spotlessly clean naked babies are brought to have their eyes washed out with boric acid.

Cholai, the young teacher who barely knows how to write but is working hard to keep the children's minds "clear" until the government can send a real teacher, comes to ask me to pick out a new song from a little interdenominational songbook which he got from the American forces. It is not at all difficult to explain to a man who stands barefoot in the sea, searing the side of his canoe with a torch of coconut leaves, what the International Seminar for Mental Health and Infant Development of last summer was about. While we were up on the mountain, I bought all the sago that tobacco would buy, until the land people closed their markets in fear of the beach and the volcano. Now every day people bring me fish, the owner of the big canoe which carried my valuables away from the village comes to make sure I know there is no charge. And all day people make and return loans, varying from two sticks to ten sticks of tobacco—fifteen cents to seventy-five cents—which I solemnly record in a big book and solemnly cancel on return. Their love of trade, of working on credit, has not abated.

There is too much to do, of course. I realize now that part of the sense of overwork in Tambunam in 1938 was because I had a fluent command of Pidgin English and a general understanding of the culture and a start on the language. This meant an immediate flow of activity which, combined with trying to reproduce the work which Madé Kaler (our Balinese secretary) and I had done together, was very tiring. The same thing, only worse, has happened here. For here I have both Pidgin and Manus and a knowledge of most of the grown people. People can be identified to me at once; I don't have to stop to have a kinship term explained. But this means that the mass of information, combined with endless reminiscing and anecdotes about everything that has happened in the last 25 years assumes rather alarming proportions, and my typing gets way behind itself. I don't dare use tape because there is no chance to work over and revise—or if one does, it takes as long. It's all rather like a family gathering with cousins one hasn't seen for 25 years, and hours of talk about the vagaries of ancestors one has hardly seen combined with, "Do you remember the time we all fell in the brook?" It is curious to see how the frightened crying of the children between a year old and two or three years has abated even among those who did not stay anywhere near me on the mountain. The tone of voice in which their elders say, *"Ndro wiyan"*—"It's all right"—has altered. In fact, this little volcanic disturbance has run true to form, a great help, not a hindrance.

Today I mapped the village and the surrounding beaches to scale, a tiring business in the hot sun, but everybody is pleased and impressed and now the two Councils and the Committee are having a long discussion as to whether they want numbers given to unoccupied house sites. I knew that by setting myself to study change, I was in a sense protecting myself from the shock which the loss of all the old cultural complexity would mean, in the disappearance of native handicrafts and costumes and all the ritual and pageantry which can make a primitive culture such a delightful aesthetic experience. But I had not guessed that there would be a sort of spiritual change which would be so gentle and so moving. It has the same sort of appeal that the first songs of a revolution have, but this has been a bloodless revolution without violence of any sort and within the law—without any change in government in the larger sense but with this tremendous increase in local organization and autonomy.

The children are even gayer and more delightful than they were 25 years ago. There is a whole bevy of babies. It's all very good.

I haven't seen Ted and Lenora since the alert, but they are coming over tomorrow. They have had a fairly intensive introduction to native life—five babies, including twins born the day after the evacuation. But I think the evacuation is going to make any difficulties of ordinary settling in in their village seem like child's play.

Balowan
August 14, 1953

I am writing from the little *"house-wind"* which has been built as a guest house on the island of Balowan, where the movement we have dubbed the NFF, the New Fellow Fashion, has progressed the most. Here a government officer has been delegated to help the natives implement their new ideals and fortunately they have found a man and his wife perfectly fitted to the task, who enjoy the isolated life and the endless problems of helping a nearly illiterate people to handle their own affairs.

Balowan is Paliau's own island, where he grew up among the gay, casual land people who had lived in fear and awe of the seafaring, bolder, blacker and much more moral Manus. Here, as a boy—or so he believes now, for here one sees the myth of the childhood of the leader being woven day by day out of almost no thread at all—he dreamt that the warfare and mutual suspicion and contempt in which the great main divisions of the peoples of the Admiralties held each other could be ended, that the names of contempt with which they spoke of each other could be abolished and that they could all be welded into one people who would act as a political unit. Under the stress of the beginning of the new movement, the sea-dwelling Manus near Balowan, the people of

Mok, moved ashore and built themselves a new village with paths edged with shells and planted with crotons, a church with a three-tiered roof and a balcony and houses carefully designed.

But it took two years after the new village was finished to get the dreamed-of local government going here and it is five years since the Peré people built their little model village, complete with dock, church, roads and signposts. And five years is about the life of a roof made of sago thatch. So today there is a race between the rate of decay of the physical embodiment of the new political dream and the ability of a well-meaning but slow-moving bureaucracy, cluttered up with dual political complications—Australian politics and United Nations politics—to move. The leaks in the church roof, the sagging house fronts in the trim little villages speak of the need for hurry. This for Bunai, Peré and Patusi, our three little villages on the South Coast.

But here in Balowan there is now a three-room school, a dispensary, a great council house, a store built with native labor and out of native funds. So I have come over to see how it is working, get some picture of what may be expected to happen in Peré, get more material on early history, for the present officer was here right after the initial cargo cult outbreak. I came over with an Australian journalist who stopped in at Peré and was on his way to Balowan, so I had a chance to see the local officials interviewed for the international press!

This was a break, for he wanted to ask many questions about what such a movement as the NFF portends for New Guinea, questions which will be asked in Australia and in the United Nations. My first break was about two weeks ago when I was called into Lorengau to answer a telephone call from New York. I was sure this would be nonsense, and it was: a publicity stunt of an advertising agency asking me whether I smoked! And for that I had to take a day's trip in a small launch in a bad sea and spend four days away from the village. However, it meant that I got into Lorengau to see a trial which I had known I wanted to see but felt just couldn't be managed—the trial of a man who had tried to murder Paliau about four months ago. This gave me a chance to study Paliau at a near distance, and then Paliau came back from Lorengau and was becalmed at Bunai for almost a week. We were able to make a recording of his present view of what happened in 1946, make films and recordings of meetings he conducted and in general get a lot done which might never have come our way at all.

Paliau, 1953.

Paliau is a man of about 45, possibly a little less, slight, pleasant, with the quiet assurance of a man who has always been able to think about what he wanted to think about and a manner which can only be described as quietly vice-regal. I have come to the conclusion that the essence of his genius is the completeness of his conception. All the people of the South Coast—and ultimately of the whole of the Admiralties—were to be welded into one unit and all the changes which would make it possible for them to belong to the modern world were to be made at once. A new kind of house, new clothes, a new calendar, a new social organization, a new form of church, a new ethic, and all the institutions necessary to support these things—a treasury, taxes, customs, a school, a hospital—all these were to be set up at once. He worked out the necessary negotiations to find space for the Manus villages on shore and supplied the design within which their entire life was rebuilt—on shore—while the Usiai (the bush people of the big island) came down to the sea coast and learned to live with the Manus and use boats.

I suspect that one of the ways in which we have steadily lost out vis-à-vis Communist-style social change in the East is that we have not only been in favor of going slowly, but we also have wanted to select which bits of our social pattern to pass on. We have never wholeheartedly accepted in entirety what the various types of reformers—missionaries, government officials, educators—have thought would be good for a backward people. But here a backward people, making the choices themselves, picked a whole pattern, each detail of which they think is right. Japan, of course, did something of the sort when the Japanese imported Western culture suddenly and in a very complete form. If distinct parts of a new pattern are learned piecemeal, all of the resistant parts of the old pattern are there to envelop, blur, obscure and distort and inevitably slow down change. At least, for the moment, that is how it all looks.

Life in Peré is ideal for work, a little tougher on the body than it is on the soul. My house is superbly placed for observation, but it is very hot. But it is seldom below 90° even at night, often 96° and often not a whisper of wind. But out on the beach which faces the reef and the open sea, on the stretch of land where they build their canoes (but where they are not permitted to build houses because the land belongs to a coconut-raising firm), they have built me a little *"house-wind."* Here the wind is so strong that working with paper is a problem, but it gives an illusion of coolness.

On days that promise to be bright and close, we pack up for the beach with typewriter, notebooks, field glasses, camera box, drinking water with lime in it, and an array of small objects like tweezers, sun glasses, tripod, the portable radio on which we get programs in Pidgin English. In all this I rather resemble the natives who often walk about in a single piece of cloth, carrying a flashlight, a cigarette lighter, a bunch of keys and a waterproof zippered tobacco pouch. Like them, I have a minimum of simple clothes and food and a disproportionate complement of modern equipment.

Here there is an embarrassment of riches: half a dozen groups of children, each group involved in complex and intricate play, people coming and going from Bunai, canoes arriving and departing, people bathing, weaving fish traps, cooking lime, each small group with a fringe of baby toddlers engaged in mimetic play, temper tantrums and every kind of byplay.

How to take few enough notes so there is some hope of writing them up? How to take notes and pictures simultaneously? How to deal with this crowded, boundaryless space in which one event flows into another in an endless stream, but single themes appear

and reappear and must be caught as they pass? So a woman walking along with what appears to be a rather inferior pinwheel on a
stick, which she is turning dissociatedly in her hand, is only explicable if one realizes that this is the remains of a set of model airplanes
built two days ago by the 12- to 14-year-olds, which now, disinte-
grated into their component parts, are either held casually in the
hands of older people or have been inherited by toddlers and are
dispersed throughout the whole group.

One has to watch long enough to see that a large series of what
look like quite different activities, performed by different groups
of children of different ages, are linked together by a complicated
set of echoes, actions that rhyme, bits of action that fall into asso-
nance and counterpoint, with single children at the same spot or
materials, such as chips from a new canoe, or an object, such as a
toy airplane stuck in the ground and left whirling alone for a
younger group to find, as the threads that bind it all together.

Out of such observations (if I can get the right units) there
ought to come the materials to show the way this very fluid, time-
oriented society works—the way one person is linked to another
through a series of repetitions and parallels in which each person
feels that he himself is the initiator, the fully autonomous, spontaneous actor and yet the whole is ordered and patterned. Twenty-
five years ago I did not find these people beautiful at all. Now the
perfect—though in some undefined way mechanical—adjustment
of their bodies to one another and to the world around them,
which is defined for each person by his own position, is aestheti-
cally satisfying and exceedingly interesting.

What does it do to a baby to have its lower jaw helped to shut
after a yawn? Why does a man verbalize his past recalcitrancy as
though it were here and now, saying: "I am lazy, I don't want to
work for the community" and so on, and then add: "That's not the
way I feel now, it's the way I felt. I say it now so I can see and hear
it and so get rid of it"? In what sense is doing something and
standing perfectly still and watching someone else doing some- •
thing the same thing? And how can one's ego be so identified with
action that whether one does, or does not, do it oneself does not,
in some sense, matter?

And so one tries to figure out how to treat this little revolution
as a microcosm of what is happening all over the world and how
to select the details of life for microscopic study.

I have never seen the newborn as at home in the world as they are able to make these babies, born very quickly with the mother on the floor and held facing the mother until the afterbirth comes, then gathered up in the prickly softness of a grass skirt, which both stimulates and shelters, washed very quickly with cups of cold water poured over it and made snug and human and content in an old woman's arms, as she sings it the lullaby—a repetitious version of the baby's own cry—which it will sleep to all through its child-hood. Eyes wide open, their cries stilled, head and hands and feet all moving in a way which masks their randomness, they look out and around themselves and it is hard to believe that they don't see a good deal.

> August 19, 1953
> Back in Peré

Each week the materials seem to organize themselves around a different theme; right now it is the senselessness of the contro-versy as to which is most important, the gifted man or the general state of the world. This is all such a pretty little microcosm in which such issues are clear and explicit.

The Pidgin ending of a letter is *Em tasol.*

> Peré
> October 2, 1953

This has been a stormy six weeks. Two attempted suicides. The birth of an anencephalic baby to the most beautiful, gentle, good parents in the village. Continued delays in the hope of getting their Council through—prolonged hanging on to the crumbling edges of a dream with fingernails that are calcium short.

I am fascinated with the type of commitment which I find I have to the accomplishment of their aspirations. I am not quite sure what it is, a reflection of a change in the whole climate of opinion in the world, or an accidental temperamental congruence, so that I feel closer to a people who believe that they can remake their culture if only they have the will to do so, or simply the human sympathy one feels for people whom one has known most of their lives. Certainly all three are factors. In 1953 we are committed to mobility within one generation and to building a world where the valuable unit is a human being and not simply membership in one kind of culture rather than another. And this means we cannot afford the aesthetic nostalgia for a "whole culture" and "cultural depth," because we can only win this temporary battle with time by putting ourselves back of human aspirations, aroused by ideas of medicine, science, literacy and human dignity, and by recognizing that the first expressions of these aspirations will sometimes seem to us grossly disharmonious—because we ourselves have so recently broken with a past we think of as more harmonious—and so also as cheap, ugly, dull and empty.

Certainly it is easier for me personally to feel committed to an endeavor of heartbreaking difficulty than to a mere desire to maintain the status quo, however balanced and charming the culture may be, as in Bali. Also, the degree of sympathy and warmth that comes with long acquaintance is hard to overestimate. I used to feel I knew many of the people with whom I worked, and often I did know them—people like Fa'amotu in Samoa and our Arapesh boys and Madé Kaler in Bali. But this is different, possibly because they are—from our point of view—not too gifted with ways of

Ted talks with John Kilipak and Peranis Cholai, the schoolteacher (left), and Raphael Manuwai by Raphael's house on the shore.

being articulate in personal relations and the long detailed knowledge of the past replaces a capacity for introspection.

When Karol Matawai, tall, violent and unruly, comes in with eyes flashing, determined to press a point of pride home, which will end with ten people going to jail on a charge which no one really wants to enforce—neither government nor natives—I find my efforts to reason with him are so tempered by the memory of the way he felt in my arms as a baby, of the way he pried his father out of a ceremony to beg a red balloon for him, that there is no irritation in my voice and my pleading succeeds. And then, because I know Kilipak—his elder brother—I know which plea will reduce his angry pride and know that if I can make him see how his younger brother's reputation will suffer, this will prevail over all his cocksure determination to have his own way.

Problems of participation, where one should interfere and where not, take on a different color when the people themselves are as anxious for guidance on *Robert's Rules of Order* as for quinine to stop malaria. The tendency toward suicide and depression, which comes with the increased internalization of conscience and self-blame for thoughts as well as acts, also involves the anthropologist in a new kind of therapeutic participation.

Of course, those of us who have worked in New Guinea always have done everything we could to save life and limb, but before the antibiotics, our capacities as lay people were much more limited. And now the request for help in school, help in meetings and help in "getting a clear idea of the road ahead" are asked in the same voice in which they once asked us to tie up a cut.

All this results in one turning over rapidly in one's mind: What will it be necessary to say to the most promising and most crucial young man in the village who is still alive because he tried to hang himself with a piece of rubber tubing left over from the war which fortunately broke? How to combine "You are the descendant of Korotan, you are a member of the clan which is the root and strength of this village, of all the Manus, the clan that is the *lapan* [the aristocrat] of all the people. You are the one who has lived close to Pokanau, the man who still remembers the old genealogies, and you have learned these too, you who best understand the new, who write better than anyone else in the village and have had the energy to organize and keep a school going without any help or materials from anyone. You are the link which will bind the past and the future together; without you the hopes of this village will lie scattered and broken." How to bring all these things together so that he will be able to conquer his self-destructive, wounded pride and decide to live? All this requires a complete involvement —perhaps involvement is always measured by one's relative ability to act and to understand—such as I used only to achieve in trying to revive a drowned child or reduce the fever of a teething baby. But it is curious and wonderful to watch the way a changing ethic means a changing type of participation.

I must stop this to get off an order to Sydney for the clothes which the village want for Christmas, when all the Manus will go to Balowan for five days' celebration and meetings. I sent for prices and samples to Sydney, for they want well-made things, not the trade goods which have traditionally been regarded as appropriate for natives. I got samples of material for the women. They stand and pick out a first choice. Then I say, "And if it isn't there any more?" and only the brightest will then really make a second choice; the others say, "Any other one in that bunch" or "Never mind, anything will be good"—a measure of the limited time per-

In my house, working with an audience of young girls.

spective within which they still say, "When the children have gone to school, then they will learn and be able to manage the new way of life."

I have to combine helping with the school with getting work done. Now we are studying maps. I mapped the village and fastened the map on my wall with the houses numbered and a list of typed names. Children studied this casually as they went in and out. Then they were given the instruction in school to make a picture of the "inside of the village." Every single one had grasped the general scheme of my diagram, but they filled in details I had left out, started numbering the houses in different ways, etc. Now they are going to draw a plan on the sand and then climb coconut palms to look down and see what a map really is.

And we have a dating scale, showing evolutionary time, time since the birth of Christ, the discovery of America, Australia and New Guinea, the two world wars and the beginning of their new era, 1946, so they can learn, as people become literate, how to borrow a time scale from those who became literate earlier. And

Pokanau and his son, Johanis Matawai, as they looked in 1929.

Pokanau makes a speech, December 1953.

to make this real, all the decades since 1890 are identified with the birth of someone in the village. In between the children do Stewart Ring Puzzle tests and Bender Gestalts and Mosaics, and so it goes.

Time, the fear that equipment will break down and the possibility that some large-scale disaster may destroy the village, these are three horsemen that ride at my heels, but I have passed the critical point in a field trip IF I had to stop now. It's a sort of reciprocal of the point of no return. . . .

VII.

FIELD VISITS IN A CHANGING WORLD
1964–1975

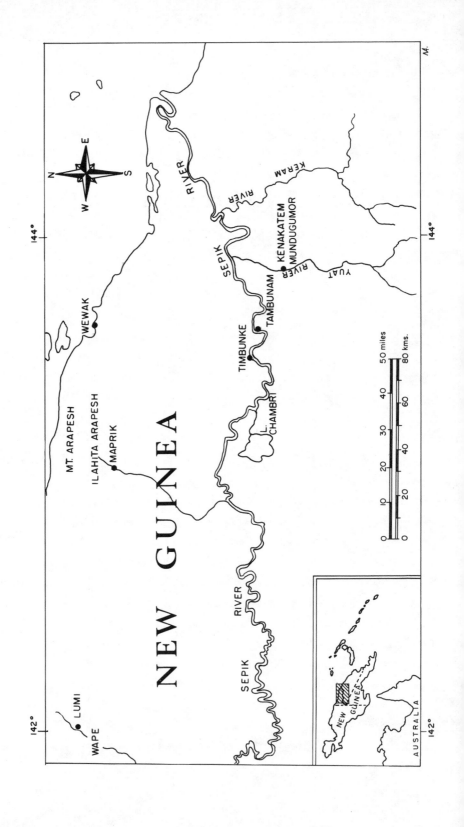

Field visits, all of them relatively brief, are an innovation made possible by modern air travel in planes ranging in size and speed from the huge 747s, in which one crosses the Pacific Ocean in a matter of hours, down to the tiny Cessnas that air-hop in minutes from one almost inaccessible place to another in Papua New Guinea. The long weeks of sea travel gave the anthropologist a period of quiet in the transition between home and the field and isolation in the field. Today one can travel halfway across the world in two days instead of two months.

Air travel has allowed me to follow the course of change in Manus for almost a quarter century. It has allowed me to participate in planning and to visit fieldworkers who are doing a major part of the research—to enjoy the ongoing process and to understand in a new way their research results. The 1953 Manus field trip was the last one on which I did a major share of the field work myself.

These field visits, for the most part, mark high points in collaboration that has extended over many years. In 1953, Rhoda Metraux, who was working in Montserrat, in the West Indies, corresponded with us in Manus about common field problems; since the 1960s she has made three field trips to Tambunam in a continuing study of the Iatmul people. Ted Schwartz initiated a major project for a survey of all the languages in the Admiralties and was joined by his new wife, Lola Romanucci-Schwartz, and their small son, Adan. Ted spent three years, 1963–1966, in the field. In 1964, Ted and Lola were in Peré when I came; in 1965, I was alone in Peré until Ted joined me there for the Christmas celebration.

In the 1960s, Barbara Heath, who had been working with the somatotype pictures we took in 1953, went to Manus several times for further work with her ophthalmologist husband, the late Scott Heath. In 1973 we also invited Lawrence Malcolm, who had been working on problems of growth, to spend some time in Peré. And in 1975, my most recent trip to Manus, Ted Schwartz preceded me to follow up on work done in 1973 by a team of his students; Barbara arrived in time to set up the camp; and, finally, Fred Roll, who has become a cooperating photographer, arrived before I left.

Air travel has made it possible, as never before, for us to share our field sites with others and in this way to expand many times over the value of what is already known. And for others to share a stage in their field work with me. In 1966 I visited Montserrat, where Rhoda Metraux was making a brief restudy. And in one crowded month in 1971, when I returned to look at the Mundugu-mor at Kenakatem, I was also able to visit Don Tuzin, among his Plains Arapesh group, and Joyce and Bill Mitchell, who were work-ing with the Wape, a mountain group, and to join Rhoda once more in the still-ongoing discussions with Iatmul experts in Tam-bunam.

Old familiarity with the ways of New Guinea, my easy knowl-edge of Pidgin English, my friendship with families in each of the villages I studied in the past and, today, the sense of what it is all about among New Guinea people who have enjoyed working with the anthropologists living in their communities—all this makes it possible for me to pick up very quickly what once it would have taken months even to approach.

Anthropology is changing even as the world changes.

Peré Village
October 23, 1964

I live neck deep in the past.

Today Lokus, who was one of my little houseboys in 1928 and Ted's cook in 1953 and is now again our chief cook and factotum —a mild, shy little old man who is about fifty, but I feel him as frail and old and his hearing and eyesight are going—Lokus came to tell me that his wife had gone to Mok to mourn for her sister's hus-band, and "You remember, Piyap, the time we came back in a canoe from Lou in 1929, it was Litauer's canoe, he was my wife's father."

Every event is tied firmly into the shared past, and I am sup-posed to remember as well as they do each detail of the long past. Faces are somewhat harder this time, especially for the men who were in their teens in 1953. The old people again recall their childhood faces and I can place them by bypassing 1953 and going back to 1928. The old women embraced me and wailed because they are old and will soon die, and my boys, now men of fifty, treat me more as an age mate and talk solemnly of the many, many years we have lived—such a long, long, long time. The kind of aging that we never see is all around me—toothlessness leading to fallen cheeks and mumbling words, people who are like walking skeletons.

The other impression is one of literally mobs of children. The village has again increased its size, as the nearby village of Patusi has moved in, packing their houses in the small bits of remaining space and along the shore so that the whole village is crowded and untidy. Pig keeping has come back and the pig pens stand again on posts over the water. The village now faces out towards the open sea, so that all day from dawn till dark there are ever-changing patterns of silhouetted figures out on the reef.

Life here on the surface is more comfortable than on my previous visits. We have two houses. Ted and Lola have the house that the former young schoolteacher, Peranis Cholai, had built for himself, with room for the baby, Adan, who is walking and dancing and babbling and screaming, Manus style, and his two nurses—Mesiang, from Bunai Village, where Ted lived in 1953, and Pwepwe, from Sori Island, where Lola spent her first months in Manus, isolated on the stormy north coast, while Ted was away on mainland New Guinea. Pwepwe is a confirmed spinster, sniffing at most of the world, and Mesiang is a soft little girl who has finished Sixth Standard and who speaks good English, but who has suffered the fate of most Manus girls who go on to higher education, and has had an illegitimate child.

My house is also the household diningroom, photography center and general meeting ground. It has a plywood floor, plywood walls to the bedroom and a real refrigerator run by kerosene in the kitchen. We also have a New Guinea-style shower, a cylinder which is filled from the top and sprinkles gently as one tugs at a chain, but I find I enjoy the cold splashing bath from a dipper, which belongs to former times and is so unsuitable in an American bathroom. Our latrine out over the water has a handsome bridge built of great old planks, the "bones of Big Manus," the canoe they were building in 1953. Intermittently, when all the various parts of battery, generator, bulbs, and so on work we have electric light,

Lola Romanucci-Schwartz with her son, Adan, about 6 months old, and Siuva Baripeo on Sori Island, 1964.

Ted Schwartz with his son, Adan, about 11 months old, at Mokereng Village, 1964.

just enough to make the old-style pressure lamp seem unbearably dim. I'd think my intolerance of the old-style lamp was age, except that Ted and Lola also find it impossible to work by it.

They have been here a month before I arrived and so—for me —it was just like slipping back into a groove which I had hardly left. The village is comfortably relaxed and very busy, between fishing and cutting timber and working thatch for the entirely new village they are building on the other side of this tiny island, on land which they purchased for some £6,000. Gambling has, for the time being, vanished. The only untoward events since I arrived have been the keening of an old woman whose son slapped her and court cases over tiny trifles—an injured key, the green coconuts that the schoolchildren ate.

All the real drama of change is going on away from here, with the 33 boys and girls who are in Lorengau, Rabaul, Lae, Port Moresby and Australia as students, teachers and nurses—all from this village where in 1953 there was no school at all except the shadow school that Peranis—with his two years of schooling—had set up "to keep the children's minds clear." The new education has opened the doors to the world, but for the girls it so far has represented almost complete catastrophe. The Manus girls have gone to school as eagerly as the boys; they are unafraid, enterprising and, coming from a society that has repudiated shame, fall easily in strange surroundings far from home. There have been only three first babies born in the village in the last 18 months; the girls either are still in school, confusing the teachers, or away at school. A few who have returned to the village are treated as damaged goods and no one wants to marry them. Meanwhile the people are beginning to demand that a training school for the various occupations be built on Manus so that the girls need not go amongst strangers.

Last time, as I approached Manus, I threaded my way through the mass of fact and fiction about Paliau. This time I found in Australia an enormous interest, knowledge about and pride in New Guinea. The New South Wales Association of University Women Graduates were considering putting a Papuan girl through college; there is talk of founding a university in New Guinea. In Port Moresby, "the House was sitting," and people had their dinner early to go and sit in the visitors' gallery of the House of Assembly, where they listened to the speeches of the newly elected native members. Paliau himself was "staying with" the director of native affairs, Mr. McCarthy. The whole society is experiencing the sense of excitement, at the top, that comes with the first breakthrough of some extreme racial-cultural barrier. I imagine something like this must have happened in the early days when Southern plantation owners first began to free and educate some of their former slaves—an upsurge of hope and release from the tension of maintaining a rigid, caste-like control. I think it is a honeymoon period that may collapse after such excitements as having Paliau and his wife to a formal naval banquet subsides.

Below this high-level official delight in the new equality, the old antagonisms still flourish and the accusations against Paliau still go on. Pressures from the United Nations are dangerously contradictory. On the one hand a demand that the people of Papua New Guinea be educated up to a high level, which can only be done by a virtual army of dedicated Australians as teachers, instructors and models, and on the other hand a demand for rapid advancement of natives into positions of authority and power, not only in political positions, but in technical fields also. The advancement of a native teacher to the position of supervisor means that the Australian white teacher, who was teaching willingly in a village school, is under pressure to take his higher qualifications elsewhere—to a high school in a city. The coincidence of poorly trained medical practitioners and attempts to eradicate malaria and get TB under control is equally unfortunate. Instead of housing all teachers in good houses of native materials, expensive prefab houses have been imported at great cost and then there is an insistence that native teachers and clerks have equally expensive houses. But this is counterpointed by a new wage scale, much higher for "Europeans" on the grounds that, come independence, the Papua New Guinea economy will not allow high wages.

But the differential effect of opening a society up at the top is very clear. Schools are set up with the expectation that children will go on from standard to standard and on to high school and beyond and lack the deadliness of the primary school from which no one is able to emerge. A whole group of maverick teachers were recruited—75 picked from 1,800 applicants—and were given a six months' crash course and sent out into the villages. There are six such teachers on the South Coast. Our own teacher in this village was once an actor and then protocol secretary for an Australian

Visiting the primary school in Peré, 1964.

The primary school children.

diplomat. Watching him teaching these children, and then watching the native teachers, has added a new dimension to my understanding of the problems of teaching the culturally deprived, whether the deprivation comes from peonage, slavery, peasanthood or an isolated primitive life. For the native teacher, it is vitally important that all the material taught is tied down to local reality —that the trees (here) are coconut palms and not unknown fir trees, that the animals are crocodiles and kangaroos, not lions and tigers. But for the teacher who speaks a world language and is part of a wider civilization, this is not the case; it is important that he should act as a whole person with reference to everything anywhere in the world—the Olympic games one minute, the Tower of London the next—for such a teacher can share with his students, as a single embodiment, the feel of a whole language and culture. . . .

Another process that has taken place a thousand times in human history is vivid here on this micro-scale. The need for the clarification of names. They have got the idea that Europeans take their father's name, so some one of the names which a man has been given at birth is randomly selected to be a man's surname. But the old custom of giving the government a false name is still around. And schoolchildren pick names at random, and the names on the famous electoral roll constructed for all New Guinea are unrecognizable and unpronounceable. So suddenly men whose identity was fast in the minutest memory of village mates and kin stand in a strange, irrational, fragmented relationship to the larger world, as letters are mailed but never arrive, bank books lie for years unclaimed, X-rays miscarry and children lose their identity as they go from school to school. We are going to try two experiments to rationalize the names in this village so that everyone will have patrilineal lineage names (which the Manus already have) so that groups of first and second patrilineal cousins will have the same surname. Then we hope to work out a simple procedure by which this can be done for all of the Admiralties, hoping that this will be a stimulus from the bottom. Meanwhile I'll try making recommendations to the New Guinea Research Unit of the Australian National University. If only we could establish a method in the world by which we could interject at the bottom the best insights from the top and so establish a circle in which people would move up from village to district to town to city and the best thinking would reach the village by a direct route. . . .

During this six weeks, I have been in the village but not of it, for life is not so set up that the people come and go freely as they do when I am working alone. Ted and Lola are working with single informants, taking texts and making tapes, in contexts where a mob of onlookers is a real disadvantage. So informal contacts with the village are discouraged; people come with messages, we are invited to meetings, people bring us fish or carvings, but no small children come and go and women stay away and are—in a new word that has come recently into Pidgin—"worried." Next year I shall spend a few weeks here by myself, in a house stripped down to bare essentials in which a crowd will do no harm, and establish a last set of close contacts on what may well be my last visit. But it is so much easier to leave and plan to come back again, that I may not say it will be my last visit. Within the enlarged village— of some 400 people—those who were children in 1928 are still closest to me, the friendships with the newcomers in 1953 seem slight in comparison.

At this point I went out to investigate a shouting row which disturbed the usual orderly sounds of a village meeting. People had decided that each clan was to clean its section of the new village, and now some were accusing others of procrastinating. Over the radio comes news of a quarrel between New South Wales and the Commonwealth Government over the control of air lines and on the Voice of America the news of the response to the Chinese explosion of a bomb. One wonders about the change of scale.

I know one thing and that is that work at any level except the fine detail of the behavior of identified persons bores me. . . . I've put a lot of time planning inventories on the basis of the old intensive work and the changes which have occurred over time as people apparently forget whole chunks of culture and then remember them again. In 1928, marriages with the land people were nothing to boast about and came up very incidentally. Today, land is valuable and everyone is raking up some Usiai ancestress. Historical origin stories may move from casual folklore filled with mythical elements to down-to-earth tales when it is necessary to present a land claim to a European court. But I never did like informant work and I know I never will—forms without flesh, no matter how many illustrations and photographs are provided. The letter I wrote Ruth Benedict about working among the Omaha still holds.

. . . But some things go on. It's a pleasure to live so close to the tides and the winds. Only this time we have an Admiralty almanac and can really find out whether it will be high water at noon on Tuesday and whether our big canoe can get through the reef. A pet eagle with a broken wing stalks about the village and a tame possum is kept for the baby's amusement. Dogs that have been miscellaneously well fed by Europeans and approximate that part of their mongrel ancestry yelp in episodic chorus. The small children still scream and scream when they are crossed. And no one ever tires of fishing!

Peré Village
December 19, 1965

This year I am living in a brand-new house in a brand-new village, with all the excitement of being the Christmas host for the last Christmas that the whole Paliau movement will ever hold as exclusively their own. Paliau's dream that all the people of Manus should be within one political unit has come true, in form at least. The old enmities—especially between adjacent villages—still smoulder, ready to burst into angry speech and blows over an injury in a soccer match. And the missions and the mission villages are still not quite sure whether Paliau is a leader who is slowly bringing his thinking and his people closer to theirs or whether he is after all Henry VIII and John Wesley rolled into one.

The village is new, sparkling with paint on the houses of those who could somehow beg, borrow, importune or in the last resort buy some corrugated iron or decorated with patterns woven in the bamboo of traditional materials. After two months of quiet, when small boys rolled hoops and had them confiscated by the school committee, the village is humming with the sounds of the returned adolescents—ukeleles and every radio and record player newly supplied with batteries. Everywhere well-dressed young people parade up and down or, abandoning their school finery, play rough and tumble games with each other. In some homes rooms have been built for the visiting children; they vary from one in which bed, chair and bench, all made by hand, are arranged to make a perfect schoolboy's room with a nicely made bed, pictures of Beatles on the wall, schoolbooks on the table and schoolbag hung in the window, to another which is a mere corner of a large barn-like room, where a suitcase with a couple of books on top signals the return of a schoolchild.

The village is alive with the delight of the visitors, the school-children and the ones who have become teachers in faraway parts of New Guinea—sometimes all alone in some small bush school among alien people only a few years away from cannibalism or headhunting. The tales they bring are mixed—stories of boarding school, examinations and prizes won for scholarship or sports and stories of the extraordinary customs of the people in the interior of New Guinea. And which is harder for them to assimilate and understand—a savage way of life, which in many respects is like that of their own grandfathers, now so enthusiastically abandoned, or a way of life which belongs to the modern world, the world of planes that fly overhead and the news that comes over the radio? For news of themselves comes over the radio too. Yesterday morning came the announcement: "At the first meeting of the new Council in Manus, Mr. Paliau Moluat, Member of the House of Assembly, was elected president."

It is a kind of paradigm of what is going on all over the world, as grandparents and parents settle for what part they themselves can play and what must be left to the comprehension of the children.

And there is worry. If the young men go away, who will care for the old? We have had a long struggle between the village as a corporate body and the members of the families with old people: Who was to build their houses, the village or the relatives? Finally Pokanau, our learned genealogist, the last of his kind, and his closest old man friend had to stage a near-death scene. Then they were brought quickly into the village, lectured for their anger, which had undoubtedly been the cause of their illnesses, and their houses went up in skeleton with relatives doing half the work and the village work force doing the other half. But their relatives-in-law will have to put up with them until after Christmas.

There is also worry because three days after the return of Posalak, our one student in Australia, the pride of his house and the whole village, a radio message came summoning him to Port Moresby for an interview. This can only mean some new scholarship or opportunity, probably for the vacation. But it is hard for his father, with his family of children all excelling in school, and for his uncle, who has prepared such a perfect room for him, to understand. . . .

Perhaps because of the three summers at the Delos Symposion on Ekistics, I think of all this in terms of the hundreds of millions of villagers all over the world who still live close together, knit together by kinship ties and old custom, under the trees their ancestors planted, whose children are preparing to live in an urban world. For the next generation, perhaps for two more generations, this will be the case; the villages must prepare the young people and let them go: as bold a venture as when Henry the Navigator sent his ships out from Portugal.

Here they let them go enthusiastically and the children return so easily to the village, re-absorbed immediately into basketball and soccer, moving in rhythm with those who have not yet been away and those who have returned for good; shy of their parents, easier with aunts and uncles and cousins. And pride helps. The representative of the United Nations, who came to visit, tells them how famous the village of Peré is (to pay me a compliment). Paliau takes it up to urge them to greater effort. And the older people say quietly: "But why not, after all it all began in Peré. Why should not

My household staff in Peré as they looked in 1928. Kapeli, Pomat, Yesa, Kilipak and Loponiu.

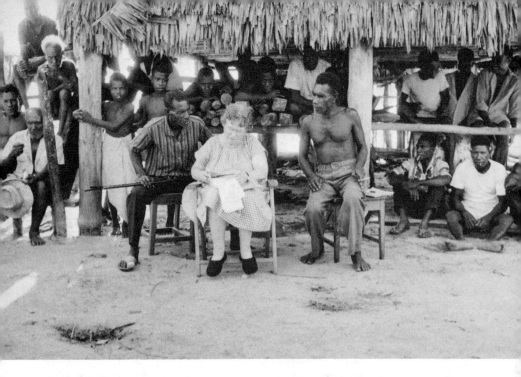

Talking with old friends in Peré, 1965. Petrus Pomat and John Kilipak, seated right and left of me, and Pokanau, seated left, holding hat.

Talking with Karol Matawai, who appears with his father on page 81, and here carries his own small son.

the origin village of the Manus people be famous throughout the world?" But it makes them a little touchy if I record court cases that put them in a bad light. Field work is a little more difficult when the fieldworker is also the chronicler of a community's success.

For the most part, I have been thinking about field work itself, what an extraordinary vocation it is, how much it demands of a young fieldworker all alone with a strange village and a set of categories, trying to match one to the other. . . . I have been able to think about all this the more vividly because this time for the first field trip since Samoa, I am all alone. All alone, it is true, in a known culture, among a people who treat me as one of themselves, whose past I know better than they do; all alone with the mass of assurances that I will be able to do the job I came to do. I measure all the factors that make this trip extremely easy for me: a house built for me by people who know I am likely to break my ankle, equipment all set up from the Schwartzes' trip here, a kerosene refrigerator (unknown luxury), medicines to deal with diseases that not so long ago were intractable, a knowledge of the language and a detailed knowledge of the people—their relationships, their dispositions and their capabilities. And I realize that even so, with all that—which no beginner has—field work is a rather appalling thing to undertake. Nowhere else is a scientist asked to be vis-à-vis, and also part of, a total human society, and to conduct his studies *in vivo,* continually aware of such a complex whole.

Perhaps the task of the psychiatrist is comparably difficult, as the psychiatrist is asked to take in, hold in mind, respond to a whole individual and respond to his own responses, including those aspects of the self that are normally veiled from other eyes. Psychiatry, fully practiced, is another of the extraordinary demands we make on young people today, as extraordinary as space flight, as underwater exploration, as any of those situations in which the whole self is "our most important tool," even where the individual is linked to the whole elaborate computerized machinery of Cape Kennedy.

And we do give young anthropologists many aids, categories into which they can arrange the behavior that they witness, such as "mother-in-law avoidance," or "ambilateral kinship," or "slash-and-burn agriculture," or "nucleation." But if they are to be good fieldworkers, they know that these tools are as preliminary as the cameras they hold in their hands, meaningless if uninformed by a vivid sense of what is really going on here, now, in this particular culture.

Today we give the fieldworker a whole battery of methods, techniques, tools and theories from which to choose—more than anyone can use, just as the vivid, ongoing life of a people is more than anyone can possibly cover in the same detail, with the same vigilance, with the same attention. So the fieldworker must choose, shape, prune, discard this and collect finer detail on that, much as a novelist works who finds some minor character is threatening to swallow up the major theme or that the hero is fast taking him out of his depth. But unlike the novelist—except when the novelist feels, as sometimes happens, possessed by characters who have a life of their own—the fieldworker is wholly and helplessly dependent on what happens—on the births, deaths, marriages, quarrels, entanglements and reconciliations, depressions and elations of the one small community. . . .

You sit at night with 300 or 400 people asleep around you, the whole village silent, and wonder what is going to happen: will the baby about to be born die or be deformed in some strange way? will the mother die and precipitate a whole set of reprisals and recriminations? will a big man die? will a quarrel break the community in two? will a child drown or a canoe break up at sea? So closely are the people knit together that any event will affect the whole— an unexpected absence or illness, an unexpected visitor and the whole equilibrium is changed. One must be continually prepared for anything, everything and—perhaps most devastating—for nothing. For it is events which reveal the forms in which one is interested, for the account of which one is responsible. This existence vis-à-vis a whole community of a totally alien culture, where no slightest lift of an eyebrow or curl of a lip means what it would mean in our own, is the central experience of field work in a living culture. And viewing it from the experience of forty years and eight different cultures, I think we demand a great deal. The wonder, to me, is not that young anthropologists fail but that so many succeed.

I've been counting over also the difference between the sustenance a young anthropologist receives from the very uniqueness and historical importance of work among a primitive people never before studied and the impact of a culture-contact situation on the present-day fieldworker working with equal commitment and intensity. The traditional anthropologist has the wonderful knowledge that everything he—or she—records will be valuable—the shape of a flute, the pattern of a cat's cradle, the plot of a myth, the names of the sun and the moon and the stars, a gesture of assent or greeting, a recipe for cooked sago, the method of counting betel nut. All of it is unique. All will vanish. All was—and will be—grist to some fellow anthropologist's mill. Nothing is wasted. He has only to record accurately and organize his notes legibly; then, whether he lives or dies, what he has done makes a contribution. With this, of course, has gone the responsibility to record many things in which he is not personally interested. But the rewards are immense. In a sense, one cannot fail.

If you go to the field with a problem, the challenge of possible failure, contrapuntal to the assurance of usefulness and success, is there, too. Any field may prove to be the wrong place to do the problem you have come to do. But there is also the certainty that if you surrender fully enough to the culture, this will itself inform your further choices and provide new problems, home-grown for the fieldworker's perception.

There are rewards for the individual who likes to work alone, just one mind required to take in a culture that has been hundreds, perhaps thousands of years in the making as it is now incorporated in this community made up of people of both sexes, all ages and diverse temperaments. All the skills he can employ as a scientist and all the skills he can draw on as an artist are needed here, and he is accountable to no one except to the actuality before him. At the same time those of us who like best to work in close cooperation with others can have the excitement of participating in a team of two or three or four, or perhaps of fitting oneself into the series of minds of those who have come before and may come after, as a kind of orchestral realization of the complexity to be studied. These were—and are—the special rewards for the traditional fieldworker.

My work this field trip not only highlights all these rewards, but also underlines the differences between traditional anthropological work and work with any people who have come under the continuing influence of contemporary world culture. Uniqueness then is no longer a property of what is studied, so that the fieldworker can rely on certain results simply by being honest and industrious. Uniqueness, now, in a study like this, lies in the relationship between the fieldworker and the material. I still have the responsibility and the incentives that come from the fact that because of my long acquaintance with this village I can perceive and record aspects of this people's life that no one else can. But even so, this knowledge has a new edge. This material will be valuable only if I myself can organize it. In traditional field work, another anthropologist familiar with the area can take over one's notes and make them meaningful. But here it is my individual consciousness which provides the ground on which the lives of these people are figures. And this makes me acutely aware of how I have always worked with two incentives—the incentive to write up my work carefully, legibly (which usually meant typing) in the field, so it would be usable in case I died, and the incentive not to take risks which would interfere with my writing it all up myself which, after all, I can do better than anyone else.

How different all this is from the problems that confront the young scientist who must go out, taking all the physical and psychological risks of field work, to study *another* Caribbean village or *another* Indian village, but who is not yet uniquely in possession of the lives of any group, is deprived of the sharp perceptions provided by an integrated, unknown primitive culture, and must struggle to work out the dimensions of a problem without which funds would not have been forthcoming, fearful that the result may be "just another community study." In addition he may become entangled in the modern devious net of intelligence, counterintelligence and conflicting loyalties as well as having to cope with the difficulties of unsafe water and lack of plumbing and light, which were less of a trial to a generation familiar with such problems.

Finally, there is the way in which, when one works in a culture in which the people become literate, one's own work becomes part of their sense of their own history. For the most part, anthropologists have treated this negatively, either insisting on the anthropologist's obligation to protect the people themselves or the chances of future fieldworkers or deploring the effect that the publication of religious secrets has had on the relationship between a tribe and its anthropologists. Very few fieldworkers have written for the people whom they have studied. Yet, today, the books I have written are becoming part of the consciousness of the Manus people, particularly of the people of this village. The names of the old men who died before they were born can be supplied with visual images. The changes through which their parents have lived are there before their eyes. After the unique experience when, under Paliau's leadership, the whole village, old and young, moved together to a new form of life, they now have the unique experience of keeping their past in visible and detailed form—a form which is respected by the world into which their children are moving as students and teachers and civil servants. . . .

Now, after my two months here, Ted Schwartz, finding the people he had planned to study all scattered in a badly flooded and impassable area in the upper reaches of the Sepik River system, has come back to Manus in time to take over the camp again as a base for further work in Manus. How often this has happened to the best fieldworkers and the most carefully worked-out field work plans! It is a hazard common to all anthropological expectations about research. And a week from now I will be in Rabaul, on my way home.

Montserrat, West Indies
September 2, 1966

I am writing from a new hotel in Montserrat where some twenty little hexagonal cottages with low gray roofs cling to the hillside, safe—or at least safer, they say, than other forms of building—when hurricanes come. Seen from the curving beach below they look like science fiction objects come to life and marching down. Inside they are delightful with two nearly solid sides for beds and cupboards, a pie-shaped wedge for the shower and two sides that face the mountain and the sea entirely glass jalousies. The roof consists of radiating white rafters set against the trim, shipshape narrow boarding in an old ship's cabin style; it looks, when you lie and look up at it, rather like the base of a plant with perfectly symmetrical radial roots. The winds, which play with total capriciousness around and above individual small patches of land, blow the sounds of other people's voices out to sea or up into the mountains so that each cottage seems entirely alone. From the little veranda one can look straight up the rising land for several miles to the village where Rhoda Metraux—and Daniel and his Haitian nurse, Tulia—lived for a year in 1953–54, and Daniel, aged four, learned about time by calculating what time of day or night it was where I was in Manus on the other side of the world but in the field too.

The relationship to other people's "field" is one that isn't discussed as much as it should be in thinking about anthropology. Anthropologists are scolded—and scold each other—because they are so possessive about their own people and nobody considers the problem of how to get a good quick look at someone else's field or how exciting it is to have other people look at one's own. Because anthropologists work in such far corners of the world and travel is so difficult, visiting someone else's field is both time-consuming and expensive. At the beginning of a field trip one wants to get on with one's own work and at the end one wants to go home as quickly as possible. So very often there just isn't time. This, of course, works both ways—against visiting and being visited. Yet it is something, I think, we have neglected. We have to work with others' field material and one of the things that makes this hard to do is that our own is so live and real, while that of others is a lot of words filled in by a few photographs and a lot of vague imaginings. I know that the Trobriands—and so everything Malinowski ever wrote—are much more real to me because I once saw a canoeload of Trobrianders in the harbor in Samarai and realized how light and gay they seemed against the background of the other peoples.

But because I worked mostly in an era when transportation was very difficult, I have not very often had these visiting experiences. Cora Dubois thought that she might come to us in Bali for perhaps a month and we had a lovely little house in the palace courtyard renovated for her. But in the end she came for three days only, into which we tried to pack every kind of useful experience of feast and trance and how to make shutters that shut and how to make medicine bottles out of bamboo. It was in a sense too utilitarian for delight.

Then in 1959, when the American Anthropological Association met in Mexico City, I had a chance to see the village where Ted and Lola Schwartz were working. It was just before Christmas and there were processions in the village every night. Once we made an afternoon's expedition to Tepoztlan, where both Robert Redfield and Oscar Lewis had worked, and Ken Heyman and I had a three-day photographing bout in a nearby village that had never had an anthropologist in it at all. Back in Mexico City Oscar Lewis took me to see some of his city slum courts. None of this took very long, but I can read and listen to what Ted or Lola says about Mexico with a far greater sense of understanding.

Of course I have twice had the experience of going into a field with others who already knew it well—to Bali, in 1936, where Jane Belo and Colin McPhee and Walter Spies were already deeply at home, and to Iatmul, in 1938, to the Sepik people about whom Gregory Bateson had written and in preparation for which I was tutored in such tactful Iatmul phrases as, "No indeed, I won't go into the men's house, that is something which belongs to the men." But these were quite different experiences. Entering your own coming field, you know that every moment is laden with responsibility and are aware that first impressions are precious and fleeting.

In visiting one's only responsibility is not to get in the way, not to upset the delicate balance between the fieldworker and the village by giving the wrong gift, asking an impolitic question or showing an inappropriate eagerness. To the extent that one's presence has been explained as a "onework"—as they say in Neo-Melanesian—the responsibility for appropriate behavior is heavier. But otherwise one is free to look and listen and take it all in through one's senses so that later every word that has been—or will be—written about that field will be many times more meaningful.

I have had other brief field encounters. Visiting a desert settlement in Saudi Arabia in company with the local anthropologist gave me a slight sense of a life in which small boys sat with grown men and no women were visible. Two weeks' intensive consultation on mental health in Israel gave me the kind of understanding within which I could read—and continue to read—accounts of life in the kibbutz. Thirty years ago a visit to a reserve for Australian Aborigines with Caroline Kelly gave me a basis for comparing reservation conditions with those of the American Indians I had studied in 1930 in Nebraska.

Last year's trip to Iran made it possible for me to watch the nomadic people both in the marketplace and camped among their flocks and herds and so to have a little more understanding of what Warren and Nina Swidler were up against in living with a nomadic people in Baluchistan. And a one-day visit to a University of Washington graduate student who was studying an Iranian village brought to life the actual internal organization of the molded cluster of mud houses. Even a one-day excursion to a native village from a South African port and a chance encounter with an offering laid out in a hidden woodland shrine, while I was on a holiday in

Java, have made their contributions. In Japan, in 1958, one day in a Japanese village with a Japanese fieldworker was worth weeks of traveling without such an informed guide. Sight and sound and feel are important, but actually it is the nexus between the resident fieldworker and the visitor that is significant for anthropological work.

It is against this background of wistfulness and scant experience of field work visiting that the present ideal situation has to be appreciated. We planned many of the methods used in Montserrat and Manus in 1953 so they would be parallel. The projective tests, some of which Tao Abel gave in Montserrat and we all gave in Manus, the methods of making village plans and censuses and the question of how to deal with the horrendous problem of more notes than one could possibly write up were all discussed in letters by Rhoda and Ted and me, halfway round the world from one another. Recently we decided to use some of the 1953 Manus and Montserrat materials—mainly projective tests—in a pilot study for a new field project next year in New Guinea, where Rhoda will pick up where Gregory and I left off in 1938 in Tambunam on the Sepik River. So it became more urgent than ever that I get a chance to see "Danio Village" in Montserrat.

At first it seemed very difficult. Much that had made field work difficult in 1953, when Rhoda had a fully equipped house in the village, made it seem prohibitive now. In the village there is no place for a stranger to rest, get a meal or take shelter when it rains. In the work she was doing before I came, Rhoda would set off from Plymouth, the town, by car—because it was too expensive to set up full-scale housekeeping for a short revisit and there is now a good road that goes into the center of Danio Village—with the most appalling load: notebook, cameras and spare films, tape recorder and tapes, raincoat and sun hat, candy for the children, sandwiches and a thermos of lemonade. If all went according to plan, she might spend several hours out in a carrot field or watching a weekly baking or visiting in someone's house. It was necessary to improvise at every turn and obviously there would be no place for a visitor.

But then she found this thoroughly charming tourist hotel which had recently opened, as Montserrat is now being developed into a quiet tourist area and retirement spot for English, American and Canadian visitors. And here, from our hexagonal cottage, we

can look straight up to the high ridge where Danio Village is and almost see the people, although it is a very rough walk indeed and to reach the village by car we have to go some six miles on winding roads. And down by the shore the fishermen cast their nets and one of them has kin in Danio.

So I am astonishingly poised above, beyond, outside—yet in full view of the field. From here we can make a trip to church, to the shop in the village, to the weekly public market in town. Rhoda sits and transcribes field notes from tapes and the sound of an old woman singing or people rambling along in a dialect that I can only barely hear a little of is like a surrounding fluid as I work. And slowly some of the principal personages come to life. I am introduced to Mr. Bramble, the chief minister, in the post office. We discuss with Mr. Osborne, the merchant who built this place, how he finally dispensed with an architect and just designed it himself —a Montserrat characteristic which he shares with the country people.

My own work goes on, but always within Montserrat. . . . I have had a chance also to experience some of the extraordinary physical aspects of this island which, no matter how well they are explained, you still don't quite believe. I've had three weeks to get used to a world in which the temperature shifts from five minutes to five minutes, in which you may have your own private rainstorm beating down and half a mile away in three directions you see the bluest sky and the calmest sea and sunlight resting on the hilltops. The formation of the mountains changes all the time, as the shifting clouds bring out the different patterns, and no one knows whether it will rain here or there or nowhere at all in the next ten minutes as the sea suddenly turns winedark and threatening from your viewpoint, floating on its surface. On no island I have ever lived has there been such a simultaneity of microclimates, all visible at once.

We sit and speculate about how the character of the island may have affected the people who came to live here and how differently they fragment memory from the way most people do. Rhoda, of course, has Haiti to compare them with, and I find that in many ways Arapesh makes a better comparison than Manus, perhaps partly because we are focusing on the relationship of the people to the hilly country.

But nowhere in New Guinea is there the same kind of stillness.

On the rocky, narrow road into Danio Village.

Visiting a village house.

And observing a small boy's doll play.

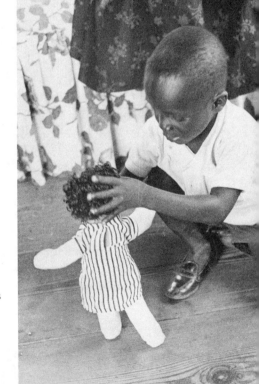

Here at night, on this isolated shore where there are no cocks to crow and the occasional sheep or goat or donkey that is tethered on the uncut lawns is taken home at night, it is impossible to tell the time of night if one awakens. There is only the sound of the sea and the little peepers who start at dusk and cry steadily till dawn. The very handsome iguanas, looking incredibly wise and ancient, climb up on the sunny verandas of cottages that are temporarily unoccupied. The beach changes overnight. When Hurricane Faith decided to pass us by and go north of Antigua, the seas pounded for two days, the soft green along the water's edge was killed in patches, now sere and brown, and the once handsome black volcanic sand (called "jet" in the brochures of the Montserrat Development Company) was buried under mountains of rancid brown seaweed. Now, a week later, only the yellow patches on the foliage remain. It is a world in which at any moment you may not be able to tell what time it is, what day it is, what season it is and, of course, whether the house you live in will be there tomorrow. When people discuss a house, one of the things they say is that it stood up through the 1924 and 1928 hurricanes but collapsed in the 1935 earthquake.

I think visiting and being visited ought to become a recognized part of anthropological professional life. It's true that films like *Dead Birds* and sound recordings like the ones Colin Turnbull brought back from his African pygmies help enormously. We can hope in time to make field records so full of sight and sound, at least, that they will live on long after the cultures they record have vanished. But in the meanwhile this kind of visit is extraordinarily rewarding.

I turn from looking across the hills to Danio Village—it's not raining there, it's pouring here—to my mixed fare of *Encounter, Counterpart, Transaction, The High Valley,* Kenneth Read's marvelous account of his field work in the highlands of New Guinea, and Chow's *Social Mobility in China.* We both stop work to discuss a promised chapter on American students' attitudes towards knowledge. Or I read a section of Goveia's *Slave Society in the British Leeward Islands at the End of the Eighteenth Century* and look up to see outside the window the first hummingbird Rhoda has ever seen in Montserrat. We suspect that the iguanas and the hummingbird are specially provided by the enterprising and innovating owner of the hotel for visitors who stay over two weeks.

"I'm going now!"

Tambunam
June 13 to July 13, 1967

At last, on an early morning in June, 1967, I was on my way up the Sepik River, in New Guinea. More than four years had gone into the planning of this trip; and now, in a small speedboat, we raced up the seventy-mile stretch of river on the final stage of the trip, from the government station at Angoram to the village of Tambunam. The sun was just beginning to dissolve the banks of mist; on both shores the flat land stretched back, green and gold, as far as the eye could see. Now we looked upon a new garden, with spirals of yam leaves climbing slender poles; now on a long bank of elephant grass, silver plumes bending to the breeze; now on a white heron, floating down to a dark beach. And on the river itself floating islands of grass, torn loose upriver, moved swiftly downstream with the current. The speedboat swerved around them, leaving a wide wake in the smooth brown water. Once we startled a crocodile—or was it only a waterlogged tree?

This was my first trip up the Sepik since 1938, when I had spent eight months living in Tambunam. This time I would stay for only a month, but with me was another anthropologist, Rhoda Metraux, who would remain for nearly a year, to take up again the study of the village people. What had changed in Tambunam since I had seen it last, and what had remained the same?

Twenty-nine years is a long time, especially in the lives of a people who die young. Months earlier I had sent a list of the men and women I had known best, and from the report sent back I knew that very many of them were dead. I knew also that the Japanese had been on the river during World War II, and that since the war, many men were engaged in crocodile-hunting for the trade. There was a mission church in Timbunke, upriver, in 1938; after the war a church and then a school were established in Tambunam. That would mean that the old ceremonial life would be gone. But I knew little else now of the village and its people.

I thought about Tambunam as it had been, the proudest and handsomest village on the river, with great houses sixty feet long and thirty feet high ranged along the river bank, deep in cool shade. Each house was supported on tremendous carved posts and had a high-pitched roof, the gables thatched in intricate patterns, with giant woven faces peering down from the eaves at passers-by.

Coconut trees were planted on built-up mounds to protect them from being washed away in the months when the river was in flood, and around these mounds the women's road wound through the village. The men had their own road, closer to the river and leading to the men's houses—their clubs, in fact—where they sat at ease among their kin and ate the bowls of boiled sago and fish brought there by their submissive, hard-working wives.

The old tradition of the village was based on headhunting. Heads had to be taken when a new house was built and when a boy became a man. In 1938 there still were men in Tambunam who wore the skin of the flying fox, permitted only to a man who had taken a head. A small boy who worked for us had lost his uncle in a headhunting raid.

Still hurrying up the river, its waters burnished by the mid-morning sun, I wondered what the fate of Tambunam was now, almost thirty years later. What would its people, almost twice as many as in 1938, have made of a world in which headhunting was only a memory and from which the spirits had departed, spirits that had formerly possessed the "trancers," who stamped up and

The shady men's road into Tambunam Village. Nowadays women and children also walk through the village on this well-swept path.

down, exhorting the men to hunt or fight? How was Tambunam making out in a world in which "business" had become an important word?

Already curio hunters had mined the river area, buying old masks and drums and carvings. And crocodiles were becoming scarce and very wary as hunters, responding to the requirements of "business," pursued them up branches of the river and through the *barets* connecting the river and inland waters. I had been told in Angoram that in the last two years river floods, the highest in living memory, had destroyed innumerable coconut trees and yam gardens, and that a devastating fire had swept the Tambunam sago patches. How, then, were the people feeding themselves and earning the money to buy food and pay their taxes? And the school children—were they now entirely cut off from the past, rootless as the grass islands floating by on the river? I felt rather as if I were hurrying to a deathbed, to record the death pangs of the Tambunams, once the fiercest, the proudest and most flamboyant people on the Sepik.

But I need not have been fearful. As the village swept into view I saw the big houses, old ones and new ones, still handsomely built and beautifully ornamented. The pride of the Tambunam people is not broken. In most of the other villages where their language is spoken, the men showed the women all the sacred, hidden things that had belonged to the men alone before they burned them and accepted the newly arrived Christian mission. By an accident of war Tambunam had been saved from this blow to pride. The village had been bombed and the great men's house, containing all its secret paraphernalia, burned to a heap of ashes. And after the war the men simply said, "It is finished." Nothing was *thrown* away, and school for the children and work away from the village have replaced the older initiation as a natural progression instead of a response to irreparable, angry loss.

Walking through the village, I discovered that the smaller men's houses still existed. They have simply been transformed into "carpenter shops." And here the older men still gather, as they always have, talking together and carving new objects, new designs and new forms, to sell abroad. The old excitement of fighting and headhunting, celebrated by a little art, has been replaced by a tremendous outburst of imaginative carving. The men have found

The pre-World War II house of Andjanavi of Wingwolimbit clan.

The new house of Mapali of Wingwolimbit clan. The face of the house is woven into the gable.

a way, based on an old tradition, of reaching out into the modern world.

It is impossible, of course, to know how long this activity can last. The destruction of the sago patches has weakened the village's self-sufficiency in food. And the men have responded with great enthusiasm to a whole series of the most modern inventions. They like outboard motors, preferably big, fifty-horsepower motors that allow them to race up and down the river on which, for long centuries, their ancestors laboriously paddled. They like transistor radios over which they can hear broadcast the music and songs of all the peoples of New Guinea who until now had been isolated for thousands of years, and they discover relationships between these different styles of singing and their own.

Although they still smoke their own home-grown tobacco, they like cigarette lighters that stay dry in the dampest weather on the river. They like watches to tell the exact time and flashlights to replace the uncertain light of palm-leaf torches. All these are expensive. Besides, children must have clothes to go to school and adults want to be dressed appropriately when they travel about. So even though they still build houses and canoes with the old materials, fish in the old way and prefer the older kinds of food, they need to earn money to live in a changing world and satisfy new ambitions.

But the bonds linking past and present are strong. This was reflected in the careful foresight with which the village prepared for my return. They had selected a house site for us within a cluster of old friends. Nginambun, my best informant, now a widow living peacefully with two co-wives of her husband, long since dead, is our next-door neighbor. On her first visit she brought the almost unrecognizable, smoke-blackened remains of the airline bag I had given her when I left all those years ago. Mbaan, who had been my linguistic informant and who is now a gentle old man revered as the wisest in ancient lore, came to watch the housebuilding, and he daily sits by the screen house, answering our questions. Kami Ashavi, who had been one of my houseboys, is now the recognized leader of his clan, and he took over the responsibility for organizing our new household, with Mbetnda, our other former houseboy, echoing his words. These are our neighbors, and they have brought their children to help in the household, to cook and carry water and chatter gaily about new things. We are picking up life just as it was laid down in 1938, when Kami Ashavi and Mbetnda went downriver with me to Wewak to see the sights and bid me goodbye.

On the first day in Tambunam I explained that I had come to see how much was different and how much the same; to learn who was still alive and who had died, and when; and to make the first contacts with the village for my younger colleague, who would stay longer and come to know them as once I had.

One of the first questions from the villagers was an unexpected one: Did we have a tape recorder? Yes, we did. This entranced them, for they want to have other people hear their songs. As once they came, eager and brimming with news of trouble and quarrels, to dictate the details of events into my typewriter, now they come every evening to sing, to chant, to play tunes on a jew's-harp, to shout totemic songs into bamboo trumpets, and then to listen to the recording and criticize the effects.

They have always been a theatrical people, carving to make a fine show and arranging elaborate dramatic performances for which their wives and mothers and uninitiated children were the only audience. And now, just as outboard motors have brought speed, flashlights a new brightness to the night and the carvers' market a new impetus to their imagination, so also radio and the anthropologist's tape recorder are providing a new setting for their gay sense of the dramatic. Without self-consciousness a man announces:

"I will now sing the song we used to sing when the heads of the slain were lined up in the men's house." And a few minutes later he tells me: "Yes, my youngest son is away at school. He is studying to be a doctor."

In the evening, their faces lighted by the warm glow of hurricane lanterns, the men sit on boxes in the front part of the house and talk about the past. Over and over again they tell about what happened when I was here before. They describe the night it rained on a crocodile hunt, when everyone rolled up the matting mosquito baskets and huddled in the wet darkness. They remember how Komankowi's baby was born with a "tail" (a bit of membrane hanging on his back, which I cut off) and tell me that he is now a married man with two children of his own. They recall the occasion when a baby refused to be born and the medium called in to help could do nothing because his possessing spirit had gone off to another man. Smilingly they speak of how I respected the taboos separating men and women and always sat properly on the periphery of sacred premises. And partly because they believe in reincarnation, they have accepted my explanation that another woman anthropologist will now take up my work here.

Kami Ashavi, given a new opportunity to exercise his considerable executive ability, announces that he will boss this new Missis, as women without a man need to be bossed. And I discover that the harsh word "boss," which came into Pidgin English from the labor lines, now refers to the man who cares for women and children. So it is said, speaking of a widow, that her brother now "bosses" her; that is, he looks after her and her children and takes care of their food and shelter and welfare.

In this society women have followed in the footsteps of their father's father's sisters, and men have taken the names belonging to their father's father, telling tales of their exploits as if they were their own. So although it is good that I have come back, it is wholly

Kami Ashavi and Mbetnda, nicknamed Simon and Peter, bring our tea to the mosquito room, 1938.

Kami Ashavi, former *luluai* of
Tambunam, blocks out a mask.

Peter Mbetnda, a war veteran,
with his schoolboy son.

I consult with Mbaan and Peter Mbetnda.

comprehensible that another woman will take up the same work
and sit among the women when in ceremonials the plumed serpent
dances, as it will again when a Tambunam man who is now in
prison returns to make a mourning feast for his dead brother.

I was surprised to find how detailed their memories were, for
they are not a people with a deep interest in fact. Plots, counter-
plots, magnificent fabrications, retrospective falsifications, yes; accurate retelling of some event, no. But as we went over all the old
events (the records of which live on in my notebooks), the retelling
took on a new significance.

What I realize now, more keenly than I ever have before, is how
the experience of the anthropologist working on a culture, and the
experience of a people for whom the passing events are the whole
of life, meet in the intensity and significance of each detail as it
happens. For a people whose lives are bounded within a few square
miles and whose relationships are confined to a few hundred men
and women and children, every birth, every death, every marriage

and every quarrel carries a tremendous burden of meaning. Every event is described again and again. Only in this way will the children learn what life is and how it is to be lived. And the young men say: "I was not born when you were here, but the older people have told us . . ."

Meanwhile, on the other side of the world, I too had relived the same moments—felt the same horror at the idea of a baby born with a tail, recalled the wetness of the rainy night at Kangleme during the crocodile hunt. All these experiences came back to me again and again as I wrote and lectured and analyzed films and photographs, extracting from each intensely observed and recorded event some meaning for the wider understanding of human culture. Although the framework appears to be so different (a primitive village of recent headhunters and a lecture room at Columbia University), there is a matching of intensity in my observation and in the Tambunam attentiveness to each detail.

With Sister Mertia, who opened the first school in Tambunam in 1953.

On this return to Tambunam it has become very clear to me that it is only through this kind of intense living in face-to-face relationships that the life and culture of a whole people can be fully experienced. It is through the records of such closely bound lives that we may hope to understand the human need for continuity, repetitive experience and intimacy. For intimacy has its source in just these familiar repetitions of laughter at old jokes, remembered anger at old quarrels, meals eaten together in the same twilight and children listening to accounts of things that happened before their parents were born, stories told and retold. And here in Tambunam, where change is still in the making, repetition binds the present to the past and to the future; repetition binds the events all of us recall to the events that now will be recorded.

Rhoda Metraux and Bill Mitchell, interview Mbaan and Tipme about a coming ceremony.

From my notes for a
New Guinea field letter
in a too-crowded month
October 1971

October 4th, Sydney, Australia, to Port Moresby, Territory of Papua New Guinea.—Sorted and packed all the things I had left here in Sydney last August. The accumulation of paper is just frightful. Left by air for Port Moresby.

October 5th, Port Moresby to Wewak.—Met at Wewak airport by Steve Seymour, the hospital administrator. Dinner with Steve, his family and Major Williams, in charge of the Army base here. Since the *kiaps* no longer do so, the Army now make extensive patrols and are the only ones to explore new country. . . .

October 6th, Wewak to Maprik, West Sepik District, for visit to Arapesh-speaking people of Ilahita.—Met at Hayfield airstrip by Don Tuzin, who drove me in his pickup truck. The drive out very bumpy and hazardous after rain; the truck kept getting stuck on the bad bush road. Ilahita had been promised a new road, but the local Member of the House of Assembly got it built through *his* village. Beverly Tuzin, Don's wife, met us at their house.

The minute we entered Ilahita, I was sure they really were Arapesh. The huge village is star-shaped out over ridges as hamlets must have grown together. There are 93 named plazas and the houses cluster around them, facing each other, making little enclosing circles. (This makes one realize how stern the layout of Tambunam is, how essentially formal in spirit.) Flying over the Maprik area, I saw from the air for the first time in my life the tall House Tambarans and the houses with slanting ridgepoles, which give an impression of kneeling, all very close together. Ilahita has modern houses, square on stilts with *pangal*—sago palm stem— walls, mostly for show or as storehouses; they sleep and store yams in the dark, slanting houses covered with unworked leaves.

Talked and talked. Watched the people. Don is a real anthropologist, concerned with anthropological problems, many of them modern—like his interest in taste and smell as categories— but deeply committed to tradition. He had gone to see Reo, who loaned him his manuscript on the Arapesh language that was found at the University of California. Has done fine work with films, stills, tapes, beautifully organized and well-thought-out notes. Beverly is trained as a nutritionist; she is slight, gentle, enjoys the village and the people. They let them wander in and out and don't interrupt what they are doing themselves. . . .

October 8th, Maprik to Lumi, West Sepik District.—The plane made a detour to pick me up at Banlip airstrip and take me—in ten minutes—to Lumi. The pilot waited and then flew out over the road to look for us. Don felt this was a tribute to me, but I think it was a tribute to his care. Joyce Mitchell met me in Lumi. Bill had to stay up in the mountains at their field site in Taute. His people were having their biggest curing ceremony with the "devil-fish" mask this weekend. This will conclude Bill's current work with the Wape.

Joyce and the children—Ned and Elizabeth—are now living in Lumi in a very trim little house that Bill designed—with indoor plumbing, all very modern. Joyce took me first to observe the teaching in a *Kisim Save*—Get Knowledge—course, where villagers with very little schooling are taught to teach literacy in Pidgin English. They were giving them the experience of being pupils but are taking them on as teachers at once—very good and worth remembering. This is a project of the Christian Missions to Many Lands, a Protestant group.

In the evening two sets of missionaries came in—Don McGregor and his wife, Aileen, Christian Brethren missionaries with linguistic training who have studied the Olo language, and Sister Mary Magdalene and Father Tom, both Australian Franciscan missionaries—and we all sat and amicably discussed missionization. McGregor has read about respecting the culture and also is inclined to find parallelisms between native beliefs and Christian beliefs; he is concerned about how much one should try to use native myths, etc. I found myself phrasing this better than ever before. You can take a lesser belief—or a human situation—and work up to a phrasing about God, but you can't work down without downgrading the more complex religion. You can start with human fatherhood and arrive at God, but not with God to explain human fatherhood. What these missionaries seem to lack is the idea that they are expanding the spiritual universe of the people. I wasn't sure I got the idea over, but on Sunday in church it was clear that Don McGregor had got the point. He preached a sermon on how he and they were "short" on a sense of universality, brotherhood beyond the village into the nation and the world.

On Saturday we went up to the hospital and saw the records

of the well-baby clinic. Perfectly beautiful—weight, inoculations, illnesses, etc.; these Joyce will use in her study of who goes—and stays—in school. Her people haven't really got to the point of having school leavers yet. In fact, these people are not much beyond the stage of the Arapesh 40 years ago—European old clothes, nominal relations to the missions, a few children in school, an occasional child who goes on to higher education, but mostly a swing between plantation work and the village. In Taute, Bill's village, the hamlets seem to take turns; a whole group of men go away together and of course have to give everything they earn to those who take care of their wives and children. . . .

On Sunday Bill arrived at noon, looking so white I was frightened, but after a few hours his tan came back. He had had no sleep and the *singsing* had meant many hours of grueling work. He feels very happy about his work—Taute was a fine choice, Joyce is well settled, the next place on the Yellow River looks good. . . .

October 11th.—Returned to Wewak by air.

October 12th, Wewak to Biwat Mission, Yuat River, East Sepik District.—I flew down in a small charter plane owned by the mission; landed easily on Biwat airstrip. The mission is where the old village of Biwat was and all four Mundugumor villages are where they were in 1932. The station is large and has a government-supported boarding school; Jan Fouary, the only foreign teacher, teaches the two upper grades. The upper river is not missionized at all, they say, and the amount of missionizing here seems rather slight. One man has seven wives, but this is rare.

Afima is dead and Omblean is said to be senile. Yeshima and his brother came to call. Yeshima is a spry little old man, doesn't speak Pidgin. His brother moved to Branda and was *luluai* there. A man came to say that he made the model crocodile for us in 1932. . . .

October 13th.—Father Wand took me down to Kenakatem in his speedboat. A crowd of people on the bank welcomed me up and said, "Come and sit down in the *house-boy.*" This is a small open house with a *limbum* sitting platform around three sides, a fire in the middle and well thatched on top. The village is filled with these little houses. . . .

Everyone more or less waited for Omblean, who, I had by now discovered, had had a stroke and was treated at the mission hospital. He approached slowly, walking with a stick, his face fuller but quite recognizable, his eyes clear. But he was hardly able to speak and his attention flickered after a minute or two. They had set me up in a folding chair I had brought and they placed a stool for him. They quite clearly have no precedent for dealing with someone in his state. He was a big man, had—still has—a big house and houses for his sons around him. They spoke of him as *longlong finis*—wholly disoriented—and yet obviously respected him and deferred to him. He sat for a while and then left. I had greeted him affectionately and he seemed to respond, but then he took no part in the conversation.

Men and women both sat around. They remembered Reo's name as Leo, but couldn't remember any name for me. Neither can I; must have been just "Missis." Where was Reo and why didn't he come back? Checked over old lists of men and women. Even with my poor pronunciation they recognized them. Afima was killed as a police-boy.

Everybody knew that Afima had worked for us. In fact, their memories are just as good as in other places; they remembered the journey to see the dying man and how we had gone to the gardens. I had an impression they could have gone on indefinitely. When I showed them the paper on "Tamberans and Tumbuans in New Guinea," they admired the flute and said they don't have any now; the only thing left is one *yakat*—a wooden mask—in Akerang, which many people have wanted to buy, but they are keeping this. Everything else is gone. They only make *singsings*—acquired from other peoples—for Christmas or on special occasions in Angoram. On the other hand, the rope inheritance pattern seems to have survived intact. . . .

I had Mrangfoh walk me through the village. We went up to the top near Akerang—the four villages are now very close, almost one village—and I wrote out names and what kinds of houses. The general effect is a series of small places. . . . I have had the house names pronounced on tape. The general appearance of the village is good—clean, well-built houses with little decoration, serrated panels under the eaves, one mask, general sense of pride in the houses. *Garamuts*—slit gongs—still here exactly as when I was here before, including one that the *luluai* had cut the tongue out of! Still use *garamuts*.

Ethos seems unchanged—cheerfully disobedient and uncooperative. Endless joking. Women and children always hitting at each

Kenakatem in a grove of coconut and betel palms, 1971.

Children by the Yuat River bank, Kenakatem.

other; children busy with little bits of leaf and wood, slap at and threaten each other, and women threaten and slap at children. Men tell the children to leave, and they don't. Women strong and immodest. Roars of laughter. . . .

October 16th.—Woke up after a series of vivid dreams more convinced than ever that the church should bring more art, more celebration, into the lives of the people. The missions ask for work, but they provide no opportunity for ritual input. Father Wand says priests have been told not to destroy native art. But it could be used for gargoyles, on banners and for processions. I cited how Bipi—in Manus—had kept carving skills alive. The church here has a lovely altar, good vestments, a statue of Our Lady—everything to make the missionaries feel at home. The only way you know you are in a native church is the very low benches and the Pidgin English missal. Just words, where the graphic and plastic arts are needed. To the Protestants I could only suggest that they expand their ethical ideals, universality and brotherhood. But for the Catholics, all the pageantry could be here. And yet art work in the classrooms is the worst kind of schoolroom drawing. Horrible!

The children are—strangely—omnivorous readers. So the best Jan can do is to feed the children's interest in reading and give the brightest ones a chance to get out. Explained to her the weaknesses of the early closed mission system and the need to get a sense of hope. But obviously there is no leverage in these villages at present except intrinsic brightness. . . .

October 17th, Biwat Mission to Tambunam Village.—Early church, second mass. Fairly large crowd of people, sang well; Father Wand shy. After Mass I made off across the airstrip and a small group came to my door with an old hook and an old mask; one of them made a speech that the hook was the last thing left of Alemi's old house. I said, "Yes, that and the old *garamuts.*" I promised to keep the hook safely in the Museum, and gave them a few sticks of tobacco. They are the least mercenary of any people I have known and, in a sense, the most sentimental.

In Father Wand's tiny speedboat to the mouth of the Yuat and up the Sepik to Tambunam. In 1932 we made the same trip—with an overnight wait in between—in two days. Father Wand insisted on taking me up to the top of the village, passing the house where Rhoda Metraux and her household and their *lauas*—sister's sons—

bearing gifts were waiting. The whole village, watching, was filled with dismay as if I were going away altogether. Our house was decorated, the grass was newly cut and an arch of sago fronds was erected on the river bank, as if for a ceremony. General impression, the village very green and many beautiful new houses.

October 18th.—RM's birthday. *Naven* ceremony in the afternoon for Meriagut's newly finished house. The women gathered down in Nginambun's house to wait; we sat nearby in the Tavireman men's house with the men. Tape and Leicas. Finally, at dusk, when all the men had drifted away, the procession arrived, headed by the *wau*, the mother's brother, with his face blackened, dressed in green leaves and with a fringe of ferns around his face. The women wore grass skirts over their clothes. The *wau* danced in front, around and up into the house wearing a woman's big carrying bag, which he later gave to his wife to carry. This was just a teaser to stimulate the owner to buy a pig for the feast. I think teasers of this sort may have replaced the old trance sessions as a way of driving people into action. . . .

Nginambun, a young woman of Tambunam, 1938. Her husband, Gawi, took her abroad to Rabaul when few New Guinea women traveled anywhere.

Nginambun plays with Kami Ashavi's baby, 1971. Her only son is a law student at the University of Papua New Guinea.

October 21st.—Visited the new school buildings across the river on clan land called Malangai. Drawings on the walls of Standard 4 of a "gorilla" in the woods that is virtually a *tumbuan*—masked figure—and of owls that become masks. Met the teachers, both men very young and uncertain. Pitiful provision wherever the Tambunam people have been involved. Yet they have contributed large numbers of valuable carvings for sale to provide for fitting out the schoolrooms. . . .

Session with Andaramai over the Masendenai land dispute and then over the history of his clan, Wingwolimbit. This was to clear up statements about the composition of the village and to work on

Pupils in Tambunam's new school, 1971.

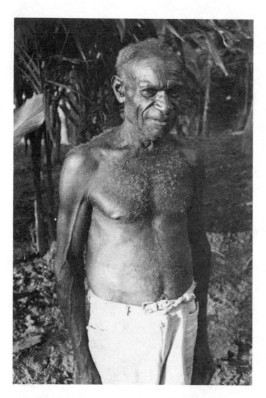

Andaramai, politician, carver, musician and expert on traditional life.

methods of eliciting this kind of material. As he described it, Tsuat-mali—the upriver Iatmul village—was simultaneously three places: (1) the place of origin of all the Iatmul people; (2) one place where his ancestors stopped on the way here; and (3) a recent settlement out of Malangai Village. He also implied that Ingai, the ancestor who migrated to Kangleme—the place in dispute with the Masendenai on the *baret* where we went on the crocodile hunt in 1938 —lived only five generations back. . . .

Discussion in the evening with RM about the different ways Gregory and I had worked and why we never had time to consult each other over details, so I have never gone over the 1938 Wompun Village *singsing* details. But we managed to work out equivalences with this year's Wompun *singsing,* in which Tambunam danced and presented the little Wompun House Tambaran with an elaborately carved ceremonial "chair." Only question left is whether a "chair" was actually carved for the 1938 *singsing*. . . .

* * *

Dancers in the Wompun *Singsing,* a ceremonial occasion, 1938.

Dancers in the Wompun *Singsing,* 1971.

Thereafter events followed in such rapid succession and discussions with Tambunam experts became so technical that we taped everything for write-up in field notes and later discussion. And my projected field letter was not written.

On October 29th, I went upriver to the mission station at Timbunke, where, in December 1932, we had spent the night on our way to Ambunti in the government pinnace. This time I talked at length with Sister Mary Anthide, in charge of the outpost hospital, and Sister Mertia, who started the Tambunam school in 1953, and the other Sisters about schools and medical care in the villages and hopes for the future.

The next morning the chartered mission airplane picked me up on Timbunke airstrip and I began the long journey that took me back to Samoa.

Peré Village
July 23, 1975

This time although I will have interesting things about change to discuss and although these Manus people continue to condense centuries into decades and decades into years, yet I am most conscious of the enormous sense of continuity as I look at old men whom I knew as children and see the grandfathers' faces reflected in their descendants. The shared memories, the shared experiences bind them together in a web that is stronger than the ancestral ghosts they fear if they do not send money and gifts home to parents who put in hard work to rear them.

It is a quiet village. Not once have we heard angry shouting voices, fighting cocks, fighting dogs, beleaguered squealing pigs. At high tide the moored canoes bump gently against each other and the thatch rustles and crackles. Every morning a procession of roosters appear on the square and crow in concert without conflict. The people are scattered again, each household secure within the space allotted for its own clan, each clan with a piece of beach where canoes can be seared with torches, outriggers mended, nets dried without the contentiousness that used to occur over the wharf in New Peré One, when the village plan had been based on social standing and officialdom rather than on kinship. Then when the village treasurers were unable to resist the importunities of their kin and the funds entrusted to their keeping dwindled and disappeared, the money was divided among the clans. Each clan was made the custodian of its own funds, responsible for its own share.

Later, when New Peré Three was designed, the clan formation was restored, with Patusi—the village that moved in and swamped New Peré Two—at the far end with a small adequate square of its own. Later still the custom grew up of each clan having one or more canteens—a small trade store that keeps tobacco, canned meat, canned fish, batteries, cookies, etc. Trade stores come to grief in New Guinea because the storekeeper gives too much credit to his kin and eventually the store goes bankrupt. Now a group of kin invest in a canteen and if they borrow it blind, there is no great

With Benedikta, widow of Poka-nau, in Peré, 1975.

harm done as they are merely recouping their investment. And actual borrowing is reduced because there is a store where things can be bought.

I realized in 1953 that as soon as money—which can be used interchangeably to buy many things in many different amounts—is introduced, it is necessary to have stores and banks. For the old protections of bartering only certain desired objects for each other, like fish for taro or yams, which kept up the supplies of different necessities, have disappeared, and also many of the traditional protections have been lost that made it possible for a man who was planning a feast to accumulate a supply which would be respected. So a store was necessary. At first a trusted individual was "the bank." People used to go and demand to see their money periodically and the man who was the bank was bound to his house, so that at first I thought he must be suffering from a depression.

Now each organization that has a fund has a savings account and a passbook, and several signatures are needed to take money out. And recently a very competent young woman, who has a degree in sociology and has studied in Australia and is now an adviser to the provincial government on the preparation of a draft constitution, has proposed a novel idea, a mobile bank—a banking official who would make periodic circuits of the outlying villages to accept deposits and provide needed cash and so cut down on expensive travel. For since the introduction of outboard motors and trucks, travel, which used to be cheap, has become very expensive.

And so the adjustments proceed, with local experimentation and today the introduction of educated young people who have been exposed to the growing world awareness of such things as the evils of a school which places excessive value on book learning and urban life or the dangers of excluding women from decisions about food as these decisions reach higher and higher levels of administration. Discussions in Rome in December 1974, on the importance of local self-sufficiency in food and the significant role played by women at the village level, which should be expressed in giving agricultural training to women as well as men, have already reached Papua New Guinea in the person of a young New Zealand woman who represents FAO and is working in the new oil palm settlement on New Britain I visited two years ago, where the people of Alitoa now live. She has introduced women into Papua

New Guinea's one agricultural college. These young people are acutely aware of the problems of relating local tradition to the "world system," facing as they do the visible presence of the Stone Age and the Electronic Age and the immediate repercussions of the worldwide energy crisis.

I am alone in the village, the first time I have been alone in a New Guinea village since 1966, when I spent many weeks here while the people were completely absorbed in preparing for the big Christmas that was to celebrate the merging of the old South Coast Council, which Paliau had started, with the new one. Everyone was exhausted in the evenings and preoccupied in the daytime. My lamp used to go out and I would rebel at the wasted time or try to read in bed with a flashlight. This year we have been going to bed early and often I have lain awake for hours, but somehow no longer rebelling, just thinking. Occasionally I turn on the flashlight and make a note of something that seems worth catching. But I am getting enough sleep, keeping up with each day's work, buffered against the welter of decisions and dilemmas which will crowd in as soon as I get back to New York. Four to five hours a day is about all I can do well on a stiff manual typewriter. Then I begin to put the carbons in backwards or make too many typos.

Being so rested—for there is a siesta at the dead center of the day—means long, very interesting novelistic dreams, pleasant to remember in the morning. The major drawbacks of field work, the press of work which means one is always behind in one's typing and the fear of getting sick and so cutting the work short, are both missing. Ted started a census and a rough map. Barbara will refine them as she measures and photographs the school children. The major things I wanted to see have happened. If I had to leave today instead of next week, no harm would be done. We know so much about these people, both in general and in detail.

Long ago I was fascinated by the idea of building a landscape of the spirit, of constructing out of remembered scenes and bits of poetry, some memorized one knew not why, a landscape within which one would live later in life. Some were figures of speech without any immediate counterpart, like

> *But a star has no roots,*
> *To and fro it floats*
> *Like a lily in the sky.*

Visitor from another land. With Barbara Heath at the Monterey, California, airport to greet her guest, John Kilipak Gizikau, 1969.

This image never came into full existence for me until I had seen the water lilies on Chambri Lake and had watched a completely rootless person float through life.

Manus—the continuity of Peré Village—is a kind of field-worker's totally reliable paradise, in the sense that I continue to find here the next thing I need to know. The wealth of evidence accumulates: Barbara's sense of their physique and of the physical continuity of biological heritages, Ted's periodic testing and precise explication of their style of thought, Lenora's sensitive awareness of the way they move and now the sophisticated comments of the educated younger generation. The world has changed, anthropology has changed and the village has changed; the people have multiplied and spread out to the far corners of New Guinea and beyond and they are helping the new institutions to flower.

Nahau, the daughter of Kampo—the leader of the Usiai village of Lahan that came down to the coast at the beginning of the Paliau Movement—asked me to write a paper for her and other young people with a comparable education. The assistant land surveyor of Papua New Guinea was sitting in her office; he comes from Patusi. So I took all that we have seen and learned, argued about and compared notes over for 47 years, all that we have subjected

Peré canoe on the way to market, 1975.

to every kind of international criticism and comment, things that have been rewritten for children's books and have been incorporated in films that are shown round the world, and I tried to put into ten pages a major piece of advice for her task of individualizing the provincial constitution. I felt a little like Papa Franz when he said that he would tell us all he knew about something—or any part of it—in 45 minutes. But it is just this process of distilling something significant and simple, shorn of extraneous detail and yet retaining its specificity, that we need to carry out.

I tried to show the failure to do just this in the United Nations reports I reproduced as an appendix to *New Lives for Old*. But the really important difference is that here I have been writing to and for Nahau—Nahau who grew up here, for whom every location, every reference to a ceremony or an event is meaningful. I have not been writing for some United Nations mission which will end up by preparing a report, like one I read in 1973, with a bunch of generalizations that would apply anywhere in the undeveloped world. Instead, this is really the devolution of decision-making to where it belongs—expertise brought to bear on the place where the knowledge originated on which it is based. Nahau knows, because she has lived it from the inside, and I know, because I have used every skill anthropology has developed to understand it, just what it means when I say that the Manus think of a village as a voluntary association of clans and sometimes single individuals and think of any boundary as something to be crossed and transcended. This is how it should be everywhere in the world: a worldwide vocabulary within which ideas can spread rapidly and suggested solutions can be broadcast, but distinctive, detailed decision-making the responsibility of each locality.

Of course, this isn't the only important thing. I can take what I learn in Manus and put it into the United Nations system also. There has to be a weaving back and forth between the highly generalized and the highly concrete, with everything changing at once. Ted spent a lot of time with the young men, talking politics, and he told me they are planning to make artificial electoral sub-provinces which will put essentially incompatible villages together.

It's been a blustery morning, windows having to be shuttered and opened, shuttered and opened, again and again. I have gone over things carefully to know which boxes contain our cameras, tape recorders, exposed film. Barbara had this all set up when I arrived on the model I established 20 years ago and she encountered first in 1966. These are the boxes—dry boxes made of light, fabricated foam with silica gel instead of ice in them—which would have to be rescued if the lamp exploded (so far, only the glass of one has burst into a hundred pieces just after it was turned out) and set this thatched house on fire or if a tidal wave threatened to wash the house away.

You go to bed each night, everything under cover and accounted for—flashlight, notebook and pencil, spectacles all handy for an emergency. And when I put my spectacles away in the middle of last night, one lens was missing. But Peranis found it this morning, lodged in a crack in the floor. The frame got bent when I stubbed my toe and fell on some gravel and knocked the plastic lens out. The rituals, the way one indicates to the village—and to Peranis who would like breakfast at 5.30, lunch at 11 and dinner at 5 o'clock if he were left to his own impatiences—that one is asleep or awake, the boiled water bottles in the kerosene refrigerator, a very modern comfort which makes it possible to keep fish two or three days and to have deliciously ice-cold pineapple, though it blows out whenever there is a wind from one direction, the place for the salt and pepper and chloroquine on the table—all these rituals are necessary because Peranis, who does not understand them thoroughly, cannot vary them.

Ted used to complain how careless and forgetful the people were, leaving ashore something needed for the engine. But they were accustomed to making anything they needed from the materials at hand, and they had not grasped all that an engine needs. So they ritually take the engine apart, put it back together and spin it in a tank of water, but do not know what they are doing. In fact you can only vary a procedure when you have completely mastered it and know which sequences are essential and which are not. If you don't know, you ignore essentials or follow procedures with too great rigidity. And isn't a religious ritual, which is efficacious in itself and therefore a mystery, just that—a procedure which must be followed rigidly because by its very nature it cannot be understood? I will now have to add to my own rituals, always take your glasses off over something on which the dislodging lens can fall and be found—the way people do their contact lenses. Peranis heard me explain to Barbara that I had lost the lens in the night, that it might be anywhere between here and the little lavatory, which has a long bridge out over the water. Peranis asked—he was picking up from English—was it just one? As I answered yes, he completed his perception, leaned down and picked up the dislodged lens, on which the light had caught.

In a way this kind of continuing field work is a symbol of the disappearance of all finality from scientific work. Not only has linearity given place to circularity and simultaneity, simple sequences of cause and effect to multiple feedback systems, but even the idea that one had "done" a kinship system or the grammar of a language. I must go back to Larry's old paper on "Structure, Function and Growth," which I sent to Gregory in the summer of 1935, the summer he and Wad had a cottage together, and they both disapproved of the paper. And the old formulations, too—modernization going in one direction only with, sometimes, the appearance of "survivals" or the return of the repressed—altogether too mechanical as well as being much too linear.

And the constitutional type problem, which has intrigued me ever since the 1924 BAAS meeting, when we had all read Jung, is now, I think, in good shape. Somatotyping is a way of describing an individual or a population in terms of identifiable components of fat, absence of fat and muscularity; there are no such types as leptosomes or mesomorphs, only individuals with certain proportions. Instead, the measurements have to be treated like the components in an IQ test where individuals can be described by an over-all Intelligence Quotient, but also differentiated by the way in which they attained that IQ score—by more or less rote memory, more or less reasoning power, a better or a poorer vocabulary. This doesn't mean that it is unimportant that the Manus are higher on mesomorphy than any other recorded population any more than it is meaningless that the Manus do very well on tests of hand-eye coordination.

But it does mean that we were premature in our thinking about the possibility of correlating some kind of bodily configuration with an innate temperament, varying in relation to particular populations and particular cultures, as we hoped to do in Chambri in 1933. It means that at best Sheldon's measurements can only be one part of what such a description of a gene configuration might turn out to be. Will it take a hundred variables—a difference as great as that between the first and second reports to the Club of Rome? But that is only a matter of three or four years. If it is true that the rate of change equals the rate of transportation (read *communication*), then it should not take that long.

But things have got clearer. And I recognize now that the gist of the argument between Ruth and me—originally Reo and me—was not whether there is a limited number of psychological types or an unlimited set of possibilities but rather, does one take the whole human race into account in building a system, so that if one part were described in sufficient and comparable detail, the rest could be derived in terms of expected properties. The unknown has to have attributes related to the known because that is the way it is set up. But anything less than the whole human race gives one either a cultural or a biological procrustean bed, as Sheldon's arbitrary scale does.

And then there is another problem, raised by present conditions in Manus. The old Manus way of life can be demonstrated to have been more conducive to the development of characteristics useful in the modern world than that of the Usiai, both as we experienced them in 1928 and as they were when they came down to the beach in 1953. They were clumsy where the Manus were agile and they lacked the Manus capacity for beautifully coordinated teamwork. But they did learn to live on the beach, to manage canoes and fishing, whereas the Manus made hardly any attempt to learn to manage the land, to plant or to move easily in the bush. So the Usiai had to be more adjustable. Today, although teachers still say that the Manus-true have an edge in learning, many Usiai are going further than any Manus has gone—and so are the North Coast Matankor.

So one is confronted by an apparent paradox. Was the very speed and unanimity of the Manus leap forward also a limitation? Their major successes today are in the field of engineering of various sorts, but not in more abstract fields. Paliau's son, who wanted to become a doctor, has settled—without a degree, at least for the time being—for an administrative clerkship; Lokus' son has been to Japan for advanced mechanical training. In contrast Gabriel Gris, a Matankor man, is chancellor of the University of Papua New Guinea, and among the Usiai, Nahau is planning to take a Ph.D.—on the Paliau Movement!—and Bernard Mino of Drano is going to the United States to study literature.

I wish somebody could take a look, today, at the Sumatrans in Indonesia and the Ibos in Nigeria—both of them groups which got an initial start at modernization ahead of others in their own area because, not having been converted to Islam, they were easier to missionize. Is the point here the old principle that the price paid for innovation is obsolescence? Or is it something about a group moving ahead uniformly and so holding each other in step—and perhaps, in a sense, holding each other back?

Just had tea at ten. Why tea? Why at ten o'clock in the morning? Part of the ritual. It used to mean at least a fifteen-minute pause in the morning that stretched from dawn to midday and some liquid, in the days when water that was filtered and boiled was still not drinkable except as very strong tea. Today it is rainwater off the tin roof of the "House-meeting" that I gave them years ago, clear, soft, delicious water that everyone can drink straight from the water tank.

Looking to the future. With Paliau and Barbara Heath in the well-baby clinic, Peré, 1975.

Appendix
A Note on Orthography and My Use
of Native Languages

During the last fifty years the spelling of place names and personal names in the Pacific has changed many times; often the very names have changed. In general I have used the spelling current at the time a letter was written. For example, here as in other publications on our work in Bali, I have retained the Dutch system of spelling and the versions of names current in the 1930s, for the sake of simple consistency.

In the Index alternative names and spellings are given so that anyone can locate at least some places which are no longer so far away as once they were and so that those who are interested in the evolution of names can trace individuals through time and different publications as, for example, the young Manus boy who was Kilipak in 1928, later became Johanis Kilipak, then John Kilipak and today calls himself John Gizikau.

In each culture in which I did research I learned the language through intensive work with native speakers, whether or not there was available linguistic material, as there was on Samoan, Manus and Balinese. The one exception was our brief field work on the Omaha reservation. In New Guinea I used the native language with women, children and all those men who did not speak adequate Pidgin English. In these letters terms in a native language are italicized and usually briefly translated.

Special problems arise in regard to Pidgin English, the lingua franca of Melanesian New Guinea. In 1928 there was no dictionary. In writing letters I used Anglicized spellings of words derived from English, rather than spelling them phonetically in the local dialect, in order to make words and phrases more easily intelligible to speakers of English. Other terms, such as *kiap* or *luluai,* with which English speakers would not be familiar, are briefly translated and Pidgin words, like occasional words in the various native languages, are italicized.

However, certain words and phrases, although they may not be found in ordinary dictionaries, have become accepted technical terms, for example, "House Tambaran" for the ubiquitous New Guinea men's cult house. Other words were long ago incorporated into the vocabulary of speakers of English in the area, for example, the terms used to designate a wide range of masculine roles, such as houseboy, cook-boy, shoot-boy, police-boy, etc. These are not italicized.

Today there are excellent dictionaries and standardized spelling for the language which is known as Melanesian Pidgin or Neo-Melanesian and is one of the languages officially recognized in Papua New Guinea. There was in the past—and still is—one great advantage in using this language. It levels the capacities of native speaker and foreign speaker—or of speakers of different native languages—as both can speak the lingua franca equally well.

References and Selected Bibliography

Abel, Theodora M., and Rhoda Metraux. 1974. *Culture and Psychotherapy.* New Haven: College and University Press.

Bateson, Gregory. 1936. *Naven.* Cambridge: Cambridge University Press. 2nd edition, 1958, Stanford: Stanford University Press.

———. 1949. "Bali: The Value System of a Steady State." In *Social Structure: Studies Presented to A. R. Radcliffe-Brown,* ed. Meyer Fortes, pp. 35–53. Oxford: Clarendon Press.

———. 1972. *Steps to an Ecology of Mind.* San Francisco: Chandler.

———, and Margaret Mead. 1942. *Balinese Character.* Special Publications of the New York Academy of Sciences, 2. New York: New York Academy of Sciences. Reissued 1962.

Belo, Jane. 1949. *Bali: Rangda and Barong.* Monographs of the American Ethnological Society, 16. New York: Augustin.

———. 1953. *Bali: Temple Festival.* Monographs of the American Ethnological Society, 22. Locust Valley, N.Y.: Augustin.

———. 1960. *Trance in Bali.* New York: Columbia University Press.

———, ed. 1970. *Traditional Balinese Culture.* New York: Columbia University Press.

Benedict, Ruth. 1934. *Patterns of Culture.* Boston: Houghton Mifflin.

Bunzel, Ruth L. 1929. *The Pueblo Potter: A Study of Creative Imagination in Primitive Art.* New York: Columbia University Press. Reprinted 1972, New York: Dover.

Chow, Yung-Teh. 1966. *Social Mobility in China.* New York: Atherton.

Foerstal, Lenora. 1977. "Cultural Influences on Perception," *Studies in the Anthropology of Visual Communication,* 4:1 (Fall).

Fortune, Reo F. 1932a. "Incest." In *Encyclopaedia of the Social Sciences,* Vol. 7, pp. 620–622. New York: Macmillan.

———. 1932b. *Omaha Secret Societies.* Columbia University Contributions to Anthropology, 14. New York: Columbia University Press.

———. 1932c. *Sorcerers of Dobu.* New York: Dutton.

———. 1935. *Manus Religion.* Philadelphia: American Philosophical Society.

———. 1939. "Arapesh Warfare," *American Anthropologist,* 41:1, 22–41.

———. 1942. *Arapesh.* Publications of the American Ethnological Society, 19. New York: Augustin.

———. 1943. "Arapesh Maternity," *Nature,* 52 (August), 164.

Golde, Peggy, ed. 1970. *Women in the Field.* Chicago: Aldine.

Goveia, Elsa V. 1965. *Slave Society in the British Leeward Islands at the End of the Eighteenth Century.* New Haven: Yale University Press.

Malinowski, Bronislaw. 1922. *Argonauts of the Western Pacific.* London: Routledge. Reprinted 1961, New York: Dutton.

McPhee, Colin. 1946. *House in Bali.* New York: John Day.

———. 1966. *Music in Bali.* New Haven: Yale University Press.

Mead, Margaret. 1928a. *Coming of Age in Samoa.* New York: Morrow.

———. 1928b. "A Lapse of Animism among a Primitive People," *Psyche,* 9:1 (July), 72–77.

———. 1930a. "An Ethnologist's Footnote to *Totem and Taboo,*" *Psychoanalytic Review,* 17:3 (July), 297–304.

———. 1930b. *Growing Up in New Guinea.* New York: Morrow.

———. 1930c. "Social Organization of Manu'a," *Bernice P. Bishop Museum Bulletin,* 76. Honolulu. Reissued 1969.

———. 1932. "An Investigation of the Thought of Primitive Children, with Special Reference to Animism," *Journal of the Royal Anthropological Institute,* 62 (January-June), 173–190.

———. 1934a. "Kinship in the Admiralty Islands," *Anthropological Papers of The American Museum of Natural History,* 34, Part 2, 183–358. New York.

———. 1934b. "Tamberans and Tumbuans in New Guinea," *Natural History,* 34:3 (May-June), 234–246.

———. 1935. *Sex and Temperament in Three Primitive Societies.* New York: Morrow.

———. 1938. "The Mountain Arapesh. I. An Importing Culture," *Anthropological Papers of The American Museum of Natural History,* 36, Part 3, 139–349. New York. Reprinted 1970, in *The Mountain Arapesh II: Arts and Supernaturalism.* Garden City, N.Y.: Natural History Press.

———. 1940. "The Mountain Arapesh. II. Supernaturalism," *Anthropological Papers of The American Museum of Natural History,* 37, Part 3, 319–451. New York. Reprinted 1970, in *The Mountain Arapesh II: Arts and Supernaturalism.* Garden City, N.Y.: Natural History Press.

———. 1947. "The Mountain Arapesh. III. Socio-Economic Life, and IV. Diary of Events in Alitoa," *Anthropological Papers of The American Museum of Natural History,* 40, Part 3, 163–419. New York. Reprinted 1971, as *The Mountain Arapesh III: Stream of Events in Alitoa.* Garden City, N.Y.: Natural History Press.

———. 1949a. *Male and Female.* New York: Morrow.

————. 1949b. "The Mountain Arapesh. V. The Record of Unabelin with Rorschach Analyses," *Anthropological Papers of The American Museum of Natural History*, 41, Part 3, 285–390. New York. Reprinted 1968, as *The Mountain Arapesh I: The Record of Unabelin with Rorschach Analyses.* New York: Natural History Press.

————. 1956. *New Lives for Old: Cultural Transformation—Manus, 1928–1953.* New York: Morrow.

————. 1959a. *An Anthropologist at Work: Writings of Ruth Benedict.* Boston: Houghton Mifflin.

————. 1959b. "Apprenticeship under Boas." In *The Anthropology of Franz Boas*, ed. Walter Goldschmidt. Memoirs of the American Anthropological Association, 89. *American Anthropologist*, 61:5, Part 2 (October), 29–45.

————. 1960. "Weaver of the Border." In *In the Company of Man*, ed. Joseph B. Casagrande, pp. 175–210. New York: Harper.

————. 1964. *Continuities in Cultural Evolution.* New Haven: Yale University Press.

————. 1972. *Blackberry Winter: My Earlier Years.* New York: Morrow.

————. 1974. "Margaret Mead." In *A History of Psychology in Autobiography*, Vol. VI, ed. Gardner Lindzey, pp. 293–326. New York: Prentice-Hall.

————. 1975. "Children's Play Style: Potentialities and Limitations of Its Use as a Cultural Indicator," *Anthropological Quarterly*, 48:3 (July), 157–181.

————, and Frances C. Macgregor. 1951. *Growth and Culture: A Photographic Study of Balinese Childhood.* New York: Putnam.

————, and Theodore Schwartz. 1960. "The Cult as a Condensed Social Process." In *Group Processes: Transactions of the Fifth Conference, October 12–15, 1958*, ed. Bertram Schaffner, pp. 85–187. New York: Josiah Macy, Jr. Foundation.

————, and Martha Wolfenstein, eds. 1956. *Childhood in Contemporary Cultures.* Chicago: University of Chicago Press.

Mershon, Katharane Edson. 1971. *Seven Plus Seven.* New York: Vantage Press.

Metraux, Rhoda. 1976. "Eidos and Change: Continuity in Process, Discontinuity in Product." In *Socialization as Cultural Communication*, ed. Theodore Schwartz, pp. 201–216. Berkeley: University of California Press.

Mitchell, William E. (Forthcoming.) *The Bamboo Fire.* New York: Norton.

Parkinson, Richard. 1907. *Dreissig Jahre in der Südsee.* Stuttgart: Strecker und Schroeder.

Read, Kenneth E. 1965. *The High Valley.* New York: Scribner.

Romanucci-Ross, Lola. 1966. "Conflits Fonciers à Mokerang village Matankor des îles de l'Amirauté," *L'Homme*, 6:2, 32–52.

————. 1969. "The Hierarchy of Resort in Curative Practices: The Admiralty Islands, Melanesia," *Journal of Health and Social Behavior*, 10:3, 201–210.

Sapir, Edward. 1921. *Language.* New York: Harcourt Brace.

Schrödinger, Erwin. 1935. *Science and the Human Temperament.* Trans. James Murphy and W. H. Johnston. New York: Norton.

Schwartz, Theodore. 1962. "The Paliau Movement in the Admiralty Islands, 1946–1954," *Anthropological Papers of The American Museum of Natural History*, 49, Part 2, 207–422. New York.

————. 1963. "Systems of Areal Integration: Some Considerations Based on the Admiralty Islands of Northern Melanesia," *Anthropological Forum*, 1:1, 56–97.

————. 1973. "Cult and Context: The Paranoid in Melanesia," *Ethos*, 1:2, 153–174.

————. 1976a. "Cargo Cult: A Melanesian Type-Response to Culture Contact." In *Responses to Change*, ed. George De Vos, pp. 157–206. New York: Van Nostrand.

————. 1976b. "Relations among Generations in Time-Limited Cultures." In *Socialization as Cultural Communication*, ed. Theodore Schwartz, pp. 217–230. Berkeley: University of California Press.

————, and Margaret Mead. 1961. "Micro- and Macro-cultural Models for Cultural Evolution," *Anthropological Linguistics*, 3:1, 1–7.

————, and Lola Romanucci-Ross. 1974. "Drinking and Inebriate Behavior in the Admiralty Islands, Melanesia," *Ethos*, 2:3, 213–231.

Sheldon, W. H. 1940. *The Varieties of Human Physique.* With collaboration of S. S. Stevens and W. B. Tucker. New York: Harper.

Thurnwald, Richard C. 1916. *Banaro Society.* Memoirs of the American Anthropological Association, 3. Lancaster, Pa.: American Anthropological Association.

Tuzin, Donald F. 1976. *The Ilahita Arapesh.* Berkeley: University of California Press.

Zoete, Beryl de, and Walter Spies. 1939. *Dance and Drama in Bali.* New York: Harper.

Acknowledgments

Acknowledgment is gratefully made to the Aldine Publishing Company for permission to reprint letters, portions of which appeared in my chapter, "Field Work in the Pacific Islands, 1925–1967," in *Women in the Field*, edited by Peggy Golde; to *Ati-Ace Newsletter* (Athens) for permission to reprint a field letter written to my family and friends; to Houghton Mifflin Company for permission to reprint portions of a letter to Ruth Benedict first published in *An Anthropologist at Work: Writings of Ruth Benedict*; and to *Redbook* magazine for permission to reprint a letter about my 1967 visit to Tambunam Village.

Acknowledgment also is made to Doubleday and Company for permission to reproduce two stanzas from "Prelude to 'Departmental Ditties' 1885," in *Rudyard Kipling's Verse*.

I wish also to thank my collaborators in field work and others whose photographs are reproduced in this volume—Gregory Bateson, Reo F. Fortune, Janet Fouary, Barbara Kirk, Alan McEwen, Rhoda Metraux, G. F. Roll and Theodore Schwartz. Thanks, finally, are owing to the American Museum of Natural History, New York, for two photographs reproduced here and to the New York Academy of Sciences for permission to reprint photographs (Plate 5, fig. 1, Plate 6, fig. 2, Plate 11, fig. 6, Plate 19, fig. 5, Plate 43, fig. 4 and Plate 72, figs. 1–6) originally published in *Balinese Character* by Gregory Bateson and myself.

Finally, I wish to thank Nicholas Amorosi for designing the six maps used in the volume.

Margaret Mead

Index

Abel, Theodora M. (Tao), clinical psychologist, member of Montserrat Expedition, 1953–1954, 287

Abelam, a people with a great artistic tradition in the Sepik area, PNG; they speak a Ndu-family language, 101

Aden, man of Alitoa, 125

Admiralty Islands, see Manus

Afima, MM's houseboy in Kenakatem, 1932, 305, 306

Aibaum, Iatmul-speaking village on Tchambuli (Chambri, PNG) Lake, 102

Aitape, town, northeast coast of New Guinea, 123, 124

Akerang, Mundugumor village on Yuat River, PNG, 306

Alemi, luluai of Kenakatem, 1932, 308

Alitoa, Mountain Arapesh village, PNG, field site, 1931–1932, 16, 101–130; see also Mountain Arapesh

Alo, eldest son of Ufuti of Vaitogi, Samoa, 32

Ambunti, government post on middle Sepik River, PNG, 140

American Anthropological Association, meeting in Mexico City, 1959, 285

American Museum of Natural History, The, New York, 95; Elmhirst Committee grant to, 95; Frederick F. Voss Anthropological and Archeological Fund, 101; MM Assistant Curator, 61; MM joins staff, 20; Rockefeller Foundation grant for Admiralty Island Expedition, 241

Amito'a, wife of Baimal of Alitoa, 121–122

Andaramai, a leading man of Iatmul village of Tambunam, 310, 312

Angoram, government post, middle Sepik River, PNG, 292, 294, 306

Arapesh, see Ilahita; Mountain Arapesh

Arapesh language, a language of the Torricelli Phylum in Northern New Guinea, 104, 107, 111

Ashavi, see Kami Ashavi

Ashcan Cats, nickname for MM's group of Barnard College friends, 41

Australian Aborigines, 286

Avangaindo, man of Tambunam, 229

Baangwin, man of Tambunam, 227

Badui, son of Balidu, about 18 years old, in Alitoa, 112

Bagoes, musician and chauffeur, Bali, 194

Baimal, man of Alitoa, 121–122

Bajoeng Gedé (Bayung Gedé), mountain village in Kintamani subdistrict, Bali, field site, 1936–1938, 164–199, 203, 215–216

Bali, island in Indonesia, formerly Netherlands East Indies, 285, map, 152; field work in 1936, 153–155, 157–216, 286; Anak Angoeng caste, 192, 193, 195, 200; Barong (masked dancers representing supernatural beast), 161, 164, 172, 185, 186; Brahmana Boda (Buddha), 208; Brahmans, 187, 193, 207; ceremonies, 172, 190, 197–198; Christmas, 195; cockfights, 172, 179–180, 181, 189; cremations, 172, 193–194, 209–211; dances, 187; Dutch government in, 171–172; Kesatrya caste, 205, 207; marriage, 187–189; Muslims in, 172; Nyepi (New Year), 158; operas, 191–192; painting, 206, 208–209; priesthood, 199; procession to the sea, 162–163; puppets, 177, 190–191; shadow plays, 190–191, 217; taboos, 164–165; trance dances, 172, 175–178; traveling shows, 185–186; wood carving, 172, 173, 206; work days

About the Author

Margaret Mead is Curator Emeritus of Ethnology, The American Museum of Natural History, New York, Adjunct Professor of Anthropology, Columbia University, and Visiting Professor of Anthropology, Department of Psychiatry, University of Cincinnati Medical College.

She began her field work in 1925 with a study of the adolescent girl in Samoa and continues to do field research among the peoples of Oceania whom she has studied over the past fifty years. Dr. Mead believes that anthropological field work with living peoples in small, bounded communities is a vital preparation for participation in the planning and development of new planetary-wide institutions.

Among her better-known books are *Coming of Age in Samoa, Sex and Temperament in Three Primitive Societies, Continuities in Cultural Evolution, Culture and Commitment* and *Blackberry Winter.*

About the Editor of This Series

Ruth Nanda Anshen, philosopher and editor, plans and edits *World Perspectives, Religious Perspectives, Credo Perspectives, Perspectives in Humanism, The Science of Culture Series* and *The Tree of Life Series.* She also writes and lectures on the relationship of knowledge to the nature and meaning of man and his existence. Dr. Anshen's book, *The Reality of the Devil: Evil in Man,* is a study in the phenomenology of evil, and is published by Harper & Row.